Investing in Shares For Dummies®

Checking Out the Ten Most Important Points about Share Investing

1. You're not buying shares; you're buying a company.

2. The only reason you buy a share is because the company is making a profit.

3. If you buy a share when the company isn't making a profit, then you're not investing; you're speculating.

4. A share (or shares in general) should never be 100 per cent of your assets.

5. In some cases (such as a severe bear market), shares aren't a good investment at all.

6. A share's price is dependent on the company, which in turn is dependent on its environment, which includes its customer base, its industry, the general economy, and politics.

7. Your common sense and logic can be just as important in choosing a good share as the advice of any investment expert.

8. Always have well-reasoned answers to questions such as 'Why are you investing in shares?' and 'Why are you investing in a particular share?'

9. If you have no idea about the prospects of a company (and sometimes even if you think you do), always use stop-loss orders.

10. Even if your philosophy is 'buy and hold for the long term', continue to monitor your shares and consider selling them if they're not appreciating or if general economic conditions have changed.

Flipping through a Mandatory Reading List for Investors

- The company's annual report
- *Standard & Poor's Share Guide*
- *The Financial Times*
- The share investing Web sites listed in Appendix A

For Dummies: Bestselling Book Series for Beginners

Investing in Shares For Dummies®

Cheat Sheet

Looking at Four Important Parts of a Company's Fundamentals

- **Earnings:** This number should be at least 10 per cent higher than the year before.
- **Sales:** This number should be higher than the year before.
- **Debt:** This number should be lower than or about the same as the year before. It should also be lower than the company's assets.
- **Equity:** This number should be higher than the year before.

Knowing the Best Financial Measures

- **Price-to-Earnings ratio (PE):** For large-cap shares, the ratio should be under 20. For all shares (including growth, small cap, and speculative issues), it shouldn't exceed 40.
- **Price to sales ratio (PSR):** The PSR should be as close to 1 as possible.
- **Return on equity (ROE):** ROE should be going up by at least 10 per cent per year.
- **Earnings growth:** Earnings should be at least 10 per cent higher than the year before. This rate should be maintained over several years.
- **Debt-to-asset ratio:** Debt should be half or less compared to assets.

Remembering Nine Events That Could Spell Trouble for Your Share

- A bear market
- Heavy insider selling
- An inquiry or investigation by the government
- Excessive government taxation
- Excessive government regulation
- Pending government intervention (for example, nationalising an industry)
- An economic slowdown or decline in the industry or sector
- National or international conflict (such as war or acts of terrorism)
- Acts of nature (such as a hurricane or tsunami)

For Dummies: Bestselling Book Series for Beginners

Investing in Shares

FOR

DUMMIES®

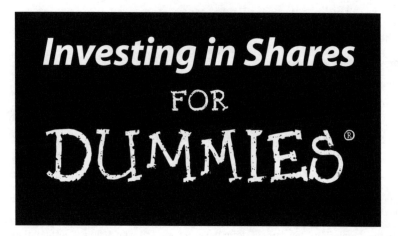

Investing in Shares
FOR
DUMMIES®

by Isabelle Kassam and Paul Mladjenovic

BICENTENNIAL
1807
WILEY
2007
BICENTENNIAL

John Wiley & Sons, Ltd

Investing in Shares For Dummies®

Published by
John Wiley & Sons, Ltd
The Atrium
Southern Gate
Chichester
West Sussex
PO19 8SQ
England

E-mail (for orders and customer service enquires): cs-books@wiley.co.uk

Visit our Home Page on www.wiley.com

Copyright © 2007 John Wiley & Sons, Ltd, Chichester, West Sussex, England

Published by John Wiley & Sons, Ltd, Chichester, West Sussex

For general information on our other products and services, please contact our Customer Care Department within the U.S. at 800-762-2974, outside the U.S. at 317-572-3993, or fax 317-572-4002.

For technical support, please visit www.wiley.com/techsupport.

Wiley also publishes its books in a variety of electronic formats. Some content that appears in print may not be available in electronic books.

British Library Cataloguing in Publication Data: A catalogue record for this book is available from the British Library

ISBN: 978-0-470-51645-4

Printed and bound in Great Britain by Bell & Bain Ltd., Glasgow

10 9 8 7 6 5 4 3 2 1

WILEY

About the Author

Isabelle Kassam is a freelance writer and media consultant who specialises in finance. She has contributed articles to *The Daily Mail, The Mirror, The Times, The Sunday Telegraph, The Independent on Sunday,* and to magazines including *Mortgage Strategy* and *Moneywise.* She also advises banks and building societies on communication with the media and with their customers. Born in Glasgow, she lives in London with her husband Kas and children Katie and Finley.

Paul Mladjenovic is a certified financial planner practitioner, writer, and public speaker who has a Web site at www.mladjenovic.com. His business, PM Financial Services, has helped people with financial and business concerns since 1981. In 1985 he achieved his CFP designation. Since 1983, Paul has taught thousands of budding investors through popular national seminars such as 'The $50 Wealthbuilder' and 'Stock Investing Like a Pro.' Paul has been quoted or referenced by many media outlets such as Bloomberg, MarketWatch, CNBC, and many financial and business publications and Web sites. As an author, he has written the books *The Unofficial Guide to Picking Stocks* (Wiley, 2000) and *Zero-Cost Marketing* (Todd Publications, 1995). In 2002, the first edition of *Stock Investing For Dummies* was ranked in the top 10 out of 300 books reviewed by Barron's. In recent years, Paul accurately forecasted many economic events, such as the rise of gold and the decline of the U.S. dollar. At press time he has been warning his students and clients about the coming decline in housing. He maintains a financial database for his readers and students at www.supermoneylinks.com.

Dedication

This book is dedicated to Kas, Katie and Finley, for letting me have all the time I spent on it, time I should have been spending with them.

– Isabelle Kassam

For my beloved Fran, Adam, Joshua, and a loving, supportive family, I thank God for you.

I also dedicate this book to the millions of investors who deserve more knowledge and information to achieve lasting prosperity.

– Paul Mladjenovic

Authors' Acknowledgments

I will always be grateful to Simon Bell at Wiley for guiding me through the process of writing my first book. His advise, cajoling and patience have been invaluable and I have learned a lot from the experience. I'd also like to thank Alison Yates at Wiley for considering me in the first place. My good friend Peter Forster is responsible for inspiring my interest in shares and thanks are also due to Tony Hazell at *The Daily Mail*, Clinton Manning at *The Mirror* and Sam Dunn of *The Independent on Sunday* for their continued support in my career. Finally, the unsung hero is David Gibson, my first editor, who spotted my potential and pushed me onto the nationals. My career would have been very different without his guidance.

– Isabelle Kassam

First and foremost, I offer my appreciation and gratitude to the wonderful people at Wiley. It has been a pleasure to work with such a top-notch organization that works so hard to create products that offer readers tremendous value and information. I wish all of you continued success! There are some notables there whom I want to single out.

The first person is Jennifer Connolly (my project editor). She is a true publishing and writing professional who has been extremely helpful, understanding, and patient. Those words are not enough to express my thanks for her fantastic guidance. May God bless her growing family! (Jennifer took over in mid-stream for the wonderful Sherri Pfouts.)

Sarah Faulkner (my copy editor) has made sure my mish-mash of content is readable and professional (no small feat). I thank her sincerely and I am grateful she worked on this book with her impressive editing skills.

My gratitude goes out to the acquisitions editor Stacy Kennedy for making this For Dummies book happen. For Dummies books don't magically appear at the bookstore, they happen due to the foresight and efforts of people like Stacy. Wiley is fortunate to have her (and the others also mentioned)!

Fran, Lipa Zyenska, you helped make those late nights at the computer more tolerable, and you helped me focus on the important things. Te amo and I thank God that you are by my side. With you and the rest of my loving family, I know that the future will be bright.

Lastly, I want to acknowledge you, the reader. Over the years, you have made the *For Dummies* books what they are today. Your devotion to these wonderful books created a foundation that played a big part in the creation of this book and many more yet to come. Thank you!

– **Paul Mladjenovic**

Publisher's Acknowledgments

We're proud of this book; please send us your comments through our Dummies online registration form located at www.dummies.com/register/.

Some of the people who helped bring this book to market include the following:

Acquisitions, Editorial, and Media Development

Project Editor: Simon Bell

Commissioning Editor: Alison Yates

Copy Editor: Kim Vernon

Technical Editor: Gavin Oldham, Chief Executive, The Share Centre www.share.co.uk

Executive Editor: Jason Dunne

Executive Project Editor: Daniel Mersey

Cover Photos: MaRoDee Photography/Alamy

Cartoons: Ed McLachlan

Composition Services

Project Coordinator:

Layout and Graphics: Carl Byers, Melissa K. Jester, Julie Trippetti, Christine Williams

Proofreaders: John Greenough, Jessica Kramer

Indexer: Donald Glassman

Publishing and Editorial for Consumer Dummies

> **Diane Graves Steele,** Vice President and Publisher, Consumer Dummies
>
> **Joyce Pepple,** Acquisitions Director, Consumer Dummies
>
> **Kristin A. Cocks,** Product Development Director, Consumer Dummies
>
> **Michael Spring,** Vice President and Publisher, Travel
>
> **Kelly Regan,** Editorial Director, Travel

Publishing for Technology Dummies

> **Andy Cummings,** Vice President and Publisher, Dummies Technology/General User

Composition Services

> **Gerry Fahey,** Vice President of Production Services
>
> **Debbie Stailey,** Director of Composition Services

Contents at a Glance

Table of Contents

Introduction

*A*lthough the stock market has served millions of investors for nearly a century, recent years have shown us that a great investing vehicle such as shares can be easily misunderstood, misused, and even abused. The great bull market of 1982–1999 came to a screeching halt in 2000. During 2000–2002, millions of investors lost a total equivalent to over 5 trillion dollars. What bothers us is that much of that loss was easily avoidable. Investors at the tail end of a bull market often think that share investing is an easy, carefree, certain way to make a quick fortune. How wrong they are! The countless stories of investors who lost tremendous amounts of money speculating in tech shares, dot-coms, and other flashy shares are lessons for all of us. Successful share investing takes diligent work and knowledge, like any other meaningful pursuit. This book can definitely help you avoid the mistakes others have made and can point you in the right direction.

Explore the pages of this book and find the topics that most interest you regarding the world of share investing. Let us assure you that we have squeezed over two decades of experience, education, and expertise between these covers. Understanding what not to do can be just as important as working out what to do. The single difference between success and failure, between gain and loss, boils down to one word: knowledge. Take this book as your first step in a lifelong learning adventure.

About This Book

The stock market has been a cornerstone of the investor's passive wealth-building programme for over a century and continues in this role. The period of 1995–2005 was one huge roller coaster ride for share investors. If it was a share chart, the graph would look like Mount Everest. Fortunes were made and lost. With just a little more knowledge and a few wealth-preserving techniques, more investors could have held onto their hard-earned stock market fortunes. With all the media attention, all the talking heads on radio and TV, and the books by investment gurus, the investing public still didn't avoid losing trillions in a historic stock market debacle. Sadly, even the so-called experts who understood shares didn't see the economic and geopolitical forces that acted like a tsunami on the market. This book also gives you a 'heads up' on those megatrends and events that will affect your share portfolio. While other books may tell you about shares, this book tells you about shares and what affects them.

This book is designed to give you a realistic approach to making money in shares. It provides the essence of sound, practical share investing strategies and insights that have been market tested and proven from nearly a hundred years of stock market history. We don't expect you to read it cover to cover, although We'd be delighted if you read every word! Instead, this book is designed as a reference tool. Feel free to read the chapters in whatever order you choose. You can flip to the sections and chapters that interest you or those that include topics that you need to know more about.

Investing in Shares For Dummies, is also a book that is quite different from the 'get rich with shares' titles that have crammed the bookshelves in recent years. It doesn't take a standard approach to the topic; it doesn't assume that shares are a sure thing and the be-all and end-all of wealth building. At times in this book, we tell you *not* to invest in shares. This book can help you succeed not only in up markets but also in down markets. Bull markets and bear markets come and go, but the informed investor can keep making money no matter what. To give you an extra edge, we have tried to include information about the investing environment for shares. Whether it is politics or hurricanes (or both), you need to know how 'the big picture' affects your share investment decisions.

Conventions Used in This Book

To make navigating through this book easier, we've established the following conventions:

- ✔ *Italic* highlights new terms that are defined.
- ✔ Monofont is used for Web addresses.
- ✔ Sidebars, shaded grey boxes of text, are filled with interesting information that isn't pertinent to your understanding of the topic, but is interesting nonetheless.

What You're Not to Read

Sidebars (grey boxes of text) in this book give you a more in-depth look at a certain topic. While they further illuminate a particular point, these sidebars aren't crucial to your understanding of the rest of the book. Feel free to read them or skip them. Of course, we'd love for you to read them all, but our feelings won't be hurt if you decide to skip them over.

The text that accompanies the Technical Stuff icon can be passed over as well. The text associated with this icon gives some technical details about share investing that are certainly interesting and informative, but you can still come away with the information you need with or without reading this text.

Foolish Assumptions

We reckon you've picked up this book for one or more of the following reasons:

- ✔ You're a beginner and want a crash course on share investing that's an easy read.

- ✔ You're already a share investor, and you need a book that allows you to read only those chapters that cover specific share investing topics of interest to you.

- ✔ You need to review your own situation with the information in the book to see if you missed anything when you invested in that hot share that your brother-in-law recommended.

- ✔ You need a great gift! When Uncle Fred is upset over his poor share picks, you can give him this book so he can get back on his financial feet. Be sure to get a copy for his broker, too. (Odds are that the broker was the one who made those picks to begin with.)

How This Book Is Organised

The information is laid out in a straightforward format. The parts progress in a logical approach that any investor interested in shares can follow very easily.

Part 1: The Essentials of Share Investing

This section is for everyone. Understanding the essentials of share investing and investing in general will only help you, especially in uncertain economic times. Shares may even touch your finances in ways not readily apparent. For example, shares are not only in individual accounts; they're also in mutual funds and pension plans.

An important point is that shares are really financial tools that are a means to an end. Investors should be able to answer the question 'Why am I considering shares at all?' Shares are a great vehicle for wealth building, but only if investors realise what they can accomplish and how to use them.

One of the essentials of share investing is understanding risk. Most people are clueless about risk. Chapter 4, on risk, is one of the most important chapters that serious share investors should read. You can't avoid every type of risk out there. (Life itself embodies risk.) However, this chapter can help you recognise it and find ways to minimise it in your share investing program.

Part II: Before You Start Buying

Once you're ready to embark on your career as a share investor, you'll need to use some resources to gather information about the shares you're interested in. Fortunately, you live in the information age. We pity the investors from the 1920s, who didn't have access to so many resources, but today's investors are in an enviable position. This part tells you where to find information and how to use it to be a more knowledgeable investor (a rarity in recent years!). For example, We explain that shares can be used for both growth and income purposes, and we discuss the characteristics of each. See Chapters 8 and 9 for more information.

When you're ready to invest, you'll invariably have to turn to a broker. There are several types, so you should know which is which. The wrong broker could make you . . . er . . . broker. Chapter 7 helps you choose.

Part III: Picking Winners

Part III is about picking good shares by using microeconomics, meaning that you look at the shares of individual companies. We explain how to evaluate a company's products, services, and other factors so that you can determine whether a company is strong and healthy.

We put a lot of emphasis on emerging sector opportunities. If we can steer you toward those segments of the stock market that show solid promise for the coming years, then that alone would make your share portfolio thrive. Putting your money into solid companies that are in thriving industries has been the hallmark of superior share investing throughout history. It's no different now. Check out Chapter 13 if you want to know more about emerging sector opportunities.

Where do you turn to find out about a company's financial health? In Chapter 11, we show you the documents you should review to make a more informed decision. Once you find the information, you'll discover how to make sense of that data as well. While you're at it, check out Chapter 12 (on analysing industries).

We compare buying shares to picking goldfish. If you look at a bunch of goldfish to choose which ones to buy, you want to make sure that you pick the healthiest ones. With shares, you also need to pick companies that are healthy. Part III can help you do that.

Part IV: Investment Strategies and Tactics

Even the shares of great companies can fall in a bad investing environment. This is where you should be aware of the "macro." If shares were goldfish, the macro would be the pond or goldfish bowl. In that case, even healthy goldfish can die if the water is toxic. Therefore, you should monitor the investing environment for shares. Part IV reveals tips, strategies, and resources that you shouldn't ignore.

Once you understand shares and the economic environment in which they operate, choose the strategy and the tactics to help steer you to your wealth-building objectives. Chapter 17 reveals some of our all-time favourite techniques for building wealth and holding on to your share investment gains. (Definitely check it out.)

You may be an investor, but that doesn't mean that you have deep pockets. Chapter 18 tells you how to buy shares with lower (or no) transaction costs. If you're going to buy the shares anyway, why not save on commissions and other costs?

As an investor, you must keep an eye on what the company insiders are doing. In Chapter 19, we explain what it may mean if the company's management is buying or selling the same share that you're considering.

After you spend all your time, money, and effort to grow your money in the world of shares, you have yet another concern: holding on to your hard-earned gains. This challenge is summarised in one word: taxes. Sound tax planning is crucial for everyone who works hard. After all, taxes are the biggest expense in your lifetime (right after children!). See Chapter 20 for more information.

Part V: The Part of Tens

We wrap up the book with a hallmark of *For Dummies* books – the Part of Tens. These chapters give you a mini crash course in share investing, including ten ways to protect yourself from fraud.

In this part, we offer some clues that signal a share price increase and how to recognise the warning signs of a share poised to fall. Also review the list of ten challenges and opportunities that face share investors (Chapter 24).

Part VI: Appendixes

Don't overlook the appendixes. We pride ourselves on the resources we can provide our readers so that they can make informed investment decisions. Whether the topic is share investing terminology, economics, or avoiding capital gains taxes, we include a treasure trove of resources to help you. Whether you go to a bookstore, the library, or the Internet, Appendix A gives you some great places to turn to for help. In Appendix B, we explain financial ratios. These important numbers help you better determine whether to invest in a particular company's shares.

Icons Used in This Book

This icon flags a particular bit of advice that just may give you an edge over other investors.

When you see this icon, we're reminding you about some information that you should always keep stashed in your memory, whether you're new to investing or an old pro.

Pay special attention to this icon because the advice can prevent headaches, heartaches, and financial aches.

The text attached to this icon may not be crucial to your success as an investor, but it may enable you to talk shop with investing gurus and better understand the financial pages of your favorite business publication or Web site.

Where to Go from Here

You may not need to read every chapter to make you more confident as a share investor, so feel free to jump around to suit your personal needs. Since every chapter is designed to be as self-contained as possible, it won't do you any harm to 'cherry-pick' what you really want to read. But if you're like us, you still may want to check out every chapter because you never know when you can come across a new tip or resource that will make a profitable difference in your share portfolio. We want you to be successful so that we can brag about you in the next edition!

Part I
The Essentials of Investing in Shares

'Congratulations, you are now a fully paid-up customer of a very successful stockbroking company & forgive me once again for not standing up.'

In this part . . .

Many investors do things in reverse; they buy shares first and learn 'some lessons' afterwards. Your success is dependent on doing your homework before you invest your first pound in shares. Most investors don't realise that they should be scrutinising their own situations and financial goals at least as much as they scrutinise shares. But how else can you know which shares are right for you? Too many people risk too much simply because they don't take stock of their current needs, goals, and risk tolerance before they invest. The chapters in this part tell you what you need to know to choose the stocks that best suit you.

Chapter 1

Exploring the Basics

· ·

· ·

*I*nvesting in shares became all the rage during the late 1990s. Everyone from postmen to pop stars got in on the act. Investors watched their share portfolios and investment funds skyrocket as the stock market reached the mania stage at the tail-end of an 18-year upswing (or *bull market*). (See Chapter 15 for more information on bull markets.) Investment activity in the United States is a great example of the popularity that stocks experienced during that period. By 1999, over half of United States households became participants in the stock market. Millions in the United Kingdom also joined the new gold rush. And millions of them lost money when the stock market fell like a stone (the *bear market* – see Chapter 15 for more on these) between 2000 and 2002. People invested. But they really didn't know exactly what they were investing in. If they'd had a rudimentary understanding of what shares really are, perhaps they could have avoided some expensive mistakes. The purpose of this book is not only to tell you about the basics of investing in shares but also to let you in on some solid strategies that can help you profit from the stock market. Before you invest your first fiver, you need to understand the basics of investing in shares.

Understanding the Basics

The basics are so basic that few people are doing them. Perhaps the most basic (and therefore most important) thing to grasp is the risk you face whenever you do anything (like putting your hard-earned money in an investment like shares). When you lose track of the basics, you lose track of why you invested to begin with. Find out more about risk (and the different kinds of risk) in Chapter 4.

In an old stand-up routine, the comic was asked 'How is your wife?' He responded 'Compared to what?' You need to apply the same attitude to stocks.

When you are asked 'how are your shares?', you may be able to say that they're doing well – especially when compared to an acceptable 'yardstick' such as an index (such as the FTSE 100). Find out more about indices in Chapter 5.

The bottom line is that the first thing you do when investing in shares is not send your money straight into a stockbroker's account or go to a Website to click 'buy shares'. The first thing you do is find out as much as you can about what shares are and how you can use them to boost your wealth.

Getting Prepared before You Get Started

Gathering information is critical to your plans for investing in shares. You need to gather information on the shares you are planning to buy twice: before you invest . . . and after. You obviously should become more informed before you invest your first fiver. But you also need to stay informed about what's happening to the company whose shares you are buying, about the industry or sector that company is in and about the economy in general. To find the best information sources, check out Chapter 6.

When you are ready to invest, you need an account with a stockbroker. How do you know which broker to use and whether to go online or use paper certificates? Chapter 7 provides some answers and resources to help you choose a broker.

Knowing How to Pick Winners

Once you get past the basics, you can get to the 'meat' of picking shares. Successful share picking is not mysterious, but it does take some time, effort, and analysis. This may sound like a lot of work but it's worth it, because shares are a convenient and important part of most investors' portfolios. Read the following section and be sure to 'leap frog' to the relevant chapters to get the inside scoop on 'hot shares'.

Recognising the value of shares

Imagine that you like eggs and you're willing to buy them at the supermarket. In this example, the eggs are like companies, and the prices represent the prices that you would pay for the companies' shares. The supermarket is the stock market. What if two brands of eggs are similar, but one costs £1 while the other costs £1.50? Which would you choose? Odds are that you would look at both brands, judge their quality, and, if they were indeed similar, take the cheaper eggs. The eggs at £1.50 are overpriced. The same principle applies to shares. What if you compare two companies that are similar in every respect but have different share prices? All things being equal, the cheaper price has greater value for the investor. But the egg example has another side.

What if the quality of the two brands of eggs is significantly different but their prices are the same? If one brand of eggs is old, of poor quality, and priced at £1 and the other brand is fresher, of superior quality, and also priced at £1, which would you buy? Of course, you'd take the good brand because they're better eggs. Perhaps the lesser eggs are an acceptable purchase at 50 pence, but they're definitely overpriced at £1. The same example works with shares. A badly run company isn't a good choice if you can buy a better company in the marketplace at the same – or a better – price.

Comparing the value of eggs may seem overly simplistic, but doing so does cut to the heart of investing in shares. Eggs and egg prices can be as varied as companies and share prices. As an investor, you must make it your job to find the best value for your investment cash. (Otherwise you get egg on your face. We bet you saw that one coming.)

Understanding how market capitalisation affects share values

You can determine the value of a company (and thus the value of its shares) in many ways. The most basic way to measure this value is to look at a company's market value, also known as market capitalisation (or market cap). *Market capitalisation* is simply the value you get when you multiply all the number of outstanding shares of a particular company by the price of a single share.

Calculating the market cap is easy. It's the number of shares outstanding multiplied by the current share price. If the company has 1 million shares outstanding and its share price is £10, the market cap is £10 million.

Small cap, mid cap, and large cap aren't references to headgear; they're references to how large the company is as measured by its market value. Here are the five basic categories of market capitalisation:

- ✔ **Fledglings** shares are sometimes known as *tiddlers*. They are small and risky.

- ✔ **Small caps:** These shares may fare better than the fledglings and still have plenty of growth potential. The key word is 'potential'.

- ✔ **Mid caps:** For many investors, this category offers a good compromise between small caps and blue chips. They offer much of the safety of the big companies while retaining a part of the growth potential of small caps.

- ✔ **Blue chips:** These are the established heavy hitters and are ideal for conservative stock investors who want steady appreciation with greater safety. These companies tend to be represented in the FTSE 100 Index. We explain more about indices in Chapter 5.

From a safety point of view, the company's size and market value do matter. All things being equal, large cap companies are considered safer than small cap companies. However, small caps shares have greater potential for growth. Compare these companies to trees: Which tree is stronger – a sturdy oak tree or a newly planted sapling? In a great storm, the oak has a chance of survival, while the young tree has a rough time. But you also have to ask yourself which tree has more opportunity for growth. The oak may not have much growth left, but the sapling has plenty of growth to look forward to.

For investment beginners, comparing market cap to trees isn't so far-fetched. You want your money to grow without becoming dead wood.

Although market capitalisation is important to consider, don't invest (or not invest) just based on market capitalisation only. It's just one measure of value. As a serious investor, you need to look at numerous factors that can help you determine whether any given share is a good investment. Keep reading – this book is full of information to help you decide.

Sharpening your investment skills

Investors who analyse the company can better judge the value of the shares and profit from buying and selling them. Your greatest asset in investing is knowledge (and a little common sense). To succeed in the world of share investment, keep in mind the following key success factors:

✔ **Analyse yourself.** What do you want to accomplish through your investment in shares? What are your investment goals? Chapter 2 can help you figure this out.

✔ **Know where to get information.** The decisions you make about your money and the shares to invest in require quality information. If you want help with information sources, turn to Chapter 3.

✔ **Understand why you want to invest in shares.** Are you seeking appreciation (capital gains) or income (dividends)? Look at Chapters 8 and 9 for information on these topics.

✔ **Do your research.** Look at the company whose shares you're considering, to see whether it's a profitable company worthy of your investment cash. Chapters 10 and 11 help you scrutinise the company.

✔ **Choosing a winning share also means that you choose a winning industry.** You frequently see share prices of mediocre companies in 'hot' industries rise higher and faster than solid companies in floundering industries. Therefore, choosing the industry is important. Find out more about analysing industries in Chapter 12.

✔ **Understand how the world affects your shares.** Shares succeed or fail in large part due to the environment in which they operate. Economics and politics make up that world, so you should know something about them. Chapter 14 covers these topics, but also take a look at Chapter 2.

✔ **Understand and identify megatrends.** Doing so makes it easier for you to make money. This edition spends more time and provides more resources helping you see the opportunities in emerging sectors and even avoid the problem areas (see Chapter 13 for details).

✔ **Use investing strategies like the experts do.** In other words, how you go about investing can be just as important as what you invest in. Chapter 16 highlights techniques for investing to help you make more money from your shares.

✔ **Keep more of the money you earn.** After all your great work in picking the right shares and making big money, you should know about keeping more of the fruits of your investing. We cover the taxation of share investment in Chapter 20.

✔ **Sometimes, what people tell you to do with shares is not as revealing as what people are actually doing.** This is why we like to look at company insiders before we buy or sell that particular share. To find out more about insider buying and selling– not to be confused with 'insider dealing' which is illegal – read Chapter 19.

Stock market schizophrenia

Have you ever noticed a share going up even though the company is reporting terrible results? How about seeing a share nosedive despite the fact that the company is doing well? What's going on? Well, judging the direction of a share in a short-term period – over the next few days or weeks – is almost impossible.

Yes, in the short term, investing in shares is irrational. The price of a share and the value of its company seem disconnected and almost schizophrenic. The key phrase to remember is 'short term'. A share's price and the company's value become more logical over an extended period

of time. The longer a share is in the public view, the more rational the performance of the share's price. In other words, a good company continues to draw attention to itself; so, more people want its shares, and the share price rises to better match the value of the company. Conversely, a bad company doesn't hold up to continued scrutiny over time. As more and more people see that the company isn't doing well, the share price declines. In the long run, a company's share price and its value eventually tell the same story.

Actually, every chapter in the book offers you valuable guidance on an essential aspect of the fantastic world of shares. The knowledge you pick up and apply from these pages has been tested over nearly a century of share picking. The investment experience of the past – the good, the bad, and some of the ugly – is here for your benefit. Use this information to make a lot of money (and make me proud!). And don't forget to check out the Appendices!

Boning Up on Strategies and Tactics

Successful investing isn't just what you invest in, it's also the way you invest. We are big on strategies such as trailing stop losses. You can find out more in Chapter 17.

Buying shares doesn't always mean that you must visit a stockbroker or that it has to be hundreds of shares. You can buy shares for pennies and use programmes such as dividend reinvestment plans. Chapter 18 tells you more.

Getting Good Tips

Protecting yourself from the risk of losing money (known as *downside exposure*) is what separates investors from gamblers, and Chapter 21 gives you ten warning signs of a share's decline. We know that when we see some of the signs that (at the least) we need to put on a stop loss order (Chapter 17) so that we can sleep at night. Sometimes the return *on* your money is not as good as the return *of* your money.

If shares give off 'negative signals', then it follows that they give off 'positive' ones as well. Chapter 22 gives you ten of the best signs that are commonly seen before a share is ready to rise. What better time to jump in?

You should be aware about the risks of fraud. It's tough enough to make money from shares in an honest market. Yet we must always be aware of those that would take our hard-earned money from us without our consent. That's why we include Chapter 23 – because there's always a chance of encountering problems when you are dealing with humanity.

Chapter 24 is (I believe) one of the best chapters in the book. You really need to understand if the environment for a particular share is good or bad. The best shares in the world sink in a tough market while the worst shares can go up in a jubilant and rising market. Ideally, you avoid those shares that are in the tough market and find good shares in a good market. This chapter points you in the direction of those markets.

Chapter 2

Sizing Up Your Current Finances and Setting Goals

In This Chapter
- ▶ Preparing your personal balance sheet
- ▶ Looking at your cash flow statement
- ▶ Determining your financial goals

*Y*es, you want to make big money. Or maybe you just want to get back the big cash you lost in the stock market debacle of 2000–2003. Either way, you want your money to grow so that you can have a better life. But before you make reservations for that Caribbean cruise you're dreaming about, you have to map out how you intend to get there. Shares can be a great component of most wealth-building programs, but you must first do some homework on a topic that you should be very familiar with – yourself. That's right. Understanding your current financial situation and clearly defining your financial goals are the first steps to successful investing.

This chapter is undoubtedly one of the most important chapters in this book. At first, you may think it's a chapter more suitable for some general book on personal finance. Wrong! Unsuccessful investors' greatest weakness is not understanding their financial situation and how shares fit in. Often, People should stay out of the stock market if they aren't prepared for the responsibilities of investing in shares – regularly reviewing the company's financial statements and tracking the company's progress. Very often, investors aren't aware of the pitfalls of investing in shares during *bear markets*, periods in which share prices fall generally. Check out Chapter 15 for more on bear markets.

Investing in shares requires balance. Investors sometimes tie up too much money in shares, putting themselves at risk of losing a significant portion of their wealth if the market plunges. Then again, other investors place little or no money in shares, and miss out on excellent opportunities to grow their wealth. Investors should make shares a part of their portfolios, but the operative word is *part*. You should only let shares take up a *portion* of your money. A disciplined investor also has money in bank accounts, bonds, and other assets that offer growth or income opportunities. Diversification is key to minimising risk. (For more on risk, see Chapter 4.)

Establishing a Starting Point

Whether you already own shares or you're looking to get into shares, you need to find out how much money you can afford to invest in them. No matter what you hope to accomplish with your share investment plan, the first step you should take as a budding investor is figuring out how much you own and how much you owe. To do this, prepare and review your personal *balance sheet*. A balance sheet is simply a list of your assets, your liabilities, and what each item is currently worth, allowing you to arrive at your *net worth*. Your net worth is the total *assets* minus the total *liabilities*. These terms may sound like accounting mumbo jumbo, but knowing your net worth is important to your future financial success, so let's just get on with it. Check out the section 'Step 4: Calculating your net worth' later in this chapter for more detail.

Composing your balance sheet is simple. Grab a pencil and a piece of paper. For the computer savvy, a spreadsheet software program accomplishes the same task. Gather all your financial documents, such as bank and stockbroker statements and other such paperwork – you need figures from these documents. Then follow the steps that I outline in the following sections. Update your balance sheet at least once a year to monitor your financial progress (Is your net worth going up or not?).

A second document to prepare is an income statement. An income statement lists your total income and your total expenses to find out how well you are doing. If your total income is greater than your total expenses, then you have net income (Great!). If your total expenses meet or exceed your total income, then you're in trouble. You better start increasing your income or cutting your expenses. You want to get to the point where you have enough net income so you can use that money to fund your share purchases.

Your personal balance sheet is really no different from balance sheets that big companies prepare. (The main difference is a few noughts, but you can use my advice in this book to work on changing that.) In fact, the more you know about your own balance sheet, the easier it is to understand the balance sheet of companies in which you're seeking to invest.

Step 1: Making sure you have an emergency fund

First, list your cash on your balance sheet (see the next step for more on listing your assets). Your goal is to have, in reserve, at least three to six months' worth of your gross living expenses in cash. The cash is important because it gives you a cushion. Three to six months is usually enough to get you through the most common forms of financial disruption, such as losing your job. Finding a new job can typically take between three and six months.

If your monthly expenses (or *outgoings*) are £1,000, you should have at least £3,000, and probably closer to £6,000, in a secure, interest-bearing bank or building society account. This account is your emergency fund and not an investment. Don't use this money to buy shares – or anything else.

Too many people put themselves at risk because they don't have a basic emergency fund. You wouldn't take the risk of walking across a busy street while wearing a blindfold but in recent years, investors have done the financial equivalent. Investors borrowed too much, put too much into investments (such as shares) that they didn't understand, and had little or no savings. One of the biggest problems during 2000–2003 was that savings were sinking while debt levels were reaching new heights. Many people had to sell shares because they needed cash to pay their bills and debts.

Resist the urge to start thinking of your investment in shares as a savings account generating over 20 per cent per year. This is dangerous thinking! If your investments flop, or if you lose your job, you will struggle financially and that will hit your share portfolio (you might have to sell some shares just to get money to pay the bills). An emergency fund helps you through a temporary cash crunch.

Step 2: Listing your assets in decreasing order of liquidity

Liquid assets don't mean beer or lemonade (unless you're Scottish & Newcastle or Cadbury Schweppes). Instead, *liquidity* refers to how quickly you can convert a particular *asset* (something you own that has value) into cash. If you know the liquidity of your assets, including investments, you have some options when you need cash to buy some shares (or pay a bill). All too often, people are short of cash and have too much wealth tied up in *illiquid investments* such as property. *Illiquid* is just a fancy way of saying that you don't have the immediate cash to meet a pressing need. (We've all been there.) Review your assets and take measures to ensure that you have enough liquid assets (along with your illiquid assets).

Listing your assets in order of liquidity on your balance sheet gives you an immediate picture of which assets you can quickly convert to cash and which ones you can't. If you need money *now,* you can see that cash in your purse or wallet, your current account, and your savings account – which are at the top of the list. The items last in order of liquidity become obvious; they're things like property and other assets that you can't sell quickly.

Selling property, even in a seller's market, can take months. Investors who don't have adequate liquid assets run the danger of selling assets quickly and possibly at a loss when they scramble to accumulate cash for short-term financial obligations. For investors in shares, this scramble may include prematurely selling shares that they originally intended to hold as long-term investments.

Table 2-1 shows a typical list of assets in order of liquidity. Use it as a guide for making your own asset list.

Table 2-1	John Q. Investor: Personal Assets as of December 31, 2006	
Asset Item	**Market Value**	**Annual Growth Rate %**
Current Assets		
Cash in wallet and in current account	£150	0
Bank and building society savings accounts and National Savings certificates	£500	2%
Shares	£2,000	11%
Investment trusts	£2,400	9%
Other assets		
(Collectibles etc .)	£240	
Total current assets	**£5,290**	
Long-term assets		
Car	£1,800	-10%
Home	£150,000	5%
Buy to Let property	£125,000	6%
Personal stuff (such as jewellery)	£4,000	
Total long-term assets	**£280,800**	
Total assets	**£286,090**	

The first column of Table 2-1 describes the asset. You can quickly convert *current assets* to cash – they're more liquid; *long-term assets* have value, but you can't necessarily convert them to cash quickly – they aren't very liquid.

Please take note. We've listed shares as short-term in the table. The reason is that this balance sheet is meant to list items in order of liquidity. Liquidity is best embodied in the question 'How quickly can I turn this asset into cash?' Because a share can be sold and converted to cash very quickly, it is a good example of a liquid asset. (However, that is not the main reason for buying shares.)

The second column gives the current market value for that item. Keep in mind that this value is not the purchase price or original value; it's the amount you would realistically get if you sold the asset in the current market. The third column shows how well that investment is doing, compared to one year ago. If the percentage rate is 5 per cent, that item's value has increased by 5 per cent from a year ago. You need to know how well all your assets are doing. Why? To adjust your assets for maximum growth or to get rid of assets that are losing money. Assets that are doing well are kept (you may even increase holdings), but assets that are down in value are candidates for removal. Perhaps you can sell them and reinvest the money elsewhere. In addition, the realised loss has tax benefits (see Chapter 20).

Working out the annual growth rate (in the third column) as a percentage isn't difficult. Say that you buy 100 shares in a company called Gro-A-Lot Ltd. (GAL), and its market value on December 31, 2005, is £50 a share for a total market value of £5,000 (100 shares at £50 a share). When you check its value on December 31, 2006, you find the stock is at £60 a share (100 shares times £60 equals a total market value of £6,000). The annual growth rate is 20 per cent. You calculate this by taking the amount of the gain (£60 a share minus £50 a share = a gain of £10 a share), which is £1,000 (100 shares times the £10 gain), and dividing it by the value at the beginning of the time period – in this case a year (£5,000). In this case, you get 20 per cent (£1,000 divided by £5,000). What if GAL also generates a dividend of £2 per share during that period; now what? In that case, GAL generates a total return of 24 per cent. To calculate the total return, add the appreciation (£10 a share times 100 shares equals £1,000) and the dividend income (£2 per share times 100 shares equals £200) and divide that sum (£1,000 + £200, or £1,200) by the value at the beginning of the year (£50 a share times 100 shares or £5,000). The total is £1,200 (£1,000 of appreciation and £200 total dividends), or 24 per cent (£1,200 ÷ £5,000).

The last line lists the total for all the assets and their current market value. The third column answers the question 'How well did this particular asset grow from a year ago?'

Step 3: Listing your liabilities

Liabilities are simply the bills that you're obliged to pay. Whether it's a credit card bill or a mortgage payment, a liability is an amount of money you have to pay back eventually (with interest). If you don't keep track of your liabilities, you may end up thinking that you have more money than you really do.

Table 2-2 lists some common liabilities. Use it as a model when you list your own. You should list the liabilities according to how soon you need to pay them. Credit card balances tend to be short-term obligations, while mortgages are long-term.

Table 2-2	Listing Personal Liabilities	
Liabilities	*Amount*	*Paying Rate %*
Credit cards	£4,000	15%
Personal loans	£13,000	10%
Mortgage	£100,000	8%
Total liabilities	£117,000	

The first column in Table 2-2 names the type of debt. Don't forget to include student loans and car loans if you have them. Don't avoid listing a liability because you're embarrassed to see how much you really owe. Be honest with yourself – doing so helps you improve your financial health.

The second column shows the current value (or current balance) of your liabilities. List the most current balance to see where you stand with your creditors.

The third column reflects how much interest you're paying for carrying that debt. This information is an important reminder about how debt can damage your wealth. Borrowing on credit cards, especially store cards, can incur interest at rates of up to 30 per cent. Using a credit card to make even a small purchase costs you if you maintain a balance. Within a year, a £50 jumper at 18 per cent costs £59 when you add the interest.

If you compare your liabilities in Table 2-2 and your personal assets in Table 2-1, you may find opportunities to reduce the amount you pay in interest. Say, for example, that you pay 15 per cent on a credit card balance of £4,000 but also have a personal asset of £5,000 in a savings account that's earning 2 per cent in interest. In that case, you could consider taking £4,000 out of the savings account to pay off the credit card balance. Doing so saves you £520; the £4,000 in the bank was earning only £80 (2 per cent of £4,000), while you were paying £600 on the credit card balance (15 per cent of £4,000).

If you can't pay off high-interest debt, at least look for ways to minimise the cost of the debt. The most obvious ways include:

- Replacing high-interest cards with low-interest or no interest cards. Many companies offer incentives to consumers, including balance transfer deals when you sign up for a new card. Some cards will charge you no interest on the debt you transfer for six, nine or 12 months.

- Replacing credit card debt with an *unsecured personal loan*, a loan where you don't have to put up any collateral or other asset to secure the debt. Loan rates tend to be lower than expensive plastic credit but you will be paying for a longer term – up to five years is common. However you can get personal loans at around six to eight per cent instead of the 18 to 30 per cent you will pay on the most expensive plastic.

In 2006 more than 100,000 people went bankrupt in England and Wales compared to just under 70,000 the previous year. More and more consumers are accepting that they are taking on too much debt. Don't be one of them. Make a diligent effort to control and reduce your debt, or the debt can become too burdensome. If you don't, you may have to sell your shares just to stay liquid. And, Murphy's Law states that you *will* sell your shares at the worst possible moment. Don't go there.

I owe, I owe, so off to work I go

One reason you continue to work is probably so that you can pay your bills. But many people today are losing their jobs because their company owes too!

Debt is one of the biggest financial problems in the world today. Companies and individuals holding excessive debt contributed to the stock market's massive decline in 2000. But if individuals managed their personal liabilities more responsibly, the general economy would be much better off.

One reason the economy appeared to be doing so well during the late 1990s was the fact that individuals and organisations went on an unprecedented spending binge, financed mostly by excessive debt. The economy looked unstoppable. However, sooner or later you have to pay the piper. Share prices may go up and down, but debt stays up until it is either paid down or the debtor files for bankruptcy. UK consumer debt has surpassed a mind-boggling £1trillion, which means challenging times ahead. Yes, the stock market will be affected!

Step 4: Calculating your net worth

Your *net worth* is an indication of your total wealth. You can calculate your net worth with this basic equation: total assets (Table 2-1) minus total liabilities (Table 2-2) equals net worth (net assets or net equity).

Table 2-3 shows this equation in action with a net worth of £169,090 – a very respectable figure. For many investors, just being in a position where assets exceed liabilities (a positive net worth) is great news. Use Table 2-3 as a model to analyse your own financial situation. Your mission (if you choose to accept it – and you should) is to ensure that your net worth increases from year to year as you progress toward your financial goal.

Table 2-3	Working Out Your Personal Net Worth	
Totals	*Amounts (£)*	*Increase from Year Before*
Total assets (from Table 2-1)	£286,090	+5%
Total liabilities (from Table 2-2)	(£117,000)	-2%
Net worth (total assets minus total liabilities)	£169,090	+3%

Step 5: Analysing your balance sheet

Create a balance sheet based on the steps you've been through so far in this chapter to illustrate your current finances. Take a close look at it and try to identify any changes you can make to increase your wealth. Sometimes reaching your financial goals can be as simple as refocusing the items on your balance sheet (use Table 2-3 as a general guideline). Here are some brief points to consider:

✔ **Is the money in your emergency (or rainy day) fund sitting in an ultra safe account and earning the highest interest available?** You are likely to earn the highest interest in an online savings account with a bank or building society. But money saved in UK banks is not 100 per cent guaranteed. Money invested in National Savings Certificates is backed by the Treasury and 100 per cent safe but the interest rates are not as good as the best deals offered by banks.'

- ✔ **Can you replace depreciating assets with appreciating assets?** Say that you have two DVD players. Why not sell one and invest the proceeds? You may say, 'But I bought that one two years ago for £500, and if I sell it now, I'll only get £300'. That's your choice. You need to decide what helps your financial situation more – a £500 item that keeps shrinking in value (a *depreciating asset*) or £300 that can grow in value when invested (an *appreciating asset*).

- ✔ **Can you replace low-yield investments with high-yield investments?** Maybe you have £5,000 in a savings account earning 3 per cent. You can certainly shop around for a better rate at another bank or building society, but you can also seek alternatives that offer a higher yield, such as savings bonds or short-term bond funds.

- ✔ **Can you pay off any high-interest debt with funds from low-interest assets?** If, for example, you have £5,000 earning 2 per cent in a taxable bank account, and you have £2,500 on a credit card charging 18 per cent, you may as well pay off the credit card balance and save on the interest.

- ✔ **If you're carrying debt, are you using that money for an investment return that is greater than the interest you're paying?** Carrying a loan with an interest rate of 8 per cent is acceptable if that borrowed money is yielding more than 8 per cent elsewhere. Borrowing money to invest in the stock market is not generally advisable. But some students who don't need their cheap student loans to fund their studies – because their parents are supporting them – use the loans to invest for profit.

- ✔ **Can you sell any personal stuff for cash?** You can replace unproductive assets with cash from car boot sales and auction Websites, but be warned: The taxman is beginning to monitor these sites to tax any income.

- ✔ **Can you use your home equity to pay off consumer debt?** Borrowing against your home has more favourable interest rates but you will be repaying the debt for longer, (Be careful about your debt level. See Chapter 23 for warnings on debt and other concerns.)

Paying off consumer debt by using funds borrowed against your home is one way to wipe the slate clean. It might be a relief to get rid of your credit card balances but you will still be repaying the debt, just at a lower rate and for longer. And you might be tempted to run up the consumer debt again. You can get overburdened and experience financial ruin (not to mention home-lessness). Not a pretty picture.

The important point to remember is that you can take control of your finances with discipline (and with the advice we offer in this book).

Funding Your Shares Programme

If you're going to invest money in shares, the first thing you need is . . . money! Where can you get that money? If you're waiting for an inheritance to come through, you may have to wait a long time, considering all the advances being made in healthcare lately. What's that? You were going to invest in healthcare shares? How ironic. Yet, the challenge still comes down to how to fund your share programme.

Many investors can reallocate their investments and assets to do the trick. *Reallocation* simply means selling some investments or other assets and reinvesting that money into shares. It boils down to deciding what investment or asset you can sell or liquidate. Generally, you want to consider those investments and assets that give you a low return on your money (or no return at all). If you have a complicated mix of investments and assets, you may want to consider reviewing your options with a financial adviser. Reallocation is just part of the answer; your cashflow is the other part.

Ever wonder why there's so much month left at the end of the money? Consider your cashflow. Your *cashflow* refers to what money is coming in (income) and what money is being spent (outgoings). The net result is either a positive cashflow or a negative cashflow, depending on your cash management skills. Maintaining a positive cashflow (more money coming in than going out) helps you increase your net worth (mo' money, mo' money, mo' money!). A negative cashflow ultimately depletes your wealth and wipes out your net worth if you don't turn it around immediately. The following sections show you how to analyse your cashflow. The first step is to do a cashflow statement.

Dot-com-and-go

If you were publishing a book about negative cash flow, look for the employees of any one of a hundred dot-com companies to write it. Their qualifications include working for a company that flew sky-high in 1999 and crashed in 2000 and 2001. Some of these companies were given millions, yet they couldn't turn a profit and eventually closed for business. You may as well call them 'dot-com-and-go'. You can learn from their mistakes. (Actually, they could have learned from you.) In the same way that profit is the most essential single element in a business, a positive cash flow is important for your finances in general and for funding your share investment program in particular.

Don't confuse a cash flow statement with an income statement (also called a *profit and loss statement* or an *income and expense statement*). A cash flow statement is simple to calculate because you can easily track what goes in and what goes out.

With a cash flow statement (see Table 2-6), you ask yourself three questions:

- ✔ **What money is coming in?** In your cash flow statement, jot down all sources of income. Calculate it for the month and then for the year. Include everything, including salary, wages, interest, dividends, and so on. Add them all up and get a grand total for your income.

- ✔ **What are your outgoings?** Write down all the things that you spend money on. List all your expenses. If possible, categorise them into essential and non-essential. You can get an idea of all the expenses that you can reduce without affecting your lifestyle. But before you even try to do that, make the list of what you spend money on as complete.

- ✔ **What's left?** If your income is greater than your outgoings, and you have that emergency fund we talked about earlier in place, then you have money ready and available for investing in shares, no matter how small the amount. We've seen small fortunes built when people started to diligently invest as little as £25 to £50 a week or a month. If your outgoings are greater than your income, then you need to sharpen your pencil. Cut down on non-essential spending and/or increase your income. If your budget is a little tight, put your share investment plans on hold until your cash flow improves.

Step 1: Tallying up your income

Using Table 2-4 as a worksheet, list and calculate the money you have coming in. The first column describes the source of the money, the second column indicates the monthly amount from each respective source, and the last column indicates the amount projected for a full year. Include all income, such as wages, business income, dividends, interest income, and so on. Then project these amounts for a year (multiply by 12) and enter those amounts in the third column.

Table 2-4	Listing Your Income	
Item	*Monthly £ Amount*	*Yearly £ Amount*
Salary and wages		

(continued)

Table 2-4 *(continued)*		
Item	*Monthly £ Amount*	*Yearly £ Amount*
Interest income and dividends		
Business net (after tax) income		
Other income		
Total income		

This is the amount of money you have to work with. To ensure your financial health, don't spend more than this amount. Always be aware of and carefully manage your income.

Step 2: Adding up your outgoings

Using Table 2-5 as a worksheet, list and calculate the money that's going out. What are you spending and on what? The first column describes what the expense is, the second column indicates the monthly amount, and the third column shows that amount projected for a full year. Include all the money you spend, including credit card and other debt payments; household expenses, such as food, utility bills, and travel expenses; and money spent for non-essential expenses such as cigarettes (they're banned most places now anyway) and elephant-foot umbrella stands.

Table 2-5	Listing Your Expenses (Outgoings)	
Item	*Monthly £ Amount*	*Yearly £ Amount*
Tax		
Rent or mortgage		
Utilities		
Food		
Clothing		
Insurance (car, household, travel, and so on)		
Telephone and mobile		
Council tax		

Item	Monthly £ Amount	Yearly £ Amount
Car expenses		
Charity donations		
Hobbies		
Credit card payments		
Loan payments		
Other		
Total		

Tax is just a category in which to lump all the various taxes that you pay the government. If you are employed and pay your tax by PAYE you may not need to list much in this category. You should include all the tax you pay through the self-assessment process. If you are self-employed you will have a higher tax figure to include. . Feel free to put each individual tax on its own line if you prefer. The important thing is creating a comprehensive list that is meaningful to you. You may notice that the outgoings don't include items such as payments into pensions or ISAs or other savings vehicles. Yes, these items do impact your cash flow, but they're not expenses; the amounts that you invest (or your employer invests for you) are essentially assets that benefit your financial situation versus an expense that doesn't help you build wealth. If you pay into a company pension fund, that will probably be taken care of in the income table if you have included your *net salary* (what's left after tax and other deductions) .

Step 3: Creating a cash flow statement

Okay, you're almost to the end. The last step is creating a cash flow statement so that you can see (all in one place) how your money moves – how much comes in and how much goes out and where it goes.

Plug the amount of your total income (from Table 2-4) and the amount of your total expenses (from Table 2-5) into the Table 2-6 worksheet to see your *cash flow*. Do you have positive cash flow – more coming in than going out – so that you can start investing in shares (or other investments), or are expenses overpowering your income? Doing a cash flow statement isn't just about finding money in your financial situation to fund your shares plan. First and foremost, it's about your financial well-being. Are you managing your finances well or not?

Table 2-6	Looking at Your Cash Flow	
Item	*Monthly £ Amount*	*Yearly £ Amount*
Total income (from Table 2-4)		
Total outgoings (from Table 2-5)		
Net inflow/outflow		

2006 saw personal and business bankruptcies climb. For the bankrupts, their personal debt and expenses far exceeded any income they generated. That's another warning to watch your cash flow; keep your income growing and your expenses and debt as low as possible.

Step 4: Analysing your cash flow

Use your cash flow statement to identify sources of funds for your investment plan. The more you can increase your income and the more you can reduce your outgoings, the better. Scrutinise your data. Where can you improve the results? Here are some questions to ask yourself:

- How can you increase your income? Do you have hobbies, interests, or skills that can generate extra cash for you?
- Can you get more paid overtime at work? How about a promotion or a job change?
- Where can you cut expenses?
- Have you categorised your expenses as either 'necessary" or 'non-essential"?
- Can you lower your debt payments by switching your personal loans and credit card balances to low-cost or no cost credit?
- Have you shopped around for cheaper insurance or utility bills?
- Have you analysed how much tax you pay to ensure you are not over-paying?

Finding investment money in tax savings

Recent research has shown that the average worker in the UK pays more than half his earnings to the government in direct and indirect taxation. It is always a good idea to sit down with your accountant or financial adviser and try to find ways to reduce your tax. Running a business from home, for example, is a great way to gain new income and to write some expenses off against tax. This can result in a lower tax burden. Your accountant might have ideas that could work for you.

One tax strategy to consider is doing your investing in shares in a tax-sheltered account such as an Individual Savings Account (ISA). Again, check with your accountant or financial adviser about tax deductions and strategies that are available to you. For more on the tax implications of investing in shares, see Chapter 20.

Setting Your Sights on Your Financial Goals

Consider shares as tools for living, just like any other investment – no more, no less. They are the tools you use (one of many) to accomplish something – to achieve a goal. Yes, successfully investing in shares is the goal that you're probably aiming for if you're reading this book. However, you must complete the following sentence: 'I want to be successful in my share investing programme to accomplish . . .' You must consider investing in shares as a means to an end. When people buy a computer, they don't (or shouldn't) think of buying a computer just to have a computer. People buy a computer because doing so helps them achieve a particular result, such as being more efficient in business, playing fun games or spending hours on the internet.

Know the difference between long-term, medium-term, and short-term goals and then set some of each. Long term is a reference to projects or financial goals that need funding five or more years from now. Medium term refers to financial goals that need funding two to five years from now, while short-term goals need funding soon – less than two years from now.

In general, shares are best suited for long-term goals such as these:

- ✔ Achieving financial independence (think retirement funding)
- ✔ Paying for further education
- ✔ Paying for any long-term expenditure or project

Some categories of shares (such as conservative or blue-chip) may be suitable for medium-term financial goals. If, for example, you plan to retire four years from now, conservative shares are appropriate. If you're optimistic about the stock market and confident that share prices will rise, then go ahead and invest. However, if you're negative about the market (you're *bearish,* or you believe that share prices will decline), you may want to wait until the economy starts to forge a clear path. For more on investing in bull or bear markets, see Chapter 15.

Shares generally aren't suitable for short-term investing goals because share prices can behave irrationally in a short period of time. Shares fluctuate from day to day, so you don't know what they will be worth in the near future. You may end up with less money than you expected. For investors seeking to reliably accrue money for short-term needs, short-term savings bonds or certificates or guaranteed stock market bonds are more appropriate.

In recent years, investors have sought quick, short-term profits by trading and speculating in shares. Lured by the fantastic returns generated by the stock market in the late 1990s, investors saw shares as a get-rich-quick scheme. It is very important for you to understand the difference between *investing, saving,* and *speculating.* Which one do you want to do? Knowing the answer to this question is crucial to your goals and aspirations. Investors who don't know the difference tend to get burned. Here's some information to help you distinguish among these three actions:

- ✔ *Investing* **is the act of putting your current funds into securities or tangible assets for the purpose of gaining future appreciation, income, or both.** You need time, knowledge, and discipline to invest. The investment can fluctuate in price, but has been chosen for long-term potential.

- ✔ *Saving* **is the safe accumulation of funds for a future use.** Savings don't fluctuate and are generally free of financial risk. The emphasis is on safety and liquidity.

- ✔ *Speculating* **is the financial world's equivalent of gambling.** An investor who speculates is seeking quick profits gained from short-term price movements in that particular asset or investment.

These distinctly different concepts are often confused even among so-called financial experts. Paul knows of one financial adviser who actually put a child's university fund money into a technology fund only to lose more than £17,000 in less than ten months. This adviser thought that she was investing, but in reality, she was speculating. Isabelle knows of another investor who decided to avoid savings accounts altogether because he had a pension plan. He didn't understand the crucial difference between 'saving' and 'investing'. He eventually found out the difference; his pension was in Equitable Life – the life assurance company which had to make payout cuts because it couldn't fund its obligations – and he's now retiring on much less than he had hoped for.

Fortunately, we can learn from these situations and get back on track. That child that lost the £17,000? He is Paul's neighbour and Paul helped the father to reinvest the remaining funds. The portfolio doubled in value by the following year. It is still growing.

Chapter 3

Defining Common Approaches to Investing in Shares

In This Chapter

▶ Deciding the time frame that fits your investment strategy

▶ Looking at your reason for investing

▶ Determining your investing style

Read this chapter carefully. Millions of investors are at risk because the market sees as much mis-investing activity in shares as it does investing. We know it sounds weird, but the situation is similar to your mad Aunt Jean reversing into the garden wall when she should be heading out onto the road on her way to the shops – she knows she needs to do something, but she chooses the wrong mechanism. Shares are tools you can use to build your wealth. When used wisely, for the right purpose, and in the right environment, they do a great job. But when improperly applied, they can lead to disaster.

In this chapter, we show you how to choose the right investments, based on your short- and long-term financial goals. We also show you how to decide on your reason for investing (for growth or income) and the style of investing – cautious or aggressive – that you need to take.

Matching Shares and Strategies with Your Goals

Various shares are out there, as well as various investment approaches. The key to success in the stock market is matching the right kind of share with the right kind of investment situation. You have to choose the share and the approach that match your goals. (Refer to Chapter 2 for more on defining your financial goals.)

Before investing in a share, ask yourself, 'When do I want to reach my financial goal?' Shares are a means to an end. Your job is to figure out what that end is – or, more importantly, when that end is. Do you want to retire in ten years or next year? Must you pay for your child's university education next year or 18 years from now? The time you have before you need the money you hope to earn from investing determines what shares you should buy. Table 3-1 gives you a few guidelines for choosing the kind of shares best suited to your type of investor considering the goals that you have.

Table 3-1	Types of share, Financial Goals, and Types of Investor	
Type of Investor	*Time Frame for Financial Goals*	*Type of Stock Most Suitable*
Cautious (worries about risk)	Long term (over 5 years)	Blue chip and large-cap shares
Aggressive (high tolerance to risk)	Long term (over 5 years)	Small-cap and mid-cap shares
Cautious (worries about risk)	Medium term (2 to 5 years)	Blue chip and large-cap shares, preferably with dividends
Aggressive (high tolerance to risk)	Medium term (2 to 5 years)	Small-cap and mid-cap shares
Short term	1 to 2 years	Shares are not suitable for the short-term. Instead, look at tax efficient savings accounts such as ISAs and guaranteed investment bonds.

Dividends are payments made to an owner (unlike *interest,* which is payment to a creditor). Dividends are a great form of income, and companies that issue dividends tend to have more stable share prices as well. For more information on dividend-paying shares, see the section 'Investing for a Reason', later in this chapter, and in Chapter 9.

Table 3-1 gives you general guidelines, but keep in mind that not everyone can fit into a particular profile. Every investor has a unique situation, set of goals, and level of risk tolerance. Remember that the terms *large-cap, mid cap,* and *small-cap* refer to the size (or *market capitalisation,* also known as *market cap*) of the company. All factors being equal, large companies are safer (less risky) than small companies. For more on market caps, see the section 'Investing for Your Personal Style', later in this chapter.

Investing for the Future

Are your goals long term or short term? Answering this question is important because individual shares can be great or horrible choices, depending on the time period you want to focus on. Generally, the length of time you plan to invest in shares can be short term, medium term, or long term. The following sections outline what kinds of shares are most appropriate for each term length.

Investing in shares becomes less risky as the time frame lengthens. Share prices tend to fluctuate on a daily basis, but they have a tendency to follow an upward or downward trend over an extended period of time. Even if you invest in a share that goes down in the short term, you may see it rise and possibly go above your investment if you have the patience to wait it out and let the share price appreciate.

Focusing on the short term

Short term generally means one year or less, although some people extend the period to two years or less.

Every person has short-term goals. Some are modest, such as setting aside money for a holiday next month or paying for a new kitchen. Other short-term goals are more ambitious, such as building up a deposit for a new home within six months. Whatever the expense or purchase, you need a pre-dictable accumulation of cash soon. If your goals are essentially short-term, stay away from the stock market!

Because shares can be so unpredictable in the short term, they're a bad choice for short-term considerations. We get a kick out of market analysts on television saying things such as, 'At £10 a share, XYZ is a solid investment, and we feel that its share price should hit our target of £20 within six to nine months.' You know that an eager investor hears that and says, 'Wow, why bother with three per cent at the bank when this share will double? I better call my stockbroker. 'It may hit that target (or surpass it), or it may not. Most of the time, the share doesn't reach the target price, and the investor is dis-appointed. The share may just as easily go down. The reason that target prices are frequently (usually) missed is that the analyst is just one person and it's difficult or him or her to work out what millions of investors will do in the short-term. The short-term can be irrational because so many investors have so many reasons for buying and selling that analysis becomes difficult. If you want to use the money you invest for an important short-term need, you can't afford to lose any of it on the stock market during that time.

Short-term investing = speculating

If you look at a period of a single year, shares have a mixed-performance record compared with other investments, such as bonds or bank investments. In 1999, big-company shares grew an average of 25 per cent, and small-company shares averaged a blistering 50 to 70 per cent, but bank accounts and various bonds ranged only from 1.5 to 7 per cent. In the year 2000, the picture was different. Stock market investors lost their shirts, and cautious investors who put their money in bank and building society savings accounts and guaranteed bonds watched their money grow.

The bottom line is that investing in shares for the short term is nothing more than speculating. Your only possible strategy is luck.

Short-term share investment is highly unpredictable. You can better serve your short-term goals with stable, interest-bearing investments (like bank or building society savings accounts).

During the raging-bull market (see more about bull markets in Chapter 15) of the late 1990s, investors watched as high-profile shares went up 20 to 50 per cent in a matter of months. Who needs a savings account earning a measly interest rate when shares grow like that! Of course, when the bear market hit between 2000 and 2003 and those same shares fell 50 to 85 per cent, a savings account earning a measly interest rate suddenly didn't seem so bad.

Shares – even the best ones – fluctuate in the short term. In a negative environment, they can be volatile. No one can accurately predict the price movement (unless you have inside information), so shares are definitely inappropriate for any financial goal that you need to reach within one year. Check Table 3-1 for suggestions about your short-term strategies.

Considering medium-term goals

Medium-term refers to financial goals that you plan to reach within five years. If, for example, you want to accumulate cash as the deposit for an investment in property four years from now, growth-oriented investments may be suitable.

Although some shares *may* be appropriate for a two- or three-year period, not all shares are good medium-term investments. Different types and categories of shares exist. Some shares are fairly stable and hold their value well, such as shares in much larger or established dividend-paying companies. Other shares have prices that jump all over the place, such as the shares of untested companies that haven't been in existence long enough to develop a consistent track record.

If you plan to invest in the stock market to meet medium-term goals, consider large, established companies or dividend-paying companies in industries that provide life's essentials (such as food and drink or utilities).

Preparing for the long term

Investing in shares is best suited to making money over a long period of time. When you measure shares against other investments in terms of five to (preferably) ten or more years, they excel. Even investors who bought shares during the depths of the Great Depression saw profitable growth in their share portfolios over a ten-year period.

In fact, if you examine any ten-year period over the past 50 years, you see that shares win over other financial investments (such as bonds or bank investments) in almost every single ten-year period when measured by total return (taking into account reinvesting and compounding of capital gains and dividends). Chapters 8 and 9 cover growth and income, and Chapter 18 gives you the low-down on reinvestment and compounding. As you can see, long-term planning allows shares to shine. Of course, your work doesn't stop at deciding on a long-term investment. You still have to do your homework and choose shares wisely because, even in good times, you can lose money if you invest in companies that go out of business. Part III shows you how to evaluate specific companies and industries, and alerts you to factors in the general economy that can affect share price behaviour. Appendix A provides plenty of resources you can turn to.

Because you can choose between many different types and categories of shares, virtually any investor with a long-term perspective should add shares to his investment portfolio. Whether you want to save for a young child's university education or for future retirement goals, carefully selected shares have proven to be a superior long-term investment.

Investing for a Reason

When a woman was asked why she bungee-jumped off the bridge that spanned a massive ravine, she answered, 'Because it's fun!' When someone asked a man why he dived into a pool that was chock-full of alligators and snakes, he responded, 'Because someone pushed me'. Your investment in shares shouldn't happen unless you have a reason that you understand, like investing for growth or investing for income. Even if an adviser pushes you to invest, be sure that your adviser gives you an explanation of how his or her choice of share fits your purpose.

Paul knows of a nice, elderly lady who had a portfolio brimming with aggressive-growth shares because she had an overbearing stockbroker. Her purpose should've been cautious, and she should have chosen investments that would preserve her wealth rather than grow it. Obviously, the stockbroker's agenda got in the way. Shares are just a means to an end. Figure out your desired end and then match the means. To find out more about dealing with stockbrokers, go to Chapter 7.

Making loads of money quickly: Growth investing

When investors want their money to grow, they look for investments that appreciate in value. *Appreciate* is just another way of saying 'grow'. If you have a share that you bought for £8 a share and now its value is £30 a share, your investment has grown by £22 a share – that's appreciation. We know we would appreciate it.

Appreciation (also known as *capital gain*) is probably the number one reason why people invest in shares. Few investments have the potential to grow your wealth as conveniently as shares. If you want the stock market to make you loads of money relatively quickly (and you can assume an element of risk), head to Chapter 8, which takes an in-depth look at investing for growth.

Shares are a great way to grow your wealth, but they're not the only way. Many investors seek alternative ways to make money, but many of these alternative ways are more aggressive and carry significantly more risk. You may have heard about people who made quick fortunes in areas such as commodities (like gold, oil, or coffee), options, and other more sophisticated investment vehicles. Keep in mind that you should limit risky investments to only a portion of your portfolio, such as 10 per cent of your investible funds. Experienced investors, however, can go as high as 20 per cent. Chapter 8 goes into greater detail about growth investing.

Steadily making money: Income investing

Not all investors want to take on the risk that comes with making a killing. Some people just want to invest in the stock market as a means of providing a steady income. They don't need share values to go through the ceiling. Instead, they need shares that perform well consistently.

If your reason for investing in shares is to create income, you need to choose shares that pay dividends. Dividends are usually paid twice a year to shareholders listed on the company register.

Distinguishing between dividends and interest

Don't confuse dividends with interest. Most people are familiar with interest, because that's what's added to your money over the years in the bank. The important difference is that *interest* is paid to creditors, and *dividends* are paid to owners or shareholders (– if you own shares, you're a shareholder because your shares represent the parts of a publicly traded company that you own).

When you buy shares, you buy pieces of that company. When you put money in a bank (or when you buy bonds), you basically lend your money. You become a creditor, and the bank or bond issuer is the debtor, and as such, it must eventually pay your money back to you with interest.

Recognising the importance of an income share's yield

Investing for income means that you have to consider your investment's *yield,* the percentage return on your investment. If you want income from a stock market investment, you must compare the yield from one particular share with alternatives. Looking at the yield is a way to compare the income you expect to receive from one investment with the expected income from others. Table 3-2 shows comparative yields.

Table 3-2	Comparing the Yields of Various Investments				
Investment	*Type*	*Amount Invested*	*Pay Type*	*Payout*	*Yield*
Smith Co.	Stock	£50/share	Dividend	£2.50	5.0%
Jones Co.	Stock	£100/share	Dividend	£4.00	4.0%
Acme Bank	Bank account	£500	Interest	£25.00	5.0%
Acme Bank	Bank account	£2,500	Interest	£131.25	5.25%
Acme Bank	Bank account	£5,000	Interest	£287.50	5.75%
Brown Co.	Bond	£5,000	Interest	£300.00	6.0%

To understand how to calculate yield, you need the following formula:

Yield = Payout ÷ Investment Amount

Yield enables you to compare how much income you would get for a prospective investment compared with the income you would get from other investments. For the sake of simplicity, this exercise is based on an annual percentage yield basis (compounding would increase the yield).

Jones Co. and Smith Co. are both typical dividend-paying shares, and in the example presented by Table 3-2, presume that both companies are similar in most respects except for their differing dividends. How can you tell whether a £50 share with a £2.50 annual dividend is better (or worse) than a £100 share with a £4.00 dividend? The yield tells you.

Even though Jones Co. pays a higher dividend (£4.00), Smith Co. has a higher yield (5 per cent). Therefore, if you had to choose between those two shares as an income investor, you would choose Smith Co. Of course, if you truly want to maximise your income and don't really need your investment to appreciate a lot, you should probably choose Brown Co.'s bond because it offers a yield of 6 per cent.

A share that pays strong, regular dividends can also increase in value. They may not always have the same growth potential as growth shares, but, at the least, they have a greater potential for capital gain than a bank's savings accounts or bonds. Dividend-paying shares (investing for income) are covered in Chapter 9.

Investing in Your Personal Style

Your investing style has nothing to do with the jeans versus pinstripes debate. It refers to your approach to investing in shares. Do you want to be cautious or aggressive? Would you rather be the tortoise or the hare? Your investment personality greatly depends on your reason for investing and the term over which you're planning to invest (see the previous two sections in this chapter). The following sections outline the two most general investment styles.

Cautious investing

Cautious investing means that you put your money into something proven, tried, and true. You invest your money in safe and secure places, such as banks and government-backed securities. But how does that apply to shares? (Table 3-1 gives you suggestions.)

Cautious stock market investors want to place their money in companies that have exhibited the following qualities:

- ✔ **Proven performance:** You want companies that have shown increasing sales and earnings year after year. You don't demand anything spectacular, just a strong and steady performance.

- ✔ **Market size:** Companies should be large-cap (short for large capitalisation). Cautious investors believe that bigger is safer. Mostly they would focus on shares in the FTSE 100 (see Chapter 5 for more on the FTSE 100).

- ✔ **Market leadership:** Companies should be leaders in their industries.

- ✔ **Perceived staying power:** You want companies with the financial clout and market position to weather uncertain market and economic conditions. It shouldn't matter what happens in the economy or who gets elected.

As a cautious investor, you don't mind if the companies' share prices jump (who would?), but you're more concerned with steady growth over the long term. Shares in blue chip companies are your ideal.

Aggressive investing

Aggressive investors can plan long term or look only over the medium term, but in both cases, they want shares that are like young greyhounds – able to race ahead of the pack. Aggressive stock market investors want to invest their money in companies that have exhibited the following qualities:

- ✔ **Great potential:** The company must have superior goods, services, or smarter working practices than the competition, that suggest that it should grow quickly in future.

- ✔ **Capital gains possibility:** Dividends are not your first consideration. You may even dislike dividends. You feel that the money is better reinvested in the company. This reinvestment, in turn, can spur greater growth.

- ✔ **Innovation:** Companies should have technologies, ideas, or certain creative methods, that make them stand apart from other companies.

Aggressive investors usually seek out small capitalisation stocks, known as *small-caps,* because they have plenty of potential for growth. Take the tree example, for instance: A sturdy oak may be strong, but it may not grow much more, whereas a brand-new sapling has plenty of growth to look forward to. Why invest in stodgy, big companies when you can invest in smaller enterprises that may become the leaders of tomorrow? Aggressive investors have no problem investing in obscure companies because they hope that such companies may become another British Petroleum (BP) or Tesco. Find out more about investing for growth in Chapter 8.

Chapter 4

Assessing the Risks

*I*nvestors face many risks, many of which we cover in this chapter. The simplest definition of risk for investors is 'the possibility that your investment will lose some (or all) of its value'. Yet you don't have to fear risk if you understand and plan for it. You need to get familiar with the concept of risk. You must understand the oldest equation in the world of investing – risk versus return. This equation states the following:

> If you want a greater return on your money, you need to tolerate more risk. If you don't want to tolerate more risk, you must tolerate a lower rate of return.

This point about risk is best illustrated from a moment in one of Paul's investment seminars. One of the attendees told Paul that he had his money in the bank but was dissatisfied with the rate of return. He moaned, 'The yield on my money is pitiful! I want to put my money somewhere where it can grow.' Paul asked him, 'How about investing in common shares? Or what about growth unit trusts? They have a solid, long-term growth track record.' He responded, 'Shares? I don't want to put my money there. It's too risky!' Okay, then. If you don't want to tolerate more risk, then don't complain about earning less on your money. Risk (in all its forms) has a bearing on all your money concerns and goals. That's why it's so important that you understand risk before you invest.

We all need to remember that risk is not a four-letter word. Well, it is a four-letter word, but you know what we mean. Risk is present no matter what you do with your money. Even if you simply stick your money under the mattress, risk is involved – several kinds in fact. You have the risk of fire. What if your house burns down? You have the risk of theft. What if burglars find your stash of cash? You also have relative risk. (Your relatives may find your money!)

Be aware of the different kinds of risk, and you can easily plan around them to keep your money growing.

Exploring Different Kinds of Risk

Think about all the ways that an investment can lose money. You can list all sorts of possibilities. So many that you may think, 'Aaargh! Why invest at all?'

Don't let risk frighten you. After all, life itself is risky. Just make sure that you understand the different kinds of risk before you start navigating the investment world. Be mindful of risk and find out about the effects of risk on your investments and personal financial goals.

Financial risk

The financial risk of investing in shares is that you can lose your money if the company whose shares you buy loses money or goes belly up. This type of risk is the most obvious because companies do go bankrupt.

You can greatly enhance the chances of your financial risk paying off by doing an adequate amount of research and choosing your shares carefully (which this book helps you do – see Part III for more details). Financial risk is a real concern even when the economy is doing well. Diligent research, a little planning, and a dose of common sense help you reduce your financial risk.

In the share investing mania of the late 1990s, millions of investors (along with many well-known investment 'gurus') ignored obvious financial risks of many then-popular stocks. Investors blindly plunged their money into shares that were bad choices. Consider investors who put their money in DrKoop.com, a health information Web site, in 1999 and held on during 2000. DrKoop.com went into cardiac arrest as it collapsed from $45 a share to $2 a share by mid-2000. By the time the stock was dead on arrival, investors had lost millions.

Internet and technology shares littered the graveyard of stock market catastrophes during 2000/2001 because investors didn't see (or didn't want to see) the risks involved with companies that didn't offer a solid record of results (profits, sales, and so on). Remember that when you invest in companies without a proven track record, you're not investing, you're speculating.

Investors who did their homework regarding the financial conditions of companies such as Internet shares discovered that these companies had the hallmarks of financial risk – high debt, low (or no) earnings, and plenty of competition. They steered clear, avoiding tremendous financial loss. Investors who didn't do their homework were lured by the status of these companies – the poster children of booming Internet fortunes – and lost their shirts.

Of course, the individual investors who lost money by investing in these trendy, high-profile companies don't deserve all the responsibility for their tremendous financial losses; certain high-profile analysts and media sources also should have known better. The late 1990s may someday be a case study of how euphoria and the herd mentality (rather than good, old-fashioned research and common sense) ruled the day (temporarily). The excitement of making potential fortunes gets the best of people sometimes, and they throw caution to the wind. Historians may look back at those days and say, 'What *were* they thinking?' Achieving true wealth takes diligent work and careful analysis.

In terms of financial risk, the bottom line is . . . well . . . the bottom line! A healthy bottom line (an accounting term for the net profit a company makes) means that a company is making money. And if a company is making money, then you can make money by investing in its shares. However, if a company isn't making money, you're unlikely to make money if you invest in it (unless you can hang on until it does make money). Profit is the lifeblood of any company.

Interest rate risk

Interest rate risk may sound like an odd type of risk, but in fact, it's a common consideration for investors. Be aware that interest rates change on a regular basis, causing challenging moments. Banks set their own interest rates, but they generally follow the base rate set by The Bank of England's monetary policy committee. When the Bank of England raises or lowers interest rates, banks and building societies raise or lower interest rates on mortgages and savings accordingly. Interest rate changes affect consumers, businesses, and, of course, investors.

The scenario outlined in the following paragraphs gives you a generic introduction to the way fluctuating interest rate risk can affect investors in general.

Suppose that you buy a long-term, high-quality corporate bond and get a yield of 6 per cent. Your money is safe, and your return is locked in at 6 per cent. Great! That's a guaranteed 6 per cent. Not bad, eh? But what happens if, after you commit your money, interest rates increase to 8 per cent? You lose the opportunity to get that extra 2 per cent interest. The only way to get out of your 6 per cent bond is to sell it at current market values and use the money to reinvest at the higher rate.

The only problem with this scenario is that the 6 per cent bond is likely to drop in value because interest rates rose. Why? Say that the investor is Bob and the bond yielding 6 per cent is a corporate bond issued by Lucin-Muny (LM). According to the bond agreement, LM must pay 6 per cent (called the *face rate* or *nominal rate*) during the life of the bond and then, upon maturity, pay the principal. If Bob buys £10,000 of LM bonds on the day they are issued, he gets £600 (of interest) every year for as long as he holds the bonds. If he holds on until maturity, he gets back his £10,000 (the principal). So far so good? The plot thickens, however.

Say that he decides to sell the bond long before maturity and that, at the time of the sale, interest rates in the market have risen to 8 per cent. Now what? The reality is that no one is going to want his 6 per cent bond if the market is offering bonds at 8 per cent. What's Bob to do? He can't change the face rate of 6 per cent, and he can't change the fact that only £600 is paid each year for the life of the bond. What has to change so that current investors get the *equivalent* yield of 8 per cent? Of course, 'The bond's value has to go down'. In this example, the bond's market value needs to drop to £7,500 so that investors buying the bond get an equivalent yield of 8 per cent. (For simplicity sake, we have left out the time it takes for the bond to mature.) Here's how it works out:

New investors still get £600 annually. However, £600 is equal to 8 per cent of £7,500. Therefore, even though investors get the face rate of 6 per cent, they get a yield of 8 per cent because the actual investment amount is £7,500. In this example, no financial risk is present, but you see how interest rate risk presents itself. Bob finds out that you can have a good company with a good bond, yet you still lose £2,500 because of the change in the interest rate. Of course, if Bob doesn't sell, he doesn't realise that loss. (For more on when to sell, see Chapter 17.)

You can lose money in an apparently sound investment because of something that sounds as harmless as 'interest rates have changed.'

Understanding the adverse effects of rising interest rates

Rising and falling interest rates offer a special risk to stock market investors. Historically, rising interest rates have had an adverse effect on share prices. I outline several reasons why in the following sections.

Hurting a company's financial condition

Rising interest rates have a negative impact on companies that carry a large current debt load or that need to take on more debt because when interest rates rise, the cost of borrowing money rises, too. Ultimately, the company's profitability and ability to grow are reduced. When a company's profits (or earnings) drop, its shares becomes less desirable, and its share price falls.

Affecting a company's customers

A company's success comes when it sells its products or services. But what happens if increased interest rates negatively impact its customers (specifically, other companies that buy from it)? The financial health of its customers directly affects the company's ability to grow sales and earnings.

For a good example of this situation, consider what happened to Cisco Systems in 2000. Because a huge part of its sales went to the telecommunications industry, Cisco's profitability depended on the health of that entire industry. The telecom industry's debt ballooned to $700 billion. This debt became the telecom industry's financial Achilles heel, which, in turn, became a pain in the neck to Cisco. Because telecom companies bought less, Cisco's profits shrank. In late March <u>2000</u>, at the height of the dot-com boom, Cisco was the most valuable company in the world, with a <u>market capitalisation</u> of more than $500 billion. From March 2000 to March 2001, Cisco's share price fell by nearly 70 per cent. Cisco's share price continued to decline in late 2001 because the companies that were its customers were hurting financially. In <u>2006</u>, with a market cap of about $110 billion, Cisco is still one of the most valuable companies in the world but it hasn't recovered the – inflated value – it had at the peak of the dot-com boom.

Impacting investors' decision-making considerations

When interest rates rise, investors start to rethink their investment strategies, resulting in one of two outcomes:

- ✔ Investors may sell any shares in interest-sensitive industries that they hold. Interest-sensitive industries include utilities, property, and the financial sector. Although increased interest rates can hurt these sectors, the reverse is also generally true: Falling interest rates boost the same industries. Keep in mind that interest rate changes affect some industries more than others.

- ✔ Investors who favour increased current income (versus waiting for the investment to grow in value to sell for a gain later on) are definitely attracted to investment vehicles that offer a higher rate of return. Higher interest rates can cause investors to switch from shares to bonds or high-interest savings accounts.

Hurting share prices indirectly

High or rising interest rates can have a negative impact on any investor's total financial picture. What happens when an investor struggles with burdensome debt, such as a second mortgage or credit card debt? He or she may sell some shares in order to pay off part of the high-interest debt. Selling shares to service debt is a common practice that, when taken collectively, can hurt share prices.

Stock markets and economies around the world are currently facing one of the biggest challenges in their histories – debt. Debt in the UK is more than £1trillion and in the USA it tops Gross Domestic Product (GDP). On top of that, some of our most established financial institutions hold many trillions worth of *derivatives*. These are contracts whose worth is derived from the value of an underlying security, and can be complicated and sophisticated investment vehicles that can backfire. Derivatives have, in fact, sunk large organisations (such as Enron), and investors should be aware of them. Just check out the financial reports of any company you are interested in. (Go to Chapter 11 to find out more).

Because of the effects of interest rates on share portfolios, both direct and indirect, successful investors regularly monitor interest rates in both the general economy and in their personal situations. Although shares have proven to be a superior long-term investment (the longer the term, the better), every investor should maintain a balanced portfolio that includes other investment vehicles, such as gilts, savings bonds, and/or bank accounts.

A diversified investor has money in vehicles that do well when interest rates rise. These vehicles include savings accounts and certificates and other variable-rate investments whose interest rates rise when market rates rise. These types of investments add a measure of safety from interest rate risk to your stock portfolio.

Market risk

People talk about *the market* and how it goes up or down, making it sound like a monolithic entity instead of what it really is – a group of millions of individuals making daily decisions to buy or sell shares. No matter how modern our society and economic system, you can't escape the laws of supply and demand. When masses of people want to buy a particular share, it becomes in demand, and its price rises. That price rises higher if the supply is limited. Conversely, if no one's interested in buying a share, its price falls. Supply and demand is the nature of market risk. The price of the share you purchase can rise and fall on the fickle whim of market demand.

Millions of investors buying and selling each minute of every trading day affect the share price of your shares. This fact makes it impossible to judge which way your shares will move tomorrow or next week. This unpredictability and seeming irrationality is why shares aren't appropriate for short-term financial growth.

In April 2001, a US news programme reported that in 2000, a man with $80,000 in the bank decided to take his money and invest it in the stock market. Because he was getting married in 2001, he wanted his money to grow faster so that he could afford a nice wedding and a deposit for the couple's future home. What happened? His money shrank to $11,000, and he had to change his plans. Sometimes, 'market risk' begets 'romantic' risk.

Losing money is only part of the headache you face when your investments fall in this way; the idea of postponing a joyful event, such as a wedding or a home purchase, just adds to the pain. The gent in the preceding story could have easily minimised his losses – and the grief from his other half – with a little knowledge and discipline.

Markets are volatile by nature; they go up and down, and investments need time to grow. This poor chap (literally, now) should have been aware of the fact that shares in general aren't suitable for short-term (one year or less) goals (see Chapter 2 for more on short-term goals). Despite the fact that the companies he invested in may have been fundamentally sound, all share prices are subject to the gyrations of the marketplace and need time to trend upward.

Investing requires diligent work and research before putting your money in quality investments with a long-term perspective. Speculating is attempting to make a relatively quick profit by monitoring the short-term price movements of a particular investment. Investors seek to minimise risk, whereas speculators don't mind risk because it can also magnify profits. Speculating and investing have clear differences, but investors frequently become speculators and ultimately put themselves and their wealth at risk. Don't be one of them.

Consider the married couple nearing retirement who decided to play with their money to see about making their pending retirement more comfortable. They borrowed a sizable sum by tapping into the equity in their home to invest in the stock market. What did they do with these funds? You guessed it; they invested in the high-flying shares of the day – technology and Internet stocks. Within eight months, they lost almost all their money.

Understanding market risk is especially important for people who are tempted to put their nest eggs or emergency funds into volatile investments such as growth shares (or unit trusts that invest in growth shares or similar aggressive investment vehicles). Remember, you can lose everything.

Inflation risk

Inflation is the artificial expansion of the quantity of money so that too much money is used in exchange for goods and services. To consumers, inflation shows up in the form of higher prices for goods and services. Inflation risk is also referred to as *purchasing power risk*. This term just means that your money doesn't buy as much as it used to. For example, 50p that bought you a sandwich in 1980 barely bought you a Twix a few years later. For you, the investor, this risk means that the value of your investment (a bond, for example) may not keep up with inflation.

Say that you have money in a savings account currently earning 4 per cent. This account has flexibility – if the market interest rate goes up, the rate you earn in your account goes up. Your account is safe from both financial risk and interest rate risk. But what if inflation is running at 5 per cent? At that point you're losing money.

Tax risk

Tax (such as income tax or capital gains tax) doesn't affect your stock market investment directly. Tax can obviously affect how much of your money you get to keep. Because the entire point of investing in shares is to build wealth, you need to understand that taxes take away a portion of the wealth that you're trying to build. Taxes can be risky because if you make the wrong move with your shares (selling them at the wrong time, for example), you can end up paying higher tax than you need to. Because tax laws change so frequently, tax risk is part of the risk-versus-return equation, as well.

It pays to mug up on how tax can impact your wealth-building program before you make your investment decisions. Chapter 20 covers in greater detail the impact of tax.

Political and governmental risks

If companies were fish, politics and government policies (such as tax, laws, and regulations) would be the pond. In the same way that fish die in a toxic or polluted pond, politics and government policies can kill companies. Of course, if you own shares in a company exposed to political and governmental risks, you need to be aware of these risks. For some companies, a single new regulation or law is enough to send them into bankruptcy. For other companies, a new law may help them increase sales and profits.

What if you invest in companies or industries that become political targets? You may want to consider selling them (you can always buy them back later) or consider putting stop-loss orders on the stock (see Chapter 17). For example, tobacco companies were the targets of political firestorms that battered their share prices. Whether you agree or disagree with the political machinations of the day is not the issue. As an investor, you have to ask yourself, 'How do politics affect the market value and the current and future prospects of my chosen investment?' (See Chapter 14 for more on how politics can affect the stock market.)

Personal risks

Frequently, the risk involved with investing in the stock market may not be directly involved with the investment or factors directly related to the investment; sometimes the risk is with the investor's circumstances.

Suppose that investor Ralph puts £15,000 into a portfolio of common shares. Imagine that the market experiences a drop in prices that week and Ralph's shares drop to a market value of £14,000.

Because shares are good for the long term, this type of decrease is usually not an alarming incident. Odds are that this dip is temporary, especially if Ralph carefully chose high-quality companies. Incidentally, if a portfolio of high-quality shares _does_ experience a temporary drop in price, it can be a great opportunity to get more shares at a good price. (Chapter 17 covers orders you can place with your broker to help you do that.)

Over the long term, Ralph would probably see the value of his investment grow substantially. But, what if during a period when his shares are declining, Ralph experiences financial difficulty and needs quick cash? He may have to sell his shares to get money.

This problem occurs frequently for investors who don't have an emergency fund or a rainy day fund to handle large, sudden expenses. You never know when your company may lay you off or when your roof may leak, leaving you with a huge repair bill. Car accidents, household emergencies, and other unforeseen events are part of life's bag of surprises – for anyone. Be sure to set money aside for sudden expenses before you buy shares. Then you aren't forced to prematurely liquidate your stock market investments to pay emergency bills (Chapter 2 provides more guidance on having liquid assets for emergencies).

You probably won't get much comfort from knowing that losses from shares are tax deductible – a loss is a loss (see Chapter 20 regarding tax). However, you can avoid the kind of loss that results from prematurely having to sell your shares if you maintain an emergency cash fund. A good place for your emergency cash fund is in an instant access ISA or other savings account.

Emotional risk

What does emotional risk have to do with shares? Emotions are important risk considerations because the main decision makers are human beings. Logic and discipline are critical factors in investment success, but even the best investor can let emotions take over the reins of money management and cause loss. For stock market investing, you're likely to be sidetracked by three main emotions: greed, fear, and love. You need to understand your emotions and what kinds of risk they can expose you to. If you get too attached to a sinking share, then you don't need a book on investing in shares, you need a doctor.

Paying the price for greed

In the 1998/2000 period, millions of investors threw caution to the wind and chased highly dubious, risky dot-com shares. The pound signs popped up in their eyes (just like slot machines) when they saw that easy street was lined with dot-com shares that were doubling and tripling in a short time. Who cares about price/earnings (P/E) ratios and earnings when you can just buy shares, make a fortune, and get out with millions? (Of course, *you* care about making money with shares, so you can flip to Chapter 10 and Appendix B to find out more about P/E ratios.)

Unfortunately, the lure of easy money can easily turn healthy attitudes about growing wealth into unhealthy greed that blinds investors and discards common sense (such as investing for quick short-term gains in dubious 'hot tips', rather than doing your homework and buying shares of solid companies with strong fundamentals and a long-term focus).

Recognising the role of fear

Greed can be a problem, but fear is the other extreme. People who are fearful of loss frequently avoid suitable investments and end up settling for a low rate of return. If you have to succumb to one of these emotions, at least fear exposes you to less loss.

Investment lessons from September 11

11 September 2001, was a horrific day that is burned in our minds and won't be forgotten in our lifetime. The acts of terrorism that day took more than 3,000 lives and caused untold pain and grief. A much less important after-effect was the hard facts on investments that investors found out that day. Terrorism reminds us that risk is more real than ever and that we should never let our guard down. What can investors glean from these terrible acts? Here are a few pointers:

✔ **Diversify your portfolio.** Of course, the events of September 11 were certainly surreal and unexpected. But before the events occurred, investors should have made it a habit to assess their situations and see whether they had any vulnerabilities. Investors in shares with no money outside the stock market are always more at risk. Keeping your portfolio diversified is a time-tested strategy that is more relevant than ever before.

✔ **Review and re-allocate.** September 11 triggered declines in the overall market, but specific industries, such as airlines and hotels, were hit particularly hard. In addition, some industries, such as defense and food, saw share prices rise. Monitor your portfolio and ask yourself whether it is overly reliant on or exposed to events in specific sectors. If so, reallocate your investments to decrease your risk exposure.

✔ **Check for signs of trouble.** Techniques such as trailing stops (which I explain in Chapter 17) come in handy when your shares plummet because of unexpected events. Even if you don't use these techniques, you can make it a regular habit to analyse your shares and check for signs of trouble, such as debts or P/E ratios that are too high. If you see signs of trouble (check out Chapter 21), consider selling anyway

Looking for love in all the wrong places

Shares are dispassionate, inanimate vehicles, but people can look for love in the strangest places. Emotional risk occurs when investors fall in love with a share and refuse to sell it even when the share is plummeting and shows all the symptoms of getting worse. Emotional risk also occurs when investors are drawn to bad investment choices just because they sound good, are popular, or are pushed by family or friends. Love and attachment are great in relationships with people, but can be horrible with investments.

Minimising Your Risk

Now, before you go mad thinking that investing in shares carries so much risk that you may as well not get out of bed, take a breath. Minimising your risk is easier than you think. Although wealth building through the stock market doesn't take place without some amount of risk, you can practice the following tips to maximise your profits and still keep your money secure.

Gaining knowledge

Some people spend more time analysing a restaurant menu to choose a £10 main course than analysing where to put their next £5,000. Lack of knowledge constitutes the greatest risk for new investors, but diminishing that risk starts with gaining knowledge. The more familiar you are with the stock market – how it works, factors that affect share value, and so on – the better you can navigate around its pitfalls and maximise your profits. The same knowledge that enables you to grow your wealth also enables you to minimise your risk. Before you put your money anywhere, you want to know as much as you can. This book is a great place to start – check out Chapter 6 for a rundown of the kinds of information you want to know before you buy shares, as well as the resources that can give you the information you need to invest successfully.

Staying out . . . for now

If you don't understand shares, don't invest. we know this book is about investing in shares, and we think that most people do well to own some shares. But that doesn't mean you should be 100 per cent invested 100 per cent of the time. If you don't understand a particular share (or don't understand shares, full stop), stay away until you do understand. Instead, give yourself an imaginary sum of money, such as £100,000, give yourself reasons to invest, and just pretend. Pick a few shares that you think may increase in value and then track them for a while and see how they perform. Begin to understand how the price of a share goes up and down, and watch what happens to the shares you chose when various events take place. As you find out more about investing in shares, you get better at picking individual shares, and you haven't risked – or lost – any money during your apprenticeship period. You can look at a number of Web sites where you can do your 'imaginary' investing, including www.share.co.uk or www.fool.co.uk. You can design your own shares portfolio and see how well you do.

Getting your financial house in order

We could write a whole book on advice on what to do before you invest. The bottom line is that you want to make sure that you are, first and foremost, financially secure before you take the plunge into the stock market. If you're not sure about your financial security, look over your situation with a financial adviser. (You can find more on financial advisers in Appendix A.)

Before you buy your first share, here are a few things you can do to get your finances in order:

✔ **Have a cushion of money.** Set aside three to six months' worth of your gross living expenses somewhere safe, such as in an instant access savings account, in case you suddenly need cash for an emergency.

✔ **Reduce your debt.** Overindulging in debt is a major problem for many people in the UK with bankruptcy and home repossessions rising. Be sure that you can cope with any debts you have.

✔ **Make sure that your job is as secure as you can make it.** Are you keeping your skills up to date? Is the company you work for strong and growing? Is the industry that you work in strong and growing?

✔ **Make sure that you have adequate insurance.** You need enough insurance to cover you and your family's needs in case of illness, death, disability, and so on.

Diversifying your investments

Diversification is a strategy for reducing risk by spreading your money across different investments. It's a fancy way of saying, 'Don't put all your eggs in one basket.' But how do you go about divvying up your money and distributing it among different investments? The easiest way to understand proper diversification may be to look at what you should *not* do:

✔ **Don't put all your money in just one share.** Sure, if you choose wisely and select a hot stock, you may make a bundle, but the odds are hugely against you. Unless you're a real expert on a particular company, it's a good idea to have small portions of your money in several different shares. As a general rule, any money you tie up in a single share should be money you can do without.

✔ **Don't put all your money in one industry.** I know people who own several shares, but the shares are all in the same industry. Again, if you're an expert in that particular industry, it may work out. But just understand that you're not properly diversified. If a problem hits an entire industry, you may get hurt.

✔ **Don't put all your money in just one type of investment.** Shares may be a great investment, but you need to have money elsewhere. Bonds, bank accounts, gilts, property, and precious metals are perennial alternatives to complement your shares portfolio. Some of these alternatives can be found in unit trusts or exchange traded funds (ETFs).

Okay, now that you know what you *shouldn't* do, what *should* you do? Until you become more knowledgeable, follow this advice:

✔ **Only keep 20 per cent (or less) of your investment money in a single share.**

✔ **Invest in four or five different shares that are in different industries.** Which industries? Choose industries that offer products and services that have shown strong, growing demand. To make this decision, use your common sense (which isn't as common as it used to be). Think about the industries that people need no matter what happens in the general economy, such as food, energy, and other consumer necessities. See Chapter 12 for more information about analysing industries.

Weighing Risk Against Return

How much risk is appropriate for you, and how do you handle it? Before you try to figure out what risks accompany your investment choices, analyse yourself. Here are some points to keep in mind when weighing risk versus return in your situation:

✔ **Your financial goal:** In five minutes with a financial calculator, you can easily see how much money you're going to need to become financially independent (presuming that financial independence is your goal). Say that you need £500,000 in ten years for a worry-free retirement and that your financial assets (such as shares, bonds, and so on) are currently worth £400,000. In this scenario, your assets need to grow by only 2.25 per cent a year to hit your target. Getting investments that grow by 2.25 per cent safely is easy to do because that is a relatively low rate of return.

The important point is that in this case you don't have to knock yourself out trying to double your money with risky, high-flying investments; some run-of-the-mill savings accounts will do just fine. All too often, investors take on more risk than is necessary. Figure out what your financial goal is so that you know what kind of return you realistically need.

✔ **Your investor profile:** Are you nearing retirement, or have you just left university? Your life situation matters when it comes to looking at risk versus return. If you're just beginning your working years, you can certainly tolerate greater risk than someone facing retirement. Even if you lose big time, you still have a long time to recoup your money and get back on track. However, if you're approaching retirement, risky or aggressive investments can do much more harm than good. If you lose money, you don't have as much time to recoup your investment, and the odds are that you need the investment money (and its income-generating capacity) to cover your living expenses after you are no longer employed.

✔ **Asset allocation:** We never tell retirees to put a large portion of their retirement money into a technology share or other volatile investment. But if they still want to speculate, we don't see a problem as long as they limit such investments to 5 per cent of their total assets. As long as the bulk of their money is safe and sound in secure investments (such as gilts or savings certificates), we know we can sleep well (knowing that *they* can sleep well!).

Asset allocation beckons back to diversification. For people in their 20s and 30s, having 75 per cent of their money in a diversified portfolio of growth shares (such as mid-cap and small-cap companies) is acceptable. For people in their 60s and 70s, it's not acceptable. They may, instead, consider investing no more than 20 per cent of their money in shares (mid-caps and large-caps are preferable). Check with your financial adviser to find the right mix for your particular situation.

Chapter 5

Getting to Know the Stock Markets

. . . .

In This Chapter

▶ Defining index basics

▶ Looking at the Footsie and other indices

▶ Exploring the indices for practical use

. . . .

'**H**ow's the market doing today?' is the most common question that interested parties ask about the stock market. This is followed by, 'What did the Footsie do?' and 'How about the Dow?'. Invariably, people asking these questions want to know whether the market has risen or fallen that day. 'Well, the Footsie fell 5.3 points to 6198.6, while the Dow Jones rose 30.05 to close at a record high of 12,471.32' may be the answer nowadays. When we refer to these numbers, we are taking about *indices*, general guides to the performance of stock markets. They give you a basic idea of how well (or how badly) the overall market is doing. In this chapter, we focus our attention on these stock market indices.

Knowing How Indices Are Measured

An *index* is a statistical measure that represents the value of a batch of shares. Investors use this measure as a barometer of the overall progress of the market (or a segment of the market).

The oldest stock market index is the Dow Jones Industrial Average (DJIA or simply 'The Dow'). It was created in 1896 by Charles Henry Dow, one of the founders of Dow Jones, publisher of the Wall Street Journal, and originally covered only 12 stocks. The number of stocks covered increased to 30 in 1928, and remains the same today. Dow worked long before the age of computers, so he kept the calculation of his stock market index simple – he worked it out on a piece of paper. Dow added up the stock prices of the 12 companies and then divided the total by 12. Technically, this number is an *average* and not really an index (hence the word 'average' in the name). But for simplicity sake, we'll refer to it as an index. Today, the number gets tweaked to account for changes such as stock splits. (For more on stock splits see Chapter 19.) In the UK, the most important index is the *Footsie* or *FTSE 100*, (the Financial Times Stock Exchange 100 Index to give it its proper name), but we'll find out more about it later in this chapter.

However, you need to know that indices get calculated differently. The primary difference between an 'index' and an 'average' is the concept of *weighting*. Weighting is the relative importance of the items when they are computed within the index. Several kinds of indices exist, including:

- **Price-weighted index:** This kind of index tracks changes based on the change in the price per share.

  To give you an example, suppose that you own two shares: Share A worth £20 a share and Share B worth £40 a share. A price-weighted index allocates a greater proportion of the index to the share at £40 than to the one at £20. Therefore, if we had only these two shares in an index, the index number would reflect the £40 share as being 67 per cent (two-thirds of the number), while the £20 stock would be 33 per cent (one-third of the number).

- **Market-value weighted index:** This kind of index tracks the proportion of a share based on its market capitalisation (or market value, also called market cap). Refer back to Chapter 2 for more on market cap.

  Say that in your *portfolio* (the collection of all the different shares you own), you have 10 million £20 shares (in Company A) and one million £40 shares (in Company B). Company A's market cap is £200 million, while Company B's market cap is £40 million. Therefore, in a market-value weighted index, Company A shares represent £200 million of a total £240 million in the portfolio – 83 per cent of the index's value – because of its much larger market cap.

- **Broad-based index:** The sample portfolios in the preceding bullets show only two companies' shares – obviously not a good representative index. Most investing professionals (especially money managers and unit trusts) use a broad-based index as a benchmark against which to compare their progress. A broad-based index provides a 'snapshot' of the entire market, such as Standard & Poor's 500 (S&P 500). (See descriptions of this index under 'Further afield: international indices' later in this chapter.)

- **Composite index:** This is an index or average that is a combination of several averages or indices. An example is the FTSE All-Share.

Using the Indices

You may be wondering what to do with all the indices out there and which one or ones you should be checking out. The following sections give you an idea of how to put all the pieces together.

Tracking the indices

Investors get an instant snapshot of how well the market is doing from indices. Indices offer a quick way to compare the performance of one investor's share portfolio or unit trusts with the rest of the market. If the Footsie goes up 10 per cent in a year and your portfolio shows a cumulative gain of 12 per cent, then you know that you're doing well. Appendix A in the back of this book lists resources to help you keep up with various indices.

The problem with indices is that they can be misleading if you take them too literally as an accurate barometer of company success. The Dow, for example, has changed its list of companies many times since 1896. Had it not, the Dow's general upward trajectory in the past few decades would have been very different. Flagging companies have been dropped and replaced with others that have shown more promise. Many of the original companies in the DJIA in 1896 did go out of business, or other companies, that aren't reflected in the index, bought them out.

Investing in indices

Can you invest directly in indices? If the market is doing well but your shares are not, can you find a way to invest in the index itself? With investments based on indices, you can invest in the market in general or a particular industry.

Say that you want to invest in the Footsie. After all, why try to 'beat the market' if just matching it is sufficient to boost your wealth? Why not have a portfolio that directly mirrors the Footsie? Well, it's too impractical and expensive to invest in all 100 companies that are in the Footsie. Fortunately, you have other ways to accomplish 'investing in indices'.

Here are the best ways:

- ✔ **Tracker funds:** A tracker fund is a fund that only invests in securities (in this case, shares) that match as closely as possible the basket of shares that are in a particular index – usually the Footsie or the FTSE All-Share.

These funds can be purchased as tax-efficient Individual Savings Accounts. Financial advisers or stockbrokers can tell you more about trackers. Or you can read about them on financial websites such as www.fool.co.uk or www.ici.org.

✔ **Exchange Traded Funds (ETFs):** ETFs are also called *Contracts For Difference* (CFD) and are one of the secrets of stock market investing. An ETF can reflect a basket of shares that mirror a particular index – much like a tracker – but the ETF can be traded like a share itself. You can transact ETFs like shares in that you can buy them, sell them, or speculate that they will fall in value. You can put stop loss orders on them to sell them when they fall by a certain amount. ETFs can give you the diversification of trackers coupled with the versatility of shares. You can buy ETFs that track indices including the Footsie, the Dow, and Nasdaq. You can find out more about ETFs from a stockbroker or financial adviser.

Checking Out Major Markets

Although most people consider the Footsie, the Dow, and Nasdaq to be the stars of the financial press, you may find other indices useful to follow because they cover other significant facets of the market, such as small-cap and mid-cap stocks.

You can check out other less-sexy indices that cover specific sectors and industries. If you're investing in a telecoms or media stock, you should also check the FTSE TMT Index to compare what your stock is doing when measured against the index. You can find indices that cover industries such as transportation, retailers, computer companies, and even football clubs. These indices are mostly run by FTSE International and information on them can be found at www.ftse.com. You can find indices to consult for almost every market in the world, so if you are considering investing in a wide portfolio of shares from different countries these indices are useful. Beginners may find it easier to stick to their home markets initially.

The FTSE 100 Index

The most famous stock market barometer in the UK is the FTSE 100 Index, more commonly known as the Footsie. Its name stands for Financial Times Stock Exchange and the Footsie is one of many indices run by the Financial Times Group, publishers of the respected newspaper. When someone asks how the market is doing, most investors in the UK quote the 'Footsie'. The FTSE tracks the top 100 companies in the UK and is updated every three months. Started in January 1984 with an initial value of 1,000, the index covers the 100 largest companies traded on the London Stock Exchange (based on market capitalisation). These stocks represent about 80 per cent of the value of all trading on the exchange. Because the index is weighted by market cap, its largest component stocks have the greatest influence on the FTSE's value. The index is quite unusual in that it re-weights its component stocks daily to represent the actual state of the market. And every three months the index is fully rebalanced when companies are demoted or promoted based on their market caps.

People refer to companies in the Footsie as *blue chips*. The following list gives the current list of companies tracked and their stock exchange codes.

The Footsie has grown in popularity as a gauge of stock market activity since it was founded in 1984. Although it's an important indicator of the market's progress, it has one drawback: it tracks only 100 companies. Regardless of their prominent status in the market, the companies represented are only a sample. This means that if the biggest companies in the index – the most valuable – hit a bad patch, they can have a big impact on the index. Turmoil among banking shares during a credit crisis in September 2007 drove the Footsie lower even though only a handful of shares were directly affected.

3i (III)

Alliance & Leicester (AL)

Alliance Boots (AB)

AMVESCAP (AVZ)

Anglo American (AA)L

Antofagasta (ANTO)

Associated British Foods (ABF)

AstraZeneca (AZN)

Aviva (AV)

BAE Systems (BA)

Barclays Bank (BARC)

BG Group (BG)

BHP Billiton (BLT)

BP (BP)

Bradford & Bingley (BB)

Brambles Industries (BI)

British Airways (BAY)

British American Tobacco (BATS)

British Land Company (BLND)

British Sky Broadcasting Group (BSY)

BT Group (BT.A)

Cadbury Schweppes (CBRY)

Cairn Energy (CNE)

Capita Group (CPI)

Carnival (CCL)

Centrica (CNA)

Compass Group (CPG)

Corus Group (CS)

Diageo (DGE)

Drax Group (DRX)

DSG International (DSGI)

Enterprise Inns (ETI)

Experian (EXPN)

Friends Provident (FP)

Gallaher Group (GLH)

GlaxoSmithKline (GSK)

Hammerson (HMSO)

Hanson (HNS)

HBOS (HBOS)

Home Retail Group (HOME)

HSBC Bank(HSBA)

ICAP (IAP)

ICI (ICI)

Imperial Tobacco (IMT)

InterContinental Hotels Group (IHG)

International Power (IPR)

ITV (ITV)

J Sainsbury (SBRY)

Johnson Matthey (JMAT)

Kazakhmys (KAZ)

Kelda Group (KEL)

Kingfisher (KGF)

Land Securities Group (LAND)

Legal & General (LGEN)

Liberty International (LII)

Lloyds TSB (LLOY)

Lonmin (LMI)

Man Group (EMG)

Marks and Spencer (MKS)

Wm Morrison Supermarkets (MRW)

National Grid (NG)

Next (NXT)

Northern Rock (NRK)

Old Mutual (OML)

Pearson (PSON)

Persimmon (PSN)

Prudential (PRU)

Reckitt Benckiser (RB)

Reed Elsevier (REL)

Resolution (RSL)

Reuters Group (RTR)

Rexam (REX)

Rio Tinto Group (RIO)

Rolls-Royce Group (RR)

Royal & Sun Alliance Insurance (RSA)

Royal Bank of Scotland Group (RBS)

Royal Dutch Shell (RDSA/RDSB)

SABMiller (SAB)

Sage Group (SGE)

Scottish & Newcastle (SCTN)

Scottish & Southern Energy (SSE)

Scottish Power (SPW)

Severn Trent (SVT)

Shire Pharmaceuticals Group (SHP)

Slough Estates (SLOU)

Smith & Nephew (SN)

Smiths Group (SMIN)

Standard Chartered Bank (STAN)

Standard Life (SL)

Tate & Lyle (TATE)

Tesco (TSCO)

Unilever (ULVR)

United Utilities (UU)

Vedanta Resources (VED)

Vodafone (VOD)

Whitbread (WTB)

Wolseley (WOS)

WPP Group (WPP)

Xstrata (XTA)

Yell Group (YELL)

Serious investors look at the following indices:

- ✔ **Broad-based indices:** Indices such as the S&P 500 are more realistic gauges of the stock market's performance than the Footsie or the Dow.

- ✔ **Industry or sector indices:** These indices are better gauges of the growth (or lack of growth) of specific industries and sectors. If you buy shares in smaller companies listed on the Alternative Investment Market (AIM), then you should track the indices for AIM.

FTSE International has several indices, including the FTSE4Good which measures socially responsible company share performance, and the FTSE All-World Index covering companies whose capitalisation represents 90–95 per cent of the world's investible market capitalisation.

FTSE 100 milestones

The forerunner to the FTSE 100 was the FTSE 30 which was set up in 1935. The FTSE 30 is the oldest index in the UK but now largely redundant. Only three of its original constituents are still in the Footsie – Imperial Chemical (now called ICI), Imperial Tobacco, and Rolls Royce.

This table shows when the FTSE 100, which was started with a 1,000 point value, reached each of its milestones and how long it took to reach that point:

Milestone	Date	How long it took
1,000	Jan 3, 1984	starting point
2,000	Mar 4, 1987	three years two months
3,000	Aug 11, 1993	six years five months
4,000	Oct 2, 1996	three years one month
5,000	Aug 6, 1997	10 months
6,000	Apr 1, 1998	eight months

As you can see, the Footsie took more than three years to hit its first major milestone of 2,000. But as later milestones came along, it took less time to hit the next one, due to the fact that the higher the Footsie is in a relative sense, the easier it is to jump 1,000 points. For example, it went from 5,000 to 6,000 in only a matter of months.

The Footsie moved up and down a lot between these milestones, its progress is not always upwards. The Big Bang in 1986, when fixed commissions for stockbrokers ended, was a massive boost to share investment and the 1999 bull market also had a marked impact. But the Footsie has stalled plenty of times along the way and on occasions smaller investors have stayed away for fear of losing their capital. The Footsie reached its record high of 6,930.2 on December 30, 1999.

The FTSE 250

The FTSE 250 Index is a capitalisation-weighted index of 250 companies on the London Stock Exchange. While you may expect it to be made up of the top 250 companies, this would be a mistake. The companies are selected quarterly as being the 101st to 350th largest companies with a primary listing on the exchange. Companies that rise and fall in value can be promoted to, or demoted from, the index. Changes, when required, take place quarterly in March, June, September, and December. A number of the companies in this index are investment trusts.

The FTSE All-Share

The FTSE All-Share Index is another capitalisation-weighted (or *market value weighted*) index, comprised of companies traded on the London Stock Exchange. It covers around 700 companies and aims to represent at least 98 per cent of the capital value of UK companies.

FTSE All-Share is the aggregation of the FTSE 100 Index, FTSE 250 Index and FTSE SmallCap Index which covers smaller companies.

Even though the index covers several hundred companies, more than 80 per cent of the index by value is made up of the largest 100 companies. Medium cap companies make up around 13 per cent of the value, and smaller companies only four per cent. The power of the big companies has become increasingly concentrated in recent years. The top 10 UK companies accounted for just 23 per cent of the FTSE All-Share 10 years ago, now they account for more than 40 per cent. When the oil company Shell decided to have its full listing in the UK, rather than splitting it between London and Amsterdam, the company more than doubled its weighting in the All-Share to around 8 per cent – making it second only in size to its rival BP. FTSE International responded to this trend by launching a new series of indices, capping company weightings at 5 per cent.

Although it's a reliable indicator of the market's overall status, the FTSE All-Share also has limitations. Despite the fact that it tracks 700 companies, the top 10 companies encompass more than 40 per cent of the index's market value. This situation can be a drawback because those 10 companies have a greater influence on the All-Share's price movement than other groups of companies. The All-Share also has a heavy concentration on a limited number of sectors. Almost half of the index is focused on five sectors – oil, banks, pharmaceuticals, mining, and telecoms – even though 30 industrial sectors are represented.

Markets for Smaller Companies

Although most new investors in the UK cut their teeth on shares listed on the London Stock Exchange, there are other markets to consider. These markets allow smaller companies to trade their shares and can offer investors rich opportunities to profit from growing young firms.

The Alternative Investment Market

The Alternative Investment Market (AIM), is a market regulated by the London Stock Exchange but with less demanding rules than the main market.

No capitalisation requirements exist, and companies don't need to issue a certain number of shares. When it was launched in 1995, The aim of the AIM was to offer an easy route to market for smaller companies, but it has also attracted larger companies looking for an easier regulatory ride.

Launched in 1995, AIM has raised almost £24 billion for more than 2,200 companies. Some companies that started out on AIM have since moved on to a full LSE listing but in the last few years, significantly more companies transferred from a full listing to AIM. In 2005, 40 companies moved directly from the main market to AIM, while only two moved from AIM to the main market.

AIM has also started to become an international exchange, often due to its low-regulatory burden, especially in relation to the Sarbanes-Oxley Act – which imposes regulatory costs on companies listed in the United States. Nearly 300 foreign companies have been admitted to AIM.

The FTSE Group has three indices for measuring AIM:

- The FTSE AIM UK 50 Index
- The FTSE AIM 100 Index
- The FTSE AIM All-Share Index

Significant tax advantages exist for investors who back AIM shares. The London Stock Exchange (`www.londonstockexchange.com`) produces two guides to the tax advantages of AIM.

The PLUS Markets Group

The PLUS Markets Group (previously known as Ofex) specialises in small companies, but also houses household names such as Arsenal Football Club. It currently trades more than 850 small – and mid-cap companies with a combined market capitalisation of more than £150 billion. Companies included are from a wide range of sectors and stages of development – from start-ups to established firms. Ofex was originally founded in 1995 as a facility for trading shares in unlisted companies, but as regulation tightened it had to modernise and in 2003 Ofex Holdings became a quoted company. The company name was changed to PLUS Markets Group in November 2004.

ShareMark

ShareMark is operated by retail stockbroker The Share Centre Ltd, which is a member of the London Stock Exchange and authorised and regulated by the Financial Services Authority. ShareMark is different to other markets because it operates through an electronic auction, matching buyers and sellers at a single price, so ShareMark stocks have no *bid/offer spread* (the difference between the buying price and the selling price) on ShareMark stocks. Auctions may occur daily, weekly, monthly or quarterly depending on the needs of the company and the shareholders. Because deals are struck periodically, rather than continually, ShareMark is well suited to the needs of less frequently traded stocks.

Investors can purchase shares traded on ShareMark in much the same way as any other listed stock – through a stockbroker. The buyers and sellers set price limits for both buy and sell orders. Value orders, allowing investors to invest a pre-determined sum, can also be set. Auctions then take place after a Compliance Review, during which The Share Centre's Compliance Department audits activity and so ensures that a fair price is struck.

ShareMark was set up in 2000 as an internal trading platform when The Share Centre issued free shares to around 90,000 clients. It was opened to other companies in 2002 and is currently available to unlisted companies, funds, and dual-traded companies that are also listed on another market such as AIM.

Further afield: International indices

Investors need to remember that the whole world is a vast marketplace that interacts with and exerts tremendous influence on individual national economies and markets. Whether you have one share or one unit trust, you should keep tabs on how world markets affect your investment. The best way to get a snapshot of international markets is, of course, with indices. A few of the more widely followed international indices are:

- **The Dow Jones index (US)**. This index is called 'The Dow', for short. As mentioned earlier in the chapter, the Dow is one of the most important indices in the world.

- **Standard & Poor's 500 (S&P 500) (US)** is another important index. Created by publishing firm Standard & Poor's, this index tracks the 500 largest publicly traded companies in the US – measured by market cap. The S&P 500 is a better representative of the overall market performance than the Dow, which features only 30 companies. In the US, money managers and financial advisers watch the S&P 500 more closely than the Dow. However, like the FTSE All-Share it has its limitations. Although it tracks 500 companies, the top 50 companies encompass 50 per cent of the index's market value.

✔ **Nasdaq (US).** Nasdaq became a formalised market in 1971. The name used to stand for 'National Association of Securities Dealers Automated Quote' system, but now it's simply 'Nasdaq' (as if it's a name like Ralph or Eddie). Nasdaq indices are similar to other indices in style and structure. The only difference is that they cover companies traded on the Nasdaq. The Nasdaq has two indices (both reported in the financial pages):

- **Nasdaq Composite Index:** Most frequently quoted on the news, the Nasdaq Composite Index covers the more than 5,000 companies that trade on Nasdaq. The companies encompass a variety of industries, but the index's concentration has primarily been technology, telecom, and Internet industries. The Nasdaq Composite Index hit an all-time high of 5,048 in March 2000 before the worst bear market in its history occurred. The index dropped a whopping 60 per cent by 2003 to approximately 2,000.

- **Nasdaq 100 Index:** The Nasdaq 100 tracks the 100 largest companies in Nasdaq. This index is for investors who want to concentrate on the largest companies, which tend to be technology businesses. It provides extra representation of technology-related companies such as Microsoft, Adobe, and Symantec.

In both cases, although these indices track growth-oriented companies, the stocks of these companies are also highly volatile and carry commensurate risk. The indices themselves bear this risk out; in the bear market of 2000 and 2001 (and even extending into 2002), they fell more than 60 per cent.

✔ **Nikkei (Japan):** This index is considered Japan's version of the Dow. If you've invested in Japanese shares or in companies that do business in Japan, you want to know what's up with the Nikkei.

✔ **CAC-40 (France):** This index tracks the 40 company shares traded on the Paris Stock Exchange.

✔ **DAX (Germany):** This index tracks the 30 largest and most active shares traded on the Frankfurt Exchange.

You can track these international indices (among others) at major financial websites, such as www.ftse.com, www.bloomberg.com, and www.market watch.com. You may find international indices useful in your analysis as you watch your shares' progress. What if you have shares in a company that has most of its customers in Japan? Then the Nikkei can help you get a general snapshot of how well the major companies are doing in Japan, which in turn can be a general barometer of its economy's well-being. If your company's business partners or customers are in the Nikkei, and it's plunging, then you know it's probably 'sayonara' for the company's share price.

Part II
Before You Start Buying

In this part . . .

When you're about to begin investing in shares, you should know that different types of shares exist for different objectives. If you can at least get a share that fits your situation, you're that much ahead in the game. In this part, you can find out where to start gathering information and discover what brokers can do for you.

Chapter 6

Gathering Information

In This Chapter

▶ Using stock exchanges to get investment information

▶ Applying accounting and economic know-how to your investments

▶ Exploring financial issues

▶ Deciphering the financial pages

▶ Interpreting dividend news

▶ Recognising good (and bad) advice when you hear it

*K*nowledge and information are two critical success factors in share investment. (Isn't that true about most things in life?) People who plunge headlong into shares without sufficient knowledge of the stock market in general, and current information in particular, quickly absorb the lesson of the eager diver who didn't find out ahead of time that the pool was only an inch deep (ouch!). In their haste to avoid missing so-called golden investment opportunities, investors too often end up losing money.

Opportunities to *make* money in the stock market will always exist, no matter how well or how poorly the economy and the market are performing in general. Don't believe that there is such thing as a single (and fleeting) magical moment, and don't feel that if you let an opportunity pass you by, you'll always regret that you missed your one big chance.

For the best approach to investing in shares, you want to build your knowledge and find quality information first. Then buy shares and make your fortunes more assuredly. Basically, before you buy shares, you need to know that the company you're investing in is

▶ Financially sound and growing

▶ Offering products and services that are in demand by consumers

▶ In a strong and growing industry (and general economy)

Where do you start and what kind of information do you want to acquire? Keep reading.

Looking to Stock Exchanges for Answers

Before you invest in shares, you need to be completely familiar with the basics of investing in them. At its most fundamental, investing in shares is about using your money to buy a piece of a company that gives you value in the form of appreciation or income. Fortunately, many resources are available to help you find out about investing in shares. Some of my favourite places are the stock exchanges themselves.

Stock exchanges are organised marketplaces for the buying and selling of shares or stocks as they are known in the US (and other securities). The London Stock Exchange (LSE), the leading European exchange, provides a framework for share buyers and sellers to make their transactions. The LSE makes money not only from a piece of every transaction but also from fees (such as listing fees) charged to companies and brokers that are members of its exchanges.

The LSE is the main exchange for most investors in the UK, closely followed by the Alternative Investment Market or AIM. Investors are also finding it increasingly easier to invest in shares listed on overseas exchanges such as the New York Stock Exchange and the Nasdaq. And smaller independent exchanges such as ShareMark are springing up. Chapter 5 gives more details about all these exchanges. Because exchanges and markets benefit from the increased popularity of, and continued demand for, investing in shares , they offer a wealth of free (or low-cost) information and resources for investors. Go to the Web sites of these exchanges and you find useful resources such as:

- ✔ Tutorials on how to invest in shares, common investment strategies, and so on.

- ✔ Glossaries and free information to help you understand the language, practice, and purpose of investing in shares.

- ✔ A wealth of news, press releases, financial data, and other information about companies listed at the exchange or market, accessed usually through an on-site search engine.

- ✔ Industry analysis and news.

- ✔ Share price quotes and other market information related to the daily market movements of shares including data such as volume, new highs, new lows, and so on.

- ✔ Free tracking of your share selections (You can input a sample portfolio, or the shares you are following, to see how well you are doing.).

What each exchange/market offers keeps changing or is updated, so go and explore each at their Web sites:

- London Stock Exchange: www.londonstockexchange.com
- Alternative Investment Market: www.londonstockexchange.comwww.amex.com
- Share Centre: www.share.co.uk

Understanding Shares and the Companies They Represent

Shares represent ownership in companies. Before you buy individual shares, you want to understand the companies whose shares you're considering and find out about their operations. It may sound like a daunting task, but you can digest the point more easily when you realise that companies work similarly to how you work. They make decisions on a day-to-day basis just as you do.

Think about how you grow and prosper as an individual or as a family, and you see the same issues with companies and how they grow and prosper. Low earnings and high debt are examples of financial difficulties that can affect both people and companies. You can understand companies' finances when you take the time to pick up information in two basic disciplines: accounting and economics. These two disciplines play a significant role in understanding the performance of a company's shares.

Accounting for taste and a whole lot more

Accounting. Yuck! But face it: Accounting is the language of business, and believe it or not, you're already familiar with the most important accounting concepts! Just look at the following three essential principles:

- **Assets minus liabilities equal net worth.** In other words, take what you own (your assets), subtract what you owe (your liabilities), and the rest is yours (net worth)! Your own personal finances work the same way as Tesco's (except yours have fewer zeros at the end). See Chapter 2 to figure out how to calculate your own net worth.

A company's balance sheet shows you its net worth at a specific time (such as 31 December). The net worth of a company is the bottom line of a company's asset and liability picture, telling you whether the company is *solvent* (has the ability to pay its debts without going out of business). The net worth of a successful company is regularly growing. To see whether your company is successful, compare its net worth with the net worth from the same point a year earlier. A company that has a £4 million net worth on 31 December, 2005, and a £5 million net worth on 31 December, 2006, is doing well; its net worth has gone up 25 per cent (£1 million) in one year.

✔ **Income less expenses equal net income.** In other words, take what you make (your income), subtract what you spend (your expenses), and the remainder is your *net income* (or net profit or net earnings – your gain).

A company's profitability is the whole point of investing in its shares. As it profits, the company becomes more valuable, and in turn, its shares become more valuable. To discover a company's net income, look at its income, or *profit and loss* (P&L), statement. Try to determine whether the company uses its gains wisely, reinvesting them for continued growth or paying down debt.

✔ **Do a comparative financial analysis.** That's a mouthful, but just a fancy way of saying how a company is doing now, compared with something else (like a prior period or a similar company).

If you know that a company you're looking at had a net income of £50,000 for the year, you may ask, 'Is that good or bad?' Obviously, making a net profit is good, but you also need to know whether the profit is good compared to something else. If the company had a net profit of £40,000 the year before, you know that the company's profitability is improving. But if a similar company had a net profit of £100,000 the year before and in the current year is making £50,000, then you may want to avoid that company or see what went wrong (if anything).

Accounting can be as simple as this list. If you understand these three basic points, you're ahead of the curve (in investing in shares as well as in your personal finances). For more information on how to use a company's financial statements to pick good shares, see Chapter 11.

Understanding how economics affects shares

Economics. Double yuck! No, you aren't required to understand 'the inelasticity of demand aggregates' (thank heavens!) or 'marginal utility' (what?). But a working knowledge of basic economics is crucial (and we mean crucial) to your success and proficiency as an investor in shares. The stock market and the economy are joined at the hip. The good (or bad) things that happen to one have a direct effect on the other.

Getting the hang of the basic concepts

Alas, many investors get lost on basic economic concepts (as do some so-called experts that you see on television). Paul owes his personal investing success to his status as a student of economics. Understanding basic economics helped him (and can help you) filter the financial news to separate relevant information from the irrelevant in order to make better investment decisions. Be aware of these important economic concepts:

✔ **Supply and demand:** How can anyone possibly think about economics without thinking of the ageless concept of supply and demand? *Supply and demand* can be simply stated as the relationship between what's available (the supply) and what people want and are willing to pay for (the demand). This equation is the main engine of economic activity and is extremely important for your share investment analysis and decision-making process. I mean, do you really want to buy shares in a company that makes papier mâché umbrella stands if you find out that the company has an oversupply and nobody wants to buy them anyway?

✔ **Cause and effect:** If you pick up a prominent news report and read, 'Companies in the table industry are expecting plummeting sales,' do you rush out and invest in companies that sell chairs or manufacture tablecloths? Considering cause and effect is an exercise in logical thinking, and believe us, logic is a major component of sound economic thought.

When you read business news, play it out in your mind. What good (or bad) can logically be expected given a certain event or situation? If you're looking for an effect ('I want a share price that keeps increasing'), you also want to understand the cause. Here are some typical events that can cause a share's price to rise:

- **Positive news reports about a company:** The news may report that a company is enjoying success with increased sales or a new product.

- **Positive news reports about a company's industry:** The media may be highlighting that the industry is poised to do well.

- **Positive news reports about a company's customers:** Maybe your company is in industry A, but its customers are in industry B. If you see good news about industry B, that may be good news for your company.

- **Negative news reports about a company's competitors:** If they are in trouble, their customers may seek alternatives to buy from, including your company.

✔ **Economic effects from government actions:** Political and governmental actions have economic consequences. As a matter of fact, nothing (and I mean nothing!) has a greater effect on investing and economics than government. Government actions usually manifest themselves as taxes, laws, or regulations. They also can take on a more ominous appearance, such as war or the threat of war. Government can willfully (or even accidentally) cause a company to go bankrupt, disrupt an entire industry, or even cause a depression. Its decisions can affect money supply, credit, and all public securities markets.

What happens to the papier mâché umbrella stand industry if the government passes a 50 per cent sales tax for that industry? Such a sales tax certainly makes a product uneconomical and encourages consumers to seek alternatives to papier mâché umbrella stands. It may even boost sales for the wicker basket industry.

The opposite can be true as well. What if the government passes a tax credit that encourages the use of solar power in homes and businesses? That obviously has a positive impact on industries that manufacture or sell solar power devices. Just don't ask us what happens to solar-powered papier mâché umbrella stands.

Gaining insight from past mistakes

Because most investors ignored basic observations about economics in the late 1990s, they subsequently lost millions in their share portfolios. In the late 1990s, the world experienced the greatest expansion of debt in history, coupled with a record expansion of the money supply". The growing debt resulted in more consumer (and corporate) borrowing, spending, and investing. This activity hyper-stimulated the stock market and caused shares to rise for five continuous years.

Of course, you should always be happy to make a decent gain every year on your investments, but such returns can't always be sustained and encourage speculation. This hyper-stimulation resulted in the following:

- ✔ More and more people depleted their savings. After all, why settle for 3 per cent in the bank when you can get 25 per cent in the stock market?

- ✔ More and more people bought on credit. If the economy is booming, why not buy now and pay later? Consumer credit hit record highs.

- ✔ More and more people borrowed against their homes. (Why not borrow and get rich now? I can pay off my debt later.)

- ✔ More and more companies sold more goods as consumers took more holidays and bought bigger cars, more electronic goods, and so on. Companies then borrowed to finance expansion, open new shops, and so on.

- ✔ More and more companies went public and offered shares to take advantage of more money that was flowing to the markets from banks and other financial institutions.

It was only a matter of time before spending started to slow down because consumers and businesses became too indebted. This slowdown in turn caused the sales of goods and services to taper off. However, companies had

Know thyself

If you're reading this book, you're probably doing so because you want to become a successful investor. Granted, to be a successful investor, you have to select great shares, but having a realistic understanding of your own financial situation and goals is equally important. I recall one investor who lost £10,000 in a speculative stock. The loss wasn't that bad because he had most of his money safely tucked away elsewhere. He also understood that his overall financial situation was secure and that the money he lost was 'play' money whose loss wouldn't have a drastic effect on his life. Most of us are not like the investor who can afford to lose £10,000. Many investors often lose even more money, and the loss does have a major, negative effect on their lives. Take time to understand yourself, your own financial picture, and your personal investment goals before you decide to buy shares.

acquired too much in the way of overhead costs, capacity, and debt because they had expanded too eagerly. At this point, companies were caught in a financial bind. Too much debt and too many expenses in a slowing economy mean one thing: Profits shrink. Companies, to stay in business, had to do the logical thing – cut expenses. What is usually the biggest expense for companies? People! To stay in business, many companies started laying off employees. As a result, consumer spending dropped further because more people were laid off or had second thoughts about their own job security.

As people had little in the way of savings and too much in the way of debt, they had to sell their shares to pay their mortgages. This trend was a major reason that shares started to fall in 2000. Earnings started to drop because of shrinking sales from a sputtering economy. As earnings fell, share prices also fell.

The lessons from the 1990s are important ones for investors today:

- ✔ Shares are not a replacement for savings accounts. Always have some money in the bank.

- ✔ Shares should never occupy 100 per cent of your investment funds.

- ✔ When anyone (including an expert) tells you that the economy will keep growing indefinitely, be skeptical and read diverse sources of information.

- ✔ If shares do well in your portfolio, consider protecting your shares (both your original investment and any gains) with stop-loss orders. (See Chapter 17 for more on these strategies.)

- ✔ Keep debt and expenses to a minimum.

- ✔ Remember that if the economy is booming, a decline is sure to follow as the ebb and flow of the economy's business cycle continues.

Staying on Top of Financial News

Reading the financial news can help you decide where or where not to invest. Many newspapers, magazines, and Web sites offer great coverage of the financial world. Obviously, the more informed you are, the better, but you don't have to read everything that's written. The information explosion in recent years has gone beyond overload, and you can easily spend so much time reading that you have little time left for investing.

The most obvious publications of interest to those investing in shares are *The Financial Times* and *Investor's Chronicle*. These excellent publications report the news and stock market data on a daily and weekly basis. Some of the more obvious Web sites are www.ft.com) and Bloomberg (www.bloomberg.com). These Web sites can actually give you news and share data within 15 to 20 minutes of an event occurring. (And don't forget the exchanges' Web sites!)

Appendix A of this book provides more information on these resources along with a treasure trove of some of the best publications, resources, and Web sites to assist you.

Figuring out what a company's up to

Before you invest, you need to know what's going on with a company. When you read about a company, from the company's literature (its annual report, for example) or from media sources, be sure to get answers to some pertinent questions:

- ✔ **Is the company making more net income – income after tax – than it did last year?** You want to invest in a company that is growing.

- ✔ **Are the company's sales greater than they were the year before?** Remember, you won't make money if the company isn't making money.

- ✔ **Is the company issuing press releases on new products, services, inventions, or business deals?** All these achievements indicate a strong, vital company.

Knowing how the company is doing, no matter what's happening with the general economy, is obviously important. To better understand how companies tick, see Chapter 12.

Discovering what's new with an industry

As you consider investing in a company, make a point of knowing what's going on in that company's industry. If the industry is doing well, your company is likely to do well, too. But then again, the reverse is also true.

Yes, we have seen investors pick successful shares in a failing industry, but those cases are exceptional. By and large, investors find it easier to succeed with a share when the entire industry is doing well. As you're watching the news, reading the financial pages, or viewing financial Web sites, check to see whether the industry is strong and dynamic. See Chapter 12 for information on analysing industries.

Knowing what's happening with the economy

No matter how well or how poorly the overall economy is performing, you want to stay informed about its general progress. The value of shares is more likely to keep going up when the economy is stable or growing. The reverse is also true; if the economy is contracting or declining, the share has a tougher time keeping its value. Some basic items to keep tabs on include the following:

- ✔ **Gross domestic product (GDP):** This is roughly the total value of output for a particular nation, measured in the sterling amount of goods and services. GDP is reported quarterly, and a rising GDP bodes well for your shares. When the GDP is rising at 3 per cent or more on an annual basis, that's solid growth. If it rises at more than zero but less than 3 per cent, that's generally considered less than stellar (or mediocre). GDP below zero (or negative GDP) means that the economy is shrinking (heading into recession).

- ✔ **Economic indicators:** The Office of National Statistics produces a flood of economic statistics each month which give a snapshot of economic activity from the preceding month. Each statistic helps you understand the economy in much the same way that barometers (and windows!) help you understand what's happening with the weather. Economists don't just look at an individual statistic; they look at a set of statistics to get a more complete picture of what's happening with the economy. Chapter 14 goes into greater detail on ways that the economy affects share prices.

Seeing what the politicians and government bureaucrats are doing

Being informed about what public officials are doing is vital to your success as an investor in shares. Because governments pass many laws every year, monitoring the political landscape is critical to your success. The news media report what the Prime Minister and Parliament are doing, so always ask yourself, 'How does a new law, tax, or regulation affect my shares?' Pay particular attention to what the Chancellor of the Exchequer announces in his Budget (usually in March or April).

Because government actions have a significant effect on your investments, make sure that you know what's going on. The best way to keep up with proposed changes to laws is through the news media. Proposals are usually laid out in an initial parliamentary consultation document called a Green Paper, which is followed some months later, after consultation and amendment, by a White Paper. The White Paper contains the final suggestions to be debated and voted on by Parliament. Specialist reporters and consumer groups tend to make a noise if they find issues of interest in Green or White Papers.

Checking for trends in society, culture, and entertainment

As odd as it sounds, trends in society, popular culture, and entertainment affect your investments, directly or indirectly. For example, headlines such as 'The grey pound – how companies cater for the growing pensioner population' may give you some important information that can make or break your share portfolio. With that particular headline, you know that as more and more people age, companies that are well positioned to cater to this growing market's wants and needs will do well – meaning a successful share for you.

Keep your eyes open to emerging trends in society at large. What trends are evident now? Can you anticipate the wants and needs of tomorrow's society? Being alert, staying a step ahead of the public, and choosing shares appropriately gives you a profitable edge over other investors. If you own shares in a solid company with growing sales and earnings, other investors eventually notice your company. As more investors buy up your company's shares, you're rewarded as the share price increases.

Reading (And Understanding) the Financial Pages

The stock market data in major business publications, such as *The Financial Times,* are loaded with information that can help you become a savvy investor – *if* you know how to interpret them. You need the information in the tables for more than selecting promising investment opportunities. You also need to consult the tables after you invest to monitor how your shares are doing. If you bought HokySmoky ordinary shares last year at £12 per share and you want to know what they are worth today, check out the stock tables printed daily in the financial pages of national newspapers. You can, of course, also find this information online at some of the Web sites already mentioned.

If you look at these tables without knowing what you're looking at or why, you're doing the equivalent of reading *War and Peace* backwards through a kaleidoscope. Nothing makes sense. But we can help you make sense of it all (well, at least the tables!). Table 6-1 shows a sample table for you to refer to as you read the sections that follow.

Table 6-1			Deciphering Tables					
52-Wk High	**52-Wk Low**	**Name (Code)**	**Div**	**Vol**	**Yld**	**P/E**	**Price**	**Chg**
21.50	8.00	SkyHighPLC (SH)		3,143		76	21.25	+0.25
47.00	31.75	LowDownPLC (LD)	2.35	2,735	5.9	18	41.00	−0.50
25.00	21.00	ValueNowPLC (VN)	1.00	1,894	4.5	12	22.00	+0.10
83.00	33.00	DoinBadlyPLC (DB)		7,601			33.50	−0.75

Every newspaper's financial tables are a little different, but they give you basically the same information. Updated daily, this section is not the place to start your search for a good share; this section is usually where your search ends. The tables are the place to look when you already know what you want to buy and you're just checking to see the most recent price, or to look when you already own it and you want to check how your investment is doing.

Each item gives you some clues about the current state of affairs for that particular company. The sections that follow describe each column to help you understand what you're looking at.

52-week high

The column labeled '52-Wk High' (refer to Table 6-1) gives you the highest price that particular share has reached in the most recent 52-week period. Knowing this price lets you gauge where the share is now versus where it has been recently. SkyHigh's (SH) shares have been as high as £21.50, while their last (most recent) price is £21.25, the number listed in the 'Price' column. (Flip to the 'Price' section for more on understanding this information.) SkyHigh's shares are trading high at the moment because the company is hovering right near its overall 52-week high figure.

Now, take a look at DoinBadly's (DB) share price. It seems to have tumbled big time. Its share price has had a high in the past 52 weeks of £83, but the company is currently trading at £33.50. Something just doesn't seem right here. During the past 52 weeks, DB's share price fell dramatically. If you're thinking about investing in DB, find out why the share price fell. If the company is a strong company, it may be a good opportunity to buy shares at a lower price. If the company is having tough times, avoid it. In any case, research the company and find out why its shares have declined in value.

52-week low

The column labelled '52-Wk Low' gives you the lowest price that particular share reached in the most recent 52-week period. Again, this information is crucial to your ability to analyse shares over a period of time. Look at DB in Table 6-1, and you can see that its current trading price of £33.50 is close to its 52-week low.

Keep in mind that the high and the low prices just give you a range of how far that particular share's price has moved within the past 52 weeks. They can alert you that a company has problems, or they can tell you that a share's price has fallen enough to make it a bargain. Simply reading the 52-Wk High and 52-Wk Low columns isn't enough to determine which of those two scenarios is happening. They basically tell you to get more information before you commit your money.

Name and code

The 'Name (Code)' column is the simplest in Table 6-1. It tells you the company name (usually abbreviated) and the code assigned to the company. When you have your eye on a share as a potential purchase, get familiar with its code. Knowing the code makes it easier for you to find your company in the financial tables, which list shares in alphabetical order by the company's name. Share codes are the language of stock market investing, and you need to use them in all communications about your shares, from getting a quote from your broker to buying shares online.

Dividend

Dividends (shown under the 'Div' column in Table 6-1) are basically payments to owners (shareholders). If a company pays a dividend, this dividend is shown in the dividend column. Newspapers usually carry this column in their weekend tables. The amount you see is the annual dividend paid out on one share. If you look at LowDownPLC (LD) in Table 6-1, you can see that you get £2.35 as an annual dividend for each share that you own. Companies usually pay the dividend half-yearly as an interim dividend and a final dividend. If I own 100 shares of LD, the company pays me £235 in total per year, in two instalments – the instalments don't have to be equal. Some UK companies, especially those with business interests in the US, pay dividends four times a year. British Petroleum (BP) is one example. A healthy company strives to maintain or upgrade the dividend for shareholders from year to year. The dividend is very important to investors seeking income from their share investment. For more about investing for income, see Chapter 9. Investors buy shares in companies that don't pay dividends primarily for growth. For more information on growth shares, see Chapter 8.

Volume

Normally, when you hear the word *volume* on the news, it refers to how many shares were bought and sold for the entire market. Volume is certainly important to watch because the shares that you're investing in are somewhere in that activity. For the 'Vol' column in Table 6-1, though, the volume refers to the individual share.

Volume tells you how many shares of that particular company were traded that day. If only 100 shares are traded in a day, then the trading volume is 100. SH had 3,143 shares change hands on the trading day represented in Table 6-1.

Is that good or bad? Neither, really. Usually the business news media only mention volume for a particular company when that volume is unusually large. If a share normally has volume in the 5,000 to 10,000 range and all of a sudden has a trading volume of 87,000, then you should sit up and take notice.

Keep in mind that a low trading volume for one share may be high trading volume for another. You can't necessarily compare one share's volume against that of any other company. The large-cap stocks like BP or Tesco typically have trading volumes in the millions of shares almost every day, while less active, smaller shares may have average trading volumes in far, far smaller numbers.

The main point to remember is that trading volume that is far in excess of that share's normal range is a sign that something is going on with that company. It may be negative or positive, but something newsworthy is happening. If the news is positive, the increased volume is a result of more people buying the share. If the news is negative, the increased volume is probably a result of more people selling the share. What are the typical events that cause increased trading volume? Some positive reasons include the following:

- **Good earnings reports:** A company announces good (or better-than-expected) earnings.

- **A new business deal:** A company announces a favourable business deal, such as a joint venture, or lands a big client.

- **A new product or service:** A company's research and development department creates a potentially profitable new product.

- **Indirect benefits:** A company may benefit from a new development in the economy or from a new law passed by Parliament.

Some negative reasons for an unusually large fluctuation in trading volume for a particular share include the following:

- **Bad earnings reports:** Profit is the lifeblood of a company. When a company's profit falls or disappears, you see more volume.

- **Governmental problems:** The company is being targeted by government action (such as a lawsuit or Competition Commission probe).

- **Liability issues:** The media reports that a company has a defective product or similar problem.

- **Financial problems:** Independent analysts report that a company's financial health is deteriorating.

Check out what's happening when you hear about heavier than usual volume (especially if you already own shares in the company).

Yield

In general, yield is a return on the money you invest. However, in the tables in the financial pages, *yield* ('Yld' in Table 6-1) is a reference to the dividend yield. It shows the percentage return that the dividend pays on the share price. Yield is most important to income investors. Yield is calculated by dividing the annual dividend by the current share price. In Table 6-1, you can see that the daily yield of ValueNow (VN) is 4.5 per cent (a dividend of £1 divided by the company's share price of £22). Notice that many companies have no yield reported; because they have no dividends, yield is zero.

Keep in mind that the yield reported in the financial pages changes daily as the share price changes. Yield is always reported as if you're buying the shares that day. If you buy VN on the day represented in Table 6-1, your yield is 4.5 percent. But what if VN's share price rises to £30 the following day? Investors who buy shares at £30 per share obtain a yield of just 3.3 percent. (The dividend of £1 is then divided by the new share price, £30.) Of course, because you bought the shares at £22, you essentially locked in the prior yield of 4.5 percent. Lucky you. Pat yourself on the back.

P/E

The P/E ratio is the ratio between the share price and the company's earnings. Many investors follow P/E ratios closely and they are important barometers of value in the world of share investment. The P/E ratio (also called the 'earnings multiple' or just 'multiple') is frequently used to determine whether shares are expensive (good value). Value investors (such as Paul) find P/E ratios essential for analysing shares as potential investments. As a general rule, the P/E should be 10 to 20 for large-cap or income shares. For growth shares, a P/E no greater than 30 to 40 is preferable.

In the P/E ratios reported in the financial pages, *price* refers to the cost of a single share. *Earnings* refers to the company's reported earnings (profits) per share in the most recent 12-months. The P/E ratio is the price divided by the earnings. In Table 6-1, VN has a reported P/E of 12, which is considered a low P/E. Notice how SH has a relatively high P/E (76). This share is considered too pricey because you're paying a price equivalent to 76 times earnings. Also notice that DB has no available P/E ratio. Usually this lack of a P/E ratio indicates that the company reported a loss in the latest 12-month trading period.

Price

The 'Price' column tells you how trading ended for a particular share on the day represented by the table – usually the day before the newspaper's publication. In Table 6-1, LD ended the previous day's trading at £41. Some newspapers report the high and low for the day as well as the share's closing price for the day.

Change

The information in the 'Chg' column answers the question 'How did the share price end on the day compared with its trading price at the end of the previous trading day?' Table 6-1 shows that SH shares ended the trading day up 25 pence (at £21.25). This column tells you that SH ended the previous day at £21. On a day when VN ends the day at £22 (up 10 pence), you can tell that the previous day it ended the trading day at £21.90.

Using News about Dividends

Reading and understanding the news about dividends is essential if you're an *income investor* (someone who invests in shares as a means of generating regular income). See Chapter 9 on investing for income.

Looking at important dates

In order to understand how buying shares that pay dividends can benefit you as an investor, you need to know how companies report and pay dividends. Some important dates in the life of a dividend are as follows:

✔ **Announcement Date:** Also called the declaration date, this is when a company reports a half-yearly dividend and the subsequent payment dates. On January 15, for example, a company may report that it 'is pleased to announce an interim dividend of 50 pence per share to shareholders of record as of February 10.' If you buy the share before, on, or after the announcement date, it won't matter with regard to receiving the company's interim dividend. The date that matters is the record date (see that bullet later in this list).

✔ **Date of execution:** Not as bad as it sounds. This is the day you actually initiate the share transaction (buying or selling). If you call up a broker (or contact him or her online) today to buy a particular share, then today is the date of execution, or the date on which you execute the trade. In most cases nowadays, your broker makes the purchase on the same day. For an example, skip to the section 'Understanding why these dates matter,' later in this chapter.

✔ **Settlement date (Closing date):** The closing or settlement date is the date on which the trade is finalised, which usually happens three business days after the date of execution if you are trading online. The settlement date for paper shares (certificates) is usually ten days after the date of execution. This is the date you pay (or are paid) for and become the proud new owner (or happy seller) of the stock.

✔ **Date of record:** The date of record is used to identify which shareholders qualify to receive the declared dividend. Because shares are bought and sold every day, how does the company know which investors to pay? The company establishes a cut-off date by declaring a *date of record*. All investors who are official shareholders on the date of record receive the dividend on the payment date even if they plan to sell the shares any time between the date of record and the payment date.

✔ **Ex-dividend date:** *Ex-dividend* means *without dividend*. Because it can take three days to process a share purchase before you become an official owner of the shares, you need to pay close attention to ex-dividend dates if you are intending to gain an income from the shares. You are not be entitled to the dividend if you buy your shares in the 'ex-dividend period.' This period can be a matter of only two or three days, but buying on these days means you are not on the register of shareholders on the date of record., See the section, 'Understanding why these dates matter' to see the effect that the ex-dividend date can have.

✔ **Payment date:** The date on which a company sends its dividend cheques, or authorises electronic payments to shareholders. Finally!

For typical dividends, the events in Table 6-2 happen twice a year.

Table 6-2	The Life of the Half-yearly Dividend	
Event	*Sample Date*	*Comments*
Date of declaration	January 15	The date that the company declares the half-yearly (interim or final) dividend
Ex-dividend date	February 7	Starts the period during which, if you buy the shares, you don't qualify for the dividend

(continued)

Table 6-2 (continued)

Event	Sample Date	Comments
Date of record	February 10	The date by which you must be on the shareholders register to qualify for the dividend
Payment date	February 27	The date that payment is made (an electronic payment or dividend cheque is sent to shareholders who were on the register on February 10)

Understanding why these dates matter

Remember that typically around three business days pass between the date of execution and the closing date. Similarly about three business days usually pass between the ex-dividend date and the date of record. You need to know this if you want to qualify to receive an upcoming dividend. Timing is important, and if you understand these dates, you know when to purchase shares and whether you qualify for a dividend.

As an example, say that you want to buy shares in ValueNowPLC (VN) in time to qualify for the interim dividend of 25 pence per share. Assume that the date of record (the date by which you have to be an official owner of the shares) is February 10. You may have to execute the trade (buy the shares) no later than February 7 to be assured of the dividend. If you execute the trade on February 7 itself, the closing date should occur three days later, on February 10 – just in time for the date of record. But you should always check with your stockbroker.

What if you execute the trade on February 8, a day later? Well, the trade's closing date is February 11, which occurs *after* the date of record. Unless you have an arrangement with your stockbroker, you won't be on the register as an official shareholder on the date of record, so you won't get that interim dividend. In this example, the February 7-10 period is called the *ex-dividend period*.

Fortunately, for those people who buy shares during their brief ex-dividend period, shares actually trade at a slighter lower price to reflect the amount of the dividend. If you can't get the dividend, you may as well save on the share purchase. How's that for a silver lining?

Evaluating (Avoiding?) Investment Tips

Psssst. Have we got a share tip for you! Come closer. You know what our tip is? Research! What we're trying to tell you is to never automatically invest just because you get a hot tip from someone. Good investment selection means looking at several sources before you decide on a share. No shortcut exists. That said, getting opinions from others never hurts – just be sure to carefully analyse the information you get. In the following list, we present some important points to bear in mind as you evaluate tips and advice from others:

- **Consider the source.** Frequently, people buy shares based on the views of some market strategist or market analyst. People may see an analyst being interviewed on a television financial show and take that person's opinions and advice as valid and good. The danger here is that the analyst may be biased because of some relationship that isn't disclosed on the show.

  It happens on TV all too often. A show's host interviews analyst U.R. Kiddingme from the investment firm Foollum & Sellum. The analyst says, 'Implosion Group is a good buy with solid, long-term, upside potential.' You later find out that the analyst's employer gets investment banking fees from Implosion Group. Analysts declare their interests in research papers but these important details can be edited out of TV and newspaper interviews. And an analyst is pretty unlikely to knock a company that is helping to pay the bills.

- **Get multiple views.** Don't base your investment decisions on just one source unless you have the best reasons in the world for thinking that a particular, single source is outstanding and reliable. A better approach is to scour current issues of independent financial publications, such as *Investor's Chronicle,* and other publications (and Web sites) listed in Appendix A.

- **Gather data from the London Stock Exchange (LSE).** When you want to get more objective information about a company, why not take a look at the reports that companies must file with the London Stock Exchange? These reports are the same reports that the pundits and financial reporters read. They include annual results announcements and trading statements as well as information on directors' share dealings. Many of the announcements filed with the stock exchange are also available on the best company Web sites.

  Notices of directors' share dealings are normally filed on Reuters News Service (RNS) – a specialist news wire where all official company announcements are made public. UK companies that have dual listings in the US also have to file all their documents with the Securities and Exchange Commission (SEC).

Chapter 7

Finding a Stockbroker

· ·

· ·

*W*hen you're ready to dive in and start investing in shares, you first have to choose a stockbroker. This process is sort of like buying a car: You can do all the research in the world and know exactly what kind of car you want to buy; but you still need a venue in which to do the actual transaction. Similarly, when you want to buy shares, your task is to do all the research you can to select the company you want to invest in. Still, you need a stockbroker to actually buy the shares, whether you buy in person, over the phone or online. In this chapter, I introduce you to the intricacies of the investor/broker relationship.

For information on various types of orders you can place with a broker, such as targets and stop-loss orders, and so on, flip to Chapter 17.

Defining the Broker's Role

The broker's primary role is to serve as the vehicle through which you buy or sell shares. When we talk about brokers, we're referring to organisations such as The Share Centre, Barclays Stockbrokers, and TD Waterhouse, and many other organisations that can buy shares on your behalf. Brokers can also be individuals who work for such firms. Although you can buy some shares directly from the company that issues them (we discuss direct purchase plans in Chapter 18), to purchase most shares, you still need a broker.

Although the primary task of brokers is the buying and selling of securities, such as shares (keep in mind that the word *securities* refers to the world of financial or paper investments, and that shares are only a small part of that world), they can perform other tasks for you, including the following:

- ✔ **Providing advisory services:** Investors pay brokers a fee for investment advice. Customers also get access to the firm's research.
- ✔ **Offering limited banking services:** Brokers can offer features such as interest-bearing accounts, cheque writing, direct deposit, and pension advice.
- ✔ **Brokering other securities:** Brokers can also buy bonds, investment and unit trusts, options, Exchange Traded Funds (ETFs), and other investments on your behalf.

Personal stockbrokers make their money from individual investors like you through various fees, including the following:

- ✔ **Brokerage commissions:** This fee is for buying and/or selling shares and other securities.
- ✔ **Service charges:** These charges are for performing administrative tasks and other functions. Brokers charge fees to investors for setting up Individual Savings Accounts or other investment vehicles.

Any broker advising you on investments must be registered with the Financial Services Authority (FSA. In addition, the money you deposit with your broker will normally be held in a linked bank account, so it has the same protection as it would have if it were held in the bank. Should your broker default, you should be entitled to most of your money back through the Financial Services Compensation Scheme. However, limits exist on the scheme including a maximum of £48,000 per individual. To find out whether the broker is registered and reputable, contact the FSA. (See Appendix A for information on the FSA.)

The distinction between personal stockbrokers and institutional stockbrokers is important. Institutional brokers make money from institutions and companies through investment banking and securities placement fees (such as initial public offerings (flotations) and secondary offerings), advisory services, and other broker services. Personal stockbrokers generally offer the same services – on a smaller scale – to individuals and small businesses.

Distinguishing between advisory and execution-only brokers

Stockbrokers fall into two basic categories: advisory, and execution-only. The type you choose really depends on what type of investor you are. In a nutshell, advisory brokers are suitable for investors who need some guidance, while execution-only brokers are better for those investors who are sufficiently confident and knowledgeable about share investment to manage with minimal help.

Advisory brokers

Advisory brokers are just what the name indicates. They advise their clients, the investors who open accounts with them, on how to invest their cash. When you open an account at a brokerage firm, a representative may be assigned to your account. This representative is usually called an *account executive,* or a *financial consultant* by the brokerage firm. This person is knowledgeable about shares in particular and investing in general.

What they can do for you

Your account executive is responsible for assisting you, answering questions about your account and the shares in your portfolio, and transacting your buy and sell orders. Here are some things that advisory brokers can do for you:

- **Offer guidance and advice.** The greatest distinction between advisory and execution-only brokers is the personal attention you receive from your account rep. You get to be on a first-name basis with an advisory broker, and you disclose much information about your finances and financial goals. The rep is there to make recommendations about shares and funds that are hopefully suitable for you.

- **Provide access to research.** Advisory brokers can give you access to their investment research department, which can give you in-depth information and analysis on a particular company. This information can be very valuable, but be aware of the pitfalls. (See the section 'Judging Brokers' Recommendations,' later in this chapter.)

- **Help you achieve your investment objectives.** Beyond advice on specific investments, a good rep gets to know you and your investment goals and *then* offers advice and answers your questions about how specific investments and strategies can help you accomplish your wealth-building goals.

✔ **Make investment decisions on your behalf.** Many investors don't want to be bothered when it comes to investment decisions. Advisory brokers can actually make decisions for your account with your authorisation. This service – known as *discretionary portfolio management* – is fine, but be sure to require them to explain their choices to you.

What to watch out for

Although the advisory brokers, with their seemingly limitless assistance, can make life easy for an investor, you need to remember some important points to avoid problems:

✔ Brokers and account reps are still salespeople. No matter how well they treat you, they're still compensated based on their ability to produce revenue for the brokerage firm. They generate commissions and fees from you on behalf of the company. (In other words, they're paid to sell you things.)

✔ Whenever your rep makes a suggestion or recommendation, be sure to ask why and request a complete answer that includes the reasoning behind the recommendation. A good advisor is able to clearly explain the reasoning behind every suggestion. If you don't fully understand and agree with the advice, don't take it.

✔ Working with an advisory broker costs more than working with an execution-only broker. Execution-only brokers are paid simply for per-forming the act of buying or selling shares for you. Advisory brokers do that and more. Additionally, they provide advice and guidance. Because of that, advisory brokers are more expensive (through higher brokerage commissions and advisory fees). Also, most advisory brokers expect you to be prepared to invest a substantial lump sum just to open an account.

✔ Handing over decision-making authority to your rep can be a possible negative because letting others make financial decisions for you is always dicey – especially when they're using *your* money. If they make poor investment choices that lose you money, you may not have any recourse because you authorised them to act on your behalf.

✔ Some brokers engage in an activity called *churning*. Churning is basically buying and selling shares for the sole purpose of generating commissions. Churning is great for brokers but bad for customers. If your account shows a lot of activity, ask for justification. Commissions, especially to advisory brokers, can take a big bite out of your wealth, so don't tolerate churning or other suspicious activity.

Before you deal with any broker, advisory or otherwise, check them out by contacting the Financial Services Authority by calling 0845 606 1234 or visiting the FSA Web site at www.fsa.gov.uk. You can ask whether any complaints or penalties have been filed against that brokerage firm or the individual rep.

Examples of advisory brokers are Killik & Co and Redmayne Bentley. Some of the banks and building societies offer stockbroking services and these can be a mix of advice and execution-only. And execution-only broker The Share Centre offers an advice line where clients can dial a premium rate line to discuss potential share investments with a stockbroker direct. All brokers now have full-featured Web sites to give you further information about their services. Get as informed as possible before you open your account. An advisory broker is there to help you build wealth, not make you . . . er . . . broker.

Execution-only brokers

Perhaps you don't need any hand-holding from a broker. You know what you want, and you can make your own investment decisions. All you want is someone to transact your buy/sell orders. In that case, go with an execution-only broker. They don't offer advice or premium services – just the basics required to perform your share transactions.

Execution-only brokers are cheaper to engage than advisory brokers and the majority of their business is done online. Because you're advising yourself (or getting advice from third parties such as newsletters or independent advisors), you can save on costs that you incur when you pay for an advisory broker.

If you choose to work with an execution-only broker, you must know as much as possible about your personal goals and needs. You have a greater responsibility for conducting adequate research to make good share selections, and you must be prepared to accept the outcome, whatever that may be.

Until about 1995, most investing in shares was done with a traditional broker sitting in an office – in a bank or building society or in an independent company. Many investors posted their certificates to the relevant office with a request for them to be sold or for other shares to be bought.

When online investing started, about one trade a day was the norm. But nowadays the majority of investing – especially by execution-only brokers – is done online. By the beginning of April 2005, around 635,000 private investors had online dealing accounts. The range of investments on offer from online brokers has also expanded to include Child Trust Funds and pensions. Many have great Web sites full of analysis and information to help their clients.

What they can do for you

Execution-only brokers offer some significant advantages over advisory brokers, such as:

- ✔ **Lower cost:** This lower cost is usually the result of lower commissions, and is the primary benefit of using execution-only brokers.

- ✔ **Unbiased service:** Execution-only brokers let you simply place your buy and sell orders . Because they don't offer advice, they have no vested interest in trying to sell you any particular shares.

- ✔ **Access to information:** Established execution-only brokers offer extensive educational materials at their offices or on their Web sites.

What to watch out for

Of course, doing business with execution-only brokers also has its downside, including the following:

- ✔ **No guidance:** Because you've chosen an execution-only broker, you *know* not to expect guidance, but the broker should make this fact clear to you anyway. If you're a knowledgeable investor, the lack of advice is considered a positive thing – no interference.

- ✔ **Hidden fees:** Execution-only brokers may shout about their lower commissions, but commissions aren't their only way of making money. Many brokers charge extra for services that you may think are included, such as issuing a share certificate or preparing your annual tax statement. Ask whether they levy fees for managing ISAs or transferring shares and other securities (such as bonds) in or out of your account. And don't expect much in the way of interest on any cash sitting in your brokerage accounts.

- ✔ **Minimal customer service:** If you deal with an Internet brokerage firm, find out about its customer service capability. If you can't get through to the Web site, make sure that the firm has an alternative help line to place your order.

Choosing a Broker

Before you choose a broker, you need to analyse your personal investing style. After you know yourself and the way you invest, then you can proceed to finding the kind of broker that fits your needs. Think of it as almost like choosing shoes; if you don't know your size, you can't get a proper fit. (And you can be in for a really uncomfortable future.)

When you come to choose a broker, keep the following points in mind:

- ✔ Match your investment style with a brokerage firm that charges the least amount of money for the services you're likely to use most frequently.

- ✔ Compare all the costs of buying, selling, and holding shares and other securities through a broker. Don't compare only commissions. Compare other costs, too, such as the interest paid on cash in your account and 'hidden' service charges.

- ✔ You can find tables comparing brokers' charges and services on money Web sites such as www.moneyextra.com and www.fool.co.uk. Check out Appendix A for a list of sources that compare brokers.

Finding brokers is easy. They're listed in the Yellow Pages as well as in many investment publications and on many financial Web sites. Start your search by using the sources in Appendix A, which includes a list of the major brokerage firms.

Discovering Various Types of Brokerage Accounts

When you decide to start investing in the stock market, you have to somehow actually *pay* for the shares you buy. Most brokerage firms offer investors different types of accounts, each serving a different purpose. The following sections explain the most common types. The basic difference boils down to how you prefer to do business when it comes to buying and selling securities. If you like to see the tangible evidence of your transactions you may want to buy and sell paper share certificates – though fewer and fewer people do. But if you worry about mislaying those fading paper assets you will do better with a nominee account. Check out the section 'Nominee accounts' later in this chapter for more info.

Whichever account you want, you need to go through the same process to open one. This process includes supplying evidence of who you are and where you live so that the broker can be sure that their services are not being used for *money laundering*, the process by which money obtained through crime is returned to the legitimate economy. You may fill out an application form online but you have to send documentation – such as a passport or utility bill – and your National Insurance number. You also have to send a cheque for the minimum account balance. It can take a couple of weeks to get your account set up.

Cash accounts

A *cash account* means just what you think it means. You must deposit a sum of money along with the new account application to begin trading. The amount of your initial deposit varies from broker to broker. Most brokers have a minimum of £1,000, but you may find others that let you open an account with less than this amount. Once in a while you may see a broker offering cash accounts with a very low minimum deposit, usually as part of a promotion. Use the resources in Appendix A to help you shop around. In any case, you still need to prove your identity to have one of these accounts.

With a cash account, your money has to be deposited in the account before the closing (or settlement) date for any trade you make. The settlement occurs three business days after the date you make the trade (the date of execution) unless you are trading paper share certificates, when it may be extended to 10 days. You may be required to have the money in the account even before the date of execution. See Chapter 6 for details on these and other important dates.

In other words, if you call your broker on Monday, 10 October, and order 50 shares of CashLess PLC. at £20 per share, then on Thursday, 13 October, you better have £1,000 in cash sitting in your account (plus commission). Otherwise, the purchase doesn't go through. And you get stung for a fee for missing the settlement date.

 If you have cash in a brokerage account, check how much interest the broker pays you on the money. Most offer a pretty low rate so it's best to arrange a linked online savings account from which to transfer cash to your broker when you need it.

Nominee accounts

A *nominee account* gives you the peace of mind that your shares are in safe hands, because they are stored electronically in your brokers' computer database. You may be sent contract notes for your trades and regular statements but you no longer have to guard your fragile paper certificates against fire, theft, flood or general clumsiness. This kind of account also gives you the flexibility to buy and sell at short notice as you can arrange to sell enough shares in one company to meet the cost of buying your latest favourite share.

Most brokers don't charge you for holding shares in your account, but they may charge for collecting dividends or making transfers to other accounts. You can have one nominee account with a broker linked to other accounts such as a cash account or an ISA account where some of your shares can be held tax-free.

As well as the security of knowing exactly where your shares are, and never missing dividend payments, most nominee account holders can now get access to all the company documents that paper shareholders are entitled to. Within a few years, paper share trading will probably disappear from the UK market.

Option accounts

An *option account* gives you all the capabilities of a nominee account (which in turn also gives you the capabilities of a cash account) plus the ability to trade *options* on shares – the right to buy or sell a share based on it reaching a particular price in the future – and stock market indices. To upgrade your nominee account to an options account, the broker usually asks you to sign a statement that you're knowledgeable about options and familiar with the risks associated with them.

Options can be a very effective addition to a share investor's array of wealth-building investment tools.

Judging Brokers' Recommendations

In recent years, we've all become enamoured with a new sport: The rating of shares by brokers in financial reports in the newspapers, and on TV and radio. Frequently these reports feature a dapper market strategist talking up a particular share. Some shares have been known to jump significantly right after an influential analyst issues a buy recommendation. Analysts' speculation and opinions make for great fun, and many people take their views very seriously. However, most investors should be very wary when analysts, especially the glib ones on TV, make a recommendation. Such recommendations are often just showbiz.

Brokers issue their recommendations (advice) as a general idea of how much regard they have for a particular share. The following list presents the basic recommendations (or ratings) and what they mean to you:

- ✔ *Strong buy* and *buy:* Get in there! These ratings are the ones to get. The analyst loves this pick, and you would be very wise to get a bunch of shares. The thing to keep in mind, however, is that *buy* recommendations are probably the most common because (let's face it) brokers sell shares.

- ✔ *Accumulate* and *market perform:* An analyst who issues these types of recommendations is positive, yet unexcited, about the pick. This rating is akin to asking friends whether they like your new suit and getting the response 'it's nice' in a monotone voice. They give a polite reply, but you wish the opinion had been more enthusiastic.

✔ *Hold* **or** *neutral:* Analysts use this language when their backs are to the wall, but they still don't want to say, 'Sell that loser!' This recommendation is like your mother saying 'If you can't say anything nice, don't say anything at all.' This rating is the analyst's way of saying nothing at all.

✔ *Sell:* Many analysts should have issued this recommendation during 2000 and 2001, but few actually uttered it. What a shame. So many investors lost money because some analysts were too nice or just afraid to be honest, sound the alarm, and urge people to sell.

✔ *Avoid like the plague:* I'm just kidding about this recommendation, but we wish that this advice was available. We've seen plenty of shares that we thought were dreadful investments – shares in companies that made no money and were in a terrible financial condition that should never have been considered at all. Yet investors gobble up millions of pounds' worth of shares that eventually become worthless.

Don't get me wrong. An analyst's recommendation is certainly a better tip than what you'd get from your barber or your sister-in-law's neighbour – unless she lives next door to a billionaire – but you want to view recommendations from analysts with a healthy dose of reality. Analysts have biases because their employment depends on the very companies that are being presented. What investors need to listen to when a broker talks up a share is the reasoning behind the recommendation. In other words, why is the broker making this recommendation?

Keep in mind that analysts' recommendations can play a useful role in your personal share investing research. If you find a great share and *then* you hear analysts give glowing reports on the same share, you're on the right track! Here are some questions and points to keep in mind:

✔ **How does the analyst arrive at a rating?** The analyst's approach to evaluating a share can help you round out your research as you consult other sources such as newsletters and independent advisory services.

✔ **What analytical approach is the analyst using?** Some analysts use *fundamental analysis* (looking at the company's financial condition and factors related to its success, such as its standing within the industry and the overall market). Other analysts use *technical analysis* (looking at the company's share price history and judging past share price movements to derive some insight regarding the share's future price movement). Many analysts use a combination of the two. Is this analyst's approach similar to your approach or to those of sources that you respect or admire?

✔ **What is the analyst's track record?** Has the analyst had a consistently good record through both bull and bear markets? Starmine (www.starmine.com) is a useful source of data on analysts' recommendations, and identifies which analysts have added the most value for investors.

✔ **How does the analyst treat important aspects of the company's performance, such as sales and earnings?** How about the company's balance sheet? The essence of a healthy company is growing sales and earnings coupled with strong assets and low debt.

✔ **Is the industry that the company is in doing well?** Do the analysts give you insight on this important information? A strong company in a weak industry can't stay strong for long.

✔ **What research sources does the analyst cite?** Does the analyst quote the Treasury or industry trade groups to support his or her thesis? These sources are important because they help give a more complete picture regarding the company's prospects for success. Imagine that you decide on the shares of a strong company. But what if the government (through agencies such as the FSA) is penalising the company for negligent activity? Or what if the company's industry is shrinking or has ceased to grow (making it tougher for the company to continue growing)? The astute investor looks at a variety of sources before buying shares.

✔ **Is the analyst rational when citing a target price for a share?** When he or she says, 'We think the share will hit £100 per share within 12 months,' is this opinion presenting a rational model, such as basing the share price on a projected price/earnings ratio? The analyst must be able to provide a logical scenario about why the share has a good chance of achieving the cited target price within the time frame mentioned. You may not necessarily agree with the analyst's conclusion, but the explanation can help you decide whether the share choice was well thought out.

✔ **Does the company that is being recommended have any ties to the analyst or the analyst's firm?** During the period 2000–2002, the financial industry got bad publicity because many analysts gave positive recommendations on shares in companies that were doing business with the very firms that employed those analysts. This conflict of interest is probably the biggest reason that analysts were so wrong in their recommendations during that period. Ask your broker to disclose any conflict of interest.

The bottom line with brokerage recommendations is that you shouldn't use them to buy or sell a share. Instead, use them to confirm your own research. We know that if we buy shares based on our own research and later discover the same shares being talked up on the financial news, that's just the icing on the cake. The experts may be great to listen to, and their recommendations can augment your own opinions; however, they're no substitute for your own careful research.

Chapter 8

Investing for Growth

*W*hat's the number one reason people invest in shares? To grow their long-term wealth (also referred to as *capital appreciation*). Yes, some people invest for income (in the form of dividends), but that's a different matter, handled in Chapter 9. Investors seeking growth would rather see the money that can be distributed as dividends reinvested in the company so that (hopefully) a greater gain is achieved by seeing the share's price rise – or *appreciate*. People interested in growing their wealth see shares as one of the convenient ways to do it. Growth shares tend to be riskier than other categories of shares, but they offer excellent long-term prospects for making the big bucks. If you're the type of investor who has enough time to let somewhat-risky shares trend upward, or who has enough money so that a loss won't devastate you financially, then growth shares are definitely for you. As they say, no guts, no glory. The challenge is to work out which shares are going to make you richer quicker.

Short of starting your own business, investing in shares is the best way to profit from a business venture. We want to emphasise that to make money from shares consistently over the long haul, you must remember that you're investing in a company; buying shares is just a means for you to participate in the company's success (or failure).

What does it matter that you think of investing in shares as buying a *company* rather than buying a *share?* Invest in a share only if you're just as excited about it as you would be if you were the chief executive in charge of running the company. If you're the sole owner of the company, do you act differently than one of a legion of obscure shareholders? Of course you do. As the owner of the company, you have a greater interest in the company. You have a strong desire to know how the enterprise is doing. As you invest in shares, make believe that you're the owner, and take an active interest in the company's products, services, sales, earnings, and so on. This attitude and discipline can enhance your goals as an investor in shares. This approach is especially important if your investment goal is growth.

Becoming a Value-Oriented Growth Investor

A share is considered a growth share when it grows faster and at a higher level than the overall stock market. Basically, a growth share performs better than its peers in categories such as sales and earnings. Value shares are shares that are priced lower than the value of the company and its assets – you can identify a value share by analysing the company's fundamentals and looking at key financial ratios, such as the price-to-earnings ratio. (For more on the topic of ratios, see Appendix B.) Growth shares tend to have better prospects for growth for the immediate future (from one to four years), but value shares tend to have less risk and more steady growth over a longer term.

Over the years, a debate has quietly raged in the financial community about growth versus value investing. Some people believe that growth and value are mutually exclusive. They maintain that large numbers of people buying shares with growth as the expectation tend to drive up the share price relative to the company's current value. Growth investors, for example, aren't put off by high price to earnings (P/E) ratios. Value investors, meanwhile, are too nervous to buy shares at high P/E ratio levels. See Appendix B for more on P/E ratios.

However, you *can* have both. A value-oriented approach to growth investing serves you best. Investors looking for long-term growth spend time analysing the company's fundamentals to make sure that the company's growth prospects lie on a solid foundation. But what if you have to choose between a growth share and a value share? Which do you choose? Seek value when you are buying the share and analyse the company's prospects for growth. Growth includes but is not limited to the health and growth of the company's specific industry and the economy at large (see Chapters 12, 13, and 14).

The bottom line is that growth is much easier to achieve when you seek solid, value-oriented companies in growing industries. To better understand industries and how they affect share values, see Chapter 12.

Being a value-oriented growth investor probably has the longest history of success versus most other share investment philosophies. The track record for those people who use value-oriented growth investing is enviable. Each may have his own spin on the concepts, but all have successfully applied the basic principles of value-oriented growth investing over many years.

Getting Tips for Choosing Growth Shares

Although the information in the previous section can help you shrink your share choices from thousands of shares to maybe a few dozen or a few hundred (depending on how well the general stock market is doing), the purpose of this section is to help you cull the so-so growth shares to unearth the go-go ones. Now you can dig deeper for the biggest potential winners. Keep in mind that you probably won't find a share to satisfy all the criteria presented here. Just make sure that your selection meets as many criteria as realistically possible. But hey, if you do find a share that meets all the criteria cited, *buy it quick!*

When choosing growth shares, you should consider investing in a company only *if* it makes a profit and *if* you understand *how* it makes that profit and from *where* it generates sales. Part of your research means looking at the industry (Chapter 12) and economic trends in general.

Making the right comparison

You have to measure the growth of a company against something to figure out whether you have a growth share. Usually, you compare the growth of a company with growth from other companies in the same industry or with the stock market in general. In practical terms, when you measure the growth of a share against the stock market, you're actually comparing it against a generally accepted benchmark, such as the FTSE 100 Index, known as the Footsie, or the Dow Jones Industrial Average (DJIA). For more on the Footsie or the DJIA, see Chapter 5.

If a company has earnings growth of 15 per cent per year over three years or more, and the industry's average growth rate over the same time frame is 10 per cent, then this share qualifies as a growth share.

A growth share is so-called not only because the company is growing but also because the company is performing well with consistency. Having a single year where your earnings do well versus the Footsie's average doesn't cut it. Growth must be consistently accomplished.

Checking out a company's fundamentals

When you hear the word *fundamentals* in the world of share investment, it refers to the company's financial condition and related data. When investors (especially value investors) do *fundamental analysis,* they look at the company's fundamentals – its balance sheet, income statement, cash flow, and other operational data, along with external factors such as the company's market position, industry, and economic prospects. Essentially, the fundamentals indicate the company's financial condition. Chapter 10 goes into greater detail about analysing a company's financial condition. However, the main numbers you want to look at include the following:

- ✔ **Sales:** Are the company's sales this year surpassing last year's? As a decent benchmark, you want to see sales at least 10 per cent higher than last year. Although it may differ depending on the industry, 10 per cent is a reasonable, general 'yardstick.'

- ✔ **Earnings:** Are earnings at least 10 per cent higher than last year? Earnings should grow at the same rate as sales (or, hopefully, better).

- ✔ **Debt:** Is the company's total debt equal to or lower than the previous year? The death knell of many a company has been excessive debt.

A company's financial condition has more factors than we mention here, but these numbers are the most important. We also realise that using the 10 per cent figure may seem like an oversimplification, but you don't need to complicate matters unnecessarily. I know someone's computerised financial model may come out to 9.675 per cent or maybe 11.07 per cent, but keep it simple for now.

Looking for leaders and megatrends

A strong company in a growing industry is a common recipe for success. If you look at the history of stock market investing, this point comes up constantly. Investors need to be on the alert for *megatrends* because they help to ensure your success.

A megatrend is a major development that has huge implications for much (if not all) of society for a long time to come. Good examples are the advent of the Internet and our ageing population. Both of these trends offer significant challenges and opportunities for our economy. Take the Internet, for example. Its potential for economic application is still being developed. Millions are flocking to it for many reasons. And census data tells us that senior citizens (over 65) will be the fastest growing segment of our population during the next 20 years. How does the stock market investor take advantage of such megatrends?

In the wake of the 2000-2002 shares bear market, two megatrends hit their stride: rising energy prices and an overheated housing market. As of 2005, these two issues became major news items with tremendous ripple effects across the national economy. For the growth investor, strategy became clear. Find value-oriented companies with solid fundamentals that are well positioned to benefit from these megatrends. What's the result? From 2002-2005, many energy-related and housing-related shares skyrocketed. As oil surpassed

$65 a barrel and petrol hit 90p a litre, most oil and oil services companies saw their shares soar during that three-year time frame. Housing shares were even more impressive. Companies that catered to these industries also prospered. Building societies that had converted to PLCs posted impressive gains.

Considering a company with a strong niche

Companies that have established a strong niche are consistently profitable. Look for a company with one or more of the following characteristics:

- ✔ **A strong brand:** Companies such as Tesco or Sky come to mind. Yes, other companies out there sell food or broadcast live sport , but a business needs a lot more than a similar product to topple companies that have established an almost irrevocable identity with the public.

- ✔ **High barriers to entry:** United Parcel Service and Federal Express have set up tremendous distribution and delivery networks that competitors can't easily duplicate. High barriers to entry offer an important edge to companies that are already established.

- ✔ **Research and development (R&D):** Companies such as Pfizer and GlaxoSmithKline spend a lot of money researching and developing new pharmaceutical products. This investment becomes a new product with millions of consumers who become loyal purchasers, so these companies are going to grow.

Noticing who's buying and/or recommending the share

You can invest in a great company and still see its shares go nowhere. Why? Because what makes the share go up is demand – having more buyers than sellers of the share. If you pick a share for all the right reasons, and the market notices the share as well, that attention causes the share price to climb. The things to watch for include the following:

- ✔ **Institutional buying:** Are fund managers and pension plans buying up the share you're looking at? If so, this type of buying power can exert tremendous upward pressure on the share's price. Some resources and publications track institutional buying and how that affects any particular share. (You can find these resources in Appendix A.) Frequently, when a fund manager buys a share, others soon follow. In spite of all the talk about independent research, a herd mentality still exists.

✔ **Analysts' attention:** Are analysts talking about the share on the financial programmes? As much as you should be skeptical about an analyst's recommendation (given the stock market debacle of 2000-2002), it offers positive reinforcement for your share. Don't ever buy a share solely on the basis of an analyst's recommendation. Just know that if you buy a share based on your own research, and analysts subsequently rave about it, your share price is likely to go up. A single recommendation by an influential analyst can be enough to send a share skyward.

✔ **Newsletter recommendations:** Independent researchers usually publish newsletters. If influential newsletters are touting your choice, that praise is also good for your share. Although great newsletters are out there (find them in Appendix A), and they offer information that's as good or better than the research departments of certain brokerage firms, don't use a single tip to base your investment decision on. But it should make you feel good if the newsletters tout a share that you've already chosen.

✔ **Consumer publications:** No, you won't find investment advice here. They may seem unexpected indicators to suggest, but consumer magazines are a source that you should notice. Publications such as *Which?* regularly look at products and services and rate them for consumer satisfaction. If a company's offerings are well received by consumers, that's a strong positive for the company. This kind of attention ultimately has a positive effect on that company's shares.

Learning investing lessons from history

A growth share isn't a creature like the Loch Ness monster – always talked about but rarely seen. Growth shares have been part of the financial scene for nearly a century. Examples abound that offer rich information that you can apply to today's stock market environment. Look at past market winners, especially those of the 1970s and 1980s, and ask yourself, 'What made them profitable shares?' I mention these two decades because they offer a stark contrast to one another. The '70s were a tough, bearish decade for shares, while the '80s were booming bull times. (See Chapter 15 for details on bear and bull markets.) Being aware and acting logically are as vital to successful stock market investing as they are to any other pursuit. Over and over again, history gives you the formula for successful share investment:

✔ Pick a company that has strong fundamentals, including signs such as rising sales and earnings and low debt. (See Chapter 10.)

✔ Make sure that the company is in a growing industry. (See Chapter 12.)

✔ Be fully invested in shares during a bull market, when prices are rising in the stock market and in the general economy. (See Chapter 15.)

✔ During a bear market, switch more of your money out of growth shares (such as technology) and into defensive shares (stable and lower-risk shares, in companies such as utilities whose services we will always need).

✔ Monitor your shares. Hold on to shares that continue to grow, and sell those shares that are declining. (See Chapter 21 for warning signals to watch out for.)

Evaluating the management of a company

The management of a company is crucial to its success. Before you buy shares in a company, you want to know that the company's management is doing a great job. But how do you do that? If you call up a company and ask, it may not even return your phone call. How do you know whether management is running the company properly? The best way is to check the numbers. The following sections tell you the numbers you need to check. If the company's management is running the business well, the ultimate result is a rising share price.

Return on equity

Although you can measure how well management is doing in several ways, you can take a quick snapshot of a management team's competence by checking the company's *return on equity* (ROE). You calculate the ROE simply by dividing earnings (more commonly called operating profit) by equity (often called shareholders' funds). The resulting percentage gives you a good idea whether the company is using its equity (or net assets) efficiently and profitably. Basically, the higher the percentage, the better, but you can consider the ROE solid if the percentage is 10 per cent or higher. Keep in mind that not all industries have identical ROEs.

To find out a company's earnings, check out the company's *profit and loss account* (or P&L). The P&L is a simple financial statement that expresses the equation:

sales – expenses = net earnings (or net income or net profit).

You can see an example of a P&L in Table 8-1. (We give more details on P&L accounts in Chapter 10.)

Table 8-1	Grobaby PLCP&L Account	
	2005	*2006*
Turnover	£82,000	£90,000
Operating expenses	(£75,000)	(£78,000)
Operating profit	£7,000	£12,000

To find out a company's equity, check out that company's balance sheet. (See Chapter 10 for more details on balance sheets.) The balance sheet is actually a simple financial statement illustrating the fact that total assets minus total liabilities equal net equity. For publicly listed companies, the net assets are called *shareholders' equity* or *shareholders' funds*. Table 8-2 shows a balance sheet for Grobaby PLC.

Table 8-2	Grobaby PLC Balance Sheet	
	December 31, 2005	*December 31, 2006*
Assets	£55,000	£65,000
Liabilities	(£20,000)	(£25,000)
Shareholders' funds	£35,000	£40,000

Table 8-1 shows that Grobaby's operating profit (or earnings before any deductions such as tax or write-offs) went from £7,000 to £12,000. In Table 8-2, you can see that Grobaby increased the shareholders' funds from £35,000 to £40,000 in one year. The ROE for the year 2005 is 20 per cent (£7,000 operating profit divided by £35,000 shareholders' funds), which is a solid number. The following year, the ROE is 30 per cent (£12,000 operating profit divided by £40,000 shareholders' funds), another solid number.

Equity and earnings growth

Two additional barometers of success are a company's profit growth year on year and growth of shareholders' funds. Look at the growth in Table 8-1. Operating profit grew from £7,000 (in 2005) to £12,000 (in 2006), or a percentage increase of 71 per cent (£12,000 minus £7,000 equals £5,000, and £5,000 divided by £7,000 is 71 per cent), which is excellent. In Table 8-2, Grobaby's shareholders' funds grew by £5,000 (from £35,000 to £40,000), or 14 per cent, which is very good – the management is doing good things here.

TECHNICAL STUFF

Protecting your downside

We become as monotonous as a one-stringed guitar on one topic: trailing stop losses. (See Chapter 17 for a full explanation of trailing stop losses.) *Trailing stop losses* are stop losses (orders to sell a share once the price of the share falls below a particular price) that you arrange to change daily based on the current value of your share. We always advocate using them, especially if you're new to the game of buying growth shares. Trailing stop losses can help you, no matter how good or bad the economy is (or how good or bad the share you're investing in is).

Suppose that you had invested in Enron, a classic example of a phenomenal growth share that went bad. In 1999 and 2000, when its shares soared, investors were as happy as chocaholics at Cadbury World. Along with many investors who forgot that sound investing takes discipline and research, Enron investors thought, 'Downside risk? What downside risk?'

Here's an example of how a stop-loss order would have worked if you had invested in Enron. Suppose that you bought Enron in 2000 at $50 per share and set up a stop-loss order with your stockbroker at $45. (Remember to make it a *GTC* (or good-til-cancelled) order. If you do, the stop-loss order stays on indefinitely.) As a general rule, I like to place the stop-loss order at 10 per cent below the market value. As the shares went up, you kept the stop-loss trailing upward like a tail. (Now you know why people call it a a 'trailing' stop loss; it trails the share's price.) When Enron hit $70, your stop-loss was changed to, say, $63, and so on. At $84, your new stop-loss was at $76. Then what?

When Enron started its perilous descent, you got out at $76. The new price of $76 triggered the stop-loss, and the share was automatically sold – you stopped the loss! Actually, in this case, you can call it a 'stop and cash in the gain' order. Because you bought the shares at $50 and sold at $76, you pocketed a nice capital gain of $26 (52 per cent appreciation – a do-Enron-ron a do-Enron!). Then you safely stepped aside and watched the share continue its plunge.

But what if the market is doing well? Are trailing stop losses a good idea? Because these stop losses are placed below the share price, you're not stopping the share from rising upward indefinitely. All you're doing is protecting your investment from losses. That's discipline! The stock market of 2004–2005 was fairly good to investors as the bear market that started in 2000 took a break. If a bear market continues, trailing stop loss strategies become very useful because a potential decline in share prices becomes a greater risk.

Insider buying

Watching management as it manages the business is important, but another indicator of how well the company is doing is whether management is buying shares in the company as well. If a company is poised for growth, who knows better than management? And if management is buying up the company's shares en masse, then that's a great indicator of the share's potential. Remember, though, that managers can't base their investment decisions on information that is not already available to the public – if they did, that would be *insider trading* and could put them in jail. See Chapter 19 for more details on (legal) insider trading.

Making sure that a company continues to do well

A company's financial situation does change, and you, as a diligent investor, need to continue to look at the numbers for as long as the share is in your portfolio. You may have chosen a great share from a great company with great numbers in 2003, but chances are pretty good that the numbers have changed since then.

Great shares don't always stay that way. A great selection that you're drawn to today may become tomorrow's pariah. Information, both good and bad, moves like lightning. In late 2000, analysts considered Enron a cream-of-the-crop company, and they fell over themselves extolling its virtues. Even celebrated market strategists called Enron their number one choice in the energy sector as late as the autumn of 2001. Yet Enron shocked investors when it filed for bankruptcy in December 2001. Its share price fell from $84 in December 2000 to a staggering 26 cents a share (yikes!) in October 2001! Keep an eye on your company's numbers!

Exploring Small-caps and Speculative Shares

Everyone wants to get in early on a hot new share. Why not? You buy Fillyerboots PLC, at £1 per share and hope it zooms to £98 before lunchtime. Who doesn't want to buy a share that may become the next IBM or Microsoft? This possibility is why investors are attracted to small-caps .

Small-cap (or small-capitalisation) is a reference to the company's market size. *Small-caps* are often newer companies that have room to grow.. Investors may face more risk with small-caps, but they also have the chance for greater gains.

Out of all the types of shares, small-cap shares continue to exhibit the greatest amount of growth. In the same way that a tree planted last year has more opportunity for growth than a mature 100-year-old oak, small-caps have greater growth potential than established large-cap shares. Of course, a small-cap doesn't exhibit spectacular growth just because of its size. It grows when it does the right things, such as increasing sales and earnings by producing goods and services that customers want.

Don't rush to buy new issue shares

When a company goes public, it means that it undergoes a *flotation* or *new issue*. This is also called an initial public offering or IPO (the American term which is now also used in the UK). The *new issue* is the process by which a private firm seeks the assistance of an investment banking firm to gain financing by issuing shares that the public purchases. Flotations generate a lot of excitement, and many investors consider them to be that proverbial ground-floor opportunity. After all, some people find it appealing to get a share before its price skyrockets after investors subsequently flock to it. Why wouldn't people find new issues appealing?

New issues are not guaranteed to soar in their first year and studies periodically done by the stockbroking industry have revealed that new issue s (more times than not) decline in price during the first 12 months 60 per cent. However, your interest in new issues should be guided by your attitude to risk. If you are prepared to take the risk that a new issue will do well for you that is your choice – if not, keep your investment cash for companies that are already established. You can always wait to see how a new issue share and the company perform. Don't worry about missing that great opportunity; if it proves to be a bona fide opportunity, you can still do well with an investment after the flotation.

For every small company that becomes a FTSE 100 firm, hundreds of companies don't grow at all or go out of business. When you try to guess the next great share before any evidence of growth, you're not investing, – you're speculating. Have you heard that one before? (If not, flip to Chapter 2 for details.) Of course you have, and you'll hear it again. Don't get us wrong – speculating is not a crime. But you must recognise that you're speculating when you're doing it. If you're going to speculate in small shares hoping for the next Cisco Systems, then use the guidelines we present in the following sections to increase your chances of success.

Avoid new issues, unless . . .

New issues are the birthplace of public shares, or the proverbial ground floor. The *new issue or initial public offering (IPO)* is the first offering to the public of a company's shares. This is also referred to as 'going public.' Because a company's going public is frequently an unproven enterprise, investing in a new issue can be risky. But some investors in the UK have done very well out of them. Here are the two types of new issues:

- ✔ **Start-up new issue:** This is a company that didn't exist before the flotation. In other words, the entrepreneurs get together and create a business plan. To get the financing they need for the company, they approach an investment banker to help them go public immediately .

Although this process happened frequently during the dot.com mania, investment bankers today need to be totally convinced by the concept before they risk their reputations on an unproven formula. Bankers seek funding (selling the shares to investors) via the new issue but if it fails the confidence of investors will wane.

✔ **A private company that decides to go public:** In many cases, the new issue is for a company that already exists and is seeking expansion capital. The company may have been around for a long time as a smaller private concern, but it decides to seek funding through a new issue to grow. In the UK, several of the big flotations in recent years have been *privatisations* (of national industries such as the railways and electricity boards) and *demutualisations* (mostly building societies turning into banks).

Of these two types of new issue, which do you think is less risky? That's right! The established company going public. Why? Because the established company is already a proven business, which is a safer bet than a brand-new start-up. Successful new issues in recent years range from football clubs such as Manchester United (now in private hands again) and Celtic to the Halifax Building Society (now part of banking giant HBoS). All were established companies *before* they went public.

Great shares started as small companies going public. You may have heard the stories of Abbey National, Powergen, BT, Centrica, Aviva and hundreds of other successes. But do you remember any of the new issues that have failed? No? We didn't think so. Many new issues don't succeed. For investors, the lesson is clear: if you prefer low risks, wait until a track record appears before you invest in a company. You may be speculating rather than investing if you don't. But then some investors 'know' they are backing a winner – like the thousands of Manchester United and Celtic fans who invested in their clubs.

Is your small-cap making money?

We emphasise two points when investing in shares:

✔ Make sure that a company is established. (Being in business for at least three years is a good minimum.)

✔ Make sure that a company is profitable.

These points are especially important for investors in small shares. Plenty of start-up ventures lose money but hope to make a fortune down the road. A good example is a company in the biotechnology industry. Biotech is an exciting area, but esoteric, and companies are finding it difficult to use the technology in profitable ways. You may say, 'But shouldn't I jump in now in anticipation of future profits?' You may get lucky, but understand that when you invest in unproven, small-cap shares, you're speculating.

Investing in small-cap shares requires analysis

The only difference between a small-cap share and a large-cap share is a few zeros in their numbers and the fact that you need to do more research with small-caps. By sheer dint of size, small-caps are riskier than large-caps, so you offset the risk by accruing more information on the share in question. Plenty of information is available on large-cap shares because they're widely followed. Small-cap shares don't get as much media attention, and fewer analysts issue reports on them. Here are a few points to keep in mind:

- ✔ **Understand your investment style.** Small-cap shares may have more potential rewards, but they also carry more risk. No investor should devote a large portion of his capital to small-cap shares. If you're considering retirement money, you're better off investing in large-cap shares, Exchange-Traded Funds (ETFs), investment-grade bonds, bank accounts, and unit trusts. For example, retirement money should be in investments that are very safe or have proven track records of steady growth over an extended period of time (five years or longer).

- ✔ **Check with the Stock Exchange**. Get the financial reports that the company must file with the Stock Exchange – you can pay a subscription for the Company Report service from the Stock Exchange which gives fundamental financial data on companies. Or you can invest in the book or CD-ROM of REFS (Really Essential Financial Statistics) which is updated quarterly.

- ✔ **Check other sources.** See whether stockbrokers and independent research services, such as newspaper market columns are , following the company. If two or more different sources like the shares, then investigate further. Check the resources in Appendix A for further sources of information before you invest.

Chapter 9

Investing for Income

● ●

In This Chapter

▶ Defining income hares

▶ Selecting income shares

▶ Looking at typical income shares

● ●

*I*nvesting for income means investing in shares that provide you with regular money payments (dividends). Income shares may not offer stellar growth, but they're good for a steady infusion of money. What type of person is best suited to income shares? Income shares can be appropriate for many investors, but they're especially well suited for the following individuals:

▸ **Conservative and novice investors:** Conservative investors like to see a slow-but-steady approach to growing their money while getting regular dividend checks. Novice investors who want to start slowly also benefit from income shares.

▸ **Retirees:** Growth investing is best suited for long-term needs, while income investing is best suited to current needs. Retirees may want some growth in their portfolios, but they're more concerned with regular income that can keep pace with inflation.

▸ **Dividend reinvestment plan (DRIP) investors:** For those investors who like to compound their money with DRIPs, income shares are perfect. For more information on DRIPs, see Chapter 18.

If you have a low tolerance for risk or if your investment goal is anything less than long-term, income shares are your best bet.

Understanding Income Shares

When people talk about gaining income from shares, they're usually talking about dividends. A *dividend* is nothing more than money paid out to the owners of the company – the shareholders. You purchase dividend shares primarily for income – not for spectacular growth potential.

A dividend is quoted as an annual number but is usually paid twice a year. For example, if the company pays a dividend of £1, you're probably paid £50p each half year. If, in this example, you have 200 shares, you're paid £200 every year (if the dividend doesn't change during that period), or £100 every six months. Getting that regular dividend cheque every six months (for as long as you hold the shares) can be a nice perk.

A good income share is a share that has a higher-than-average dividend (typically 4 per cent or higher).

Dividend rates aren't guaranteed – they can go up or down, or, in some cases, the dividend can be discontinued. Fortunately, most companies that issue dividends continue them indefinitely and actually increase dividend payments from time to time. Historically, dividend increases have equalled (or exceeded) the rate of inflation.

Advantages of income shares

Income shares tend to be among the least volatile of all shares, and many investors view them as defensive shares. *Defensive shares* are shares in companies that sell goods and services that are generally needed no matter what shape the economy is in. (Don't confuse defensive shares with *defence shares,* which specialise in goods and equipment for the military.) Food, beverage, and utility companies are great examples of defensive shares. Even when the economy is experiencing tough times, people still need to eat, drink, and turn the lights on. Companies that offer relatively high dividends also tend to be large firms in established, stable industries.

Some industries in particular are known for high-dividend shares. Utilities (such as electric, gas, and water), and the energy sector (oil and gas) are places where you definitely find income shares. Yes, you can find high-dividend shares in other industries, but you find a high concentration of them in the above mentioned industries. For more details, see the sections highlighting these industries later in this chapter.

Disadvantages of income shares

Before you say, 'Income shares are great! I'll get my cheque book and buy a batch right now,' take a look at potential disadvantages (ugh!). Income shares do come with fine print.

What goes up . . .

Income shares can go down as well as up, just as any share can. Obviously, you don't mind your income shares going up in value, but they can go down just as easily. The factors that affect shares in general – politics, economic trends

(Chapter 14), industry changes (Chapter 12), and so on – affect income shares, too. Fortunately, income shares don't get hit as hard as other shares when the market is declining because high dividends tend to act as a support to the share price. Therefore, income shares' prices usually fall less dramatically than the prices of other shares in a declining market.

Interest-rate sensitivity

Income shares can be sensitive to rising interest rates. When interest rates go up, other investments (such as corporate bonds, gilts, and savings certificates) are more attractive. When your income share is yielding 4 per cent and interest rates are going to 5 per cent, 6 per cent, or higher, you may think, 'Hmmm. Why settle for a 4 per cent yield when I can get 5 per cent or better elsewhere?' As more and more investors sell their low-yield shares, the prices for those shares fall.

Another point to remember is that rising interest rates may hurt the company's financial strength. If the company has to pay more interest, that may affect the company's earnings, which in turn may affect the dividend.

Dividend-paying companies that are experiencing consistent, falling revenues tend to cut dividends. In this case, 'consistent' means beyond just a year.

Inflation eats into dividends

Although many companies raise their dividends on a regular basis, some don't. Or, if they do raise their dividends, the increases may be small. If income is your primary consideration, you want to be aware of this fact. If you're getting the same dividend year after year and this income is important to you, rising inflation becomes a problem. Say that you have XYZ shares at £10 per share with an annual dividend of 30 pence (the yield is 30 pence divided by £10, or 3 per cent). If you have a yield of 3 per cent two years in a row, how do you feel when inflation rises 6 per cent one year and 7 per cent the next year? Because inflation means that your costs are rising, inflation shrinks the value of the dividend income you receive.

As you can see, even conservative income investors can be confronted with different types of risk. (Chapter 4 covers the topic of risk in greater detail.) Fortunately, the rest of this chapter helps you carefully choose income shares so that you can minimise these potential disadvantages.

Don't forget the taxman

The government usually taxes dividends as ordinary income. Dividends from all UK companies are quoted net of tax. Companies paying dividends must first deduct one-ninth of the price and pay this in tax. See Chapter 20 for more information on taxes for investors.

Minding your dividends and interest

Dividends are sometimes confused with interest. However, *dividends* are payouts to owners, while *interest* is a payment to a creditor. A share investor is a part owner of the company he or she invests in and is entitled to dividends when they're issued. A bank, on the other hand, considers you a creditor when you open an account. The bank borrows your money and pays you interest on it.

Analysing Income Shares

Look at income shares in the same way you do growth shares when assessing the financial strength of a company. Getting nice dividends comes to a screeching halt if the company can't afford to pay them. If your budget depends on dividend income, then monitoring the company's financial strength is that much more important. You can apply the same techniques I list in Chapter 8 for assessing the financial strength of growth shares to your assessment of income shares.

Understanding your needs first

You choose income shares primarily because you want or need income now. As a secondary point, income shares have the potential for steady, long-term appreciation. So if you're investing for retirement needs that won't occur for another 20 years, maybe income shares aren't suitable for you – better to invest in growth shares because they're more likely to grow your money faster over your stated length of investment term.

If you're certain that you want income shares, do a rough calculation to work out how big a portion of your portfolio you want income shares to occupy. Suppose that you need £25,000 in investment income to satisfy your current financial needs. If you have bonds that give you £20,000 in interest income and you want the rest to come from dividends from income shares, you need to choose companies that pay you £5,000 in annual dividends. If you have £80,000 left to invest, you know that you need a portfolio of income shares that provide £5,000 in dividend income or a yield of 6.25 per cent (£5,000 divided by £80,000 equals a yield of 6.25 per cent).

Use the following table as a general guideline for understanding your need for income.

Playing it safe

If you're an investor seeking income and you're nervous about potential risks with income shares, here are some non-stock alternatives:

✔ **National Savings Certificates:** Although the interest rates are not always as good as you get from the best bank and building society accounts, these savings vehicles are guaranteed by the Treasury. They are the safest savings in the UK. They come in a variety of guises including fixed interest offers and bonds aimed at pensioners or young people. New issues are launched regularly and interest rate changes are announced in the national press.'

✔ **Bank and building society accounts:** Considered pretty safe, and backed by the Financial Services Compensation Scheme, try to have cash invested in savings accounts before you start investing in shares.

✔ **Unit trusts:** Many unit trusts, are suitable for income investors. They offer investors diversification and professional management, and investors do not need to have a large lump sum to start investing.

Item	*Your Amounts*	*Sample Amounts*
A. How much annual income do you need?		£10,000
B. The value of your portfolio (or money available for investment)		£150,000
C. Yield necessary to achieve income (divide item A by item B)		6.7%

With this simple table, you know that if you have £150,000 in income shares yielding 6.7 per cent, you receive income of £10,000 – meeting your stated financial need. You may ask, 'Why not just buy £150,000 of bonds (for instance) that yield at least 6.7 per cent?' Well, if you're satisfied with that £10,000, and inflation for the foreseeable future is zero, then you have a point. Unfortunately, inflation is probably with us for the foreseeable future. Fortunately, the steady growth that income shares provide is a benefit to you.

If you have income shares and don't have any immediate need for the dividends, consider reinvesting the dividends in the company's shares. For more details on this kind of reinvesting, see Chapter 18.

Every investor is different. If you're not sure about your current or future needs, your best choice is to consult with an independent financial adviser.

Checking out yield

Because income shares pay out dividends – income – you need to assess which shares can give you the highest income. How do you decide which shares will pay the most money? The main thing to look for in choosing income shares is *yield* (the percentage rate of return paid on a share in the form of dividends). Looking at a 'share's dividend yield is the quickest way to find out how much money you can earn from a particular income share versus other dividend-paying shares (or even other investments such as a bank account). Table 9-1 illustrates this point. Dividend yield is calculated in the following way:

Dividend yield = dividend income = share investment

The next two sections use the information in Table 9-1 to compare the yields from different investments and to see how evaluating yield can help you choose the company to earn you the most money.

Don't stop scrutinising shares after you acquire them. You may have made a great choice that gives you a great dividend, but that doesn't mean that the shares stay that way indefinitely. Monitor the company's progress for as long as it's in your portfolio. Use resources such as www.ft.com and www.fool. co.uk (see Appendix A for more resources) to track your shares and to monitor how well that particular company continues to perform.

Table 9-1	Comparing Yields			
Investment	*Type*	*Investment Amount*	*Annual Investment Income (Dividend)*	*Yield (Annual Investment Income ÷Investment Amount)*
Smith PLC	Ordinary shares	£20 per share	£1.00 per share	5%
Jones PLC	Ordinary shares	£30 per share	£1.50 per share	5%
Wilson Bank	Savings account	£1,000 deposit	£40	4%

Examining yield

Most people have no problem understanding yield when it comes to savings. If I tell you that my National Savings Certificate has an annual yield of 3.5 per cent, you can easily work out that if I deposit £1,000 in that account, a year later I have £1,035 (slightly more if you include compounding). The 'National Savings Certificate's market value in this example is the same as the deposit amount – £1,000. That makes it easy to calculate.

How about shares? When you see a share listed in the financial pages, the dividend yield is provided along with the share's price and annual dividend. The dividend yield in the financial pages is always calculated as if you bought the share on the previous day – the day before publication. Just keep in mind that, based on supply and demand, share prices change virtually every day (every minute!) that the market is open. Therefore, because the share price changes every day, the yield changes as well. So, keep the following two things in mind when examining yield:

- ✔ **The yield listed in the financial pages may not represent the yield you're receiving.** What if you bought shares in Smith PLC (see Table 9-1) a month ago at £20 per share? With an annual dividend of £1, you know that your yield is 5 per cent. But what if today Smith PLC is selling for £40 per share? If you look in the financial pages, the yield quoted would be 2.5 per cent. Gasp! Did the dividend get cut in half?! No, not really. You're still getting 5 per cent because you bought the stock at £20 rather than the current £40 price; the quoted yield is for investors who purchase Smith PLC today. Investors who buy Smith PLC shares today pay £40 and get the £1 dividend, and they're locked into the current yield of 2.5 per cent. Although Smith PLC may have been a good income investment for you a month ago, it's not such a hot pick today because the price of the shares doubled, cutting the yield in half. Even though the dividend hasn't changed, the yield changed dramatically because of the share price change.

- ✔ **Share price affects how good an investment the shares may be.** Another way to look at yield is by looking at the amount of investment. Using Smith PLC in Table 9-1 as the example, the investor who bought, say, 100 shares of Smith PLC when they were £20 per share only paid £2,000 (100 shares times £20 – leave out commissions to make the example simple). If the same share is purchased later at £40 per share, the total investment amount is £4,000 (100 shares times £40). In both cases, the investor gets a total dividend income of £100 (100 shares times £1 dividend per share). From a yield perspective, which investment is yielding more – the £2,000 investment or the £4,000 investment? Of course, it's better to get the income (£100 in this case) with the smaller investment (a 5 per cent yield is better than a 2.5 per cent yield).

Comparing yield between different shares

All things being equal, choosing Smith PLC or Jones PLC is a coin toss. Look at your situation and each company's fundamentals and prospects and something may sway you. What if Smith PLC is a motoring company and Jones PLC is a utility serving inner London. Now what? In a difficult economy, the motoring industry struggles, while utilities were generally in much better shape. In that scenario, Smith PLC's dividend would be in jeopardy while Jones PLC's dividend would be more secure. Another issue would be the dividend cover (see next section). Therefore, having the same yield is not the same as the same risk. Different companies have different risks associated with them.

Checking the company's dividend cover

You can use the *dividend cover* to work out what per cent proportion of the company's earnings are being paid out in the form of dividends. Keep in mind that companies pay dividends from their net earnings. Therefore, the company's earnings should always be higher than the dividends the company pays out. Here's how to calculate the dividend cover:

Earnings per share ÷ dividend per share = dividend cover

Say that the company CashFlow Now, PLC, (CFN) has annual earnings of £1 million. (Remember that earnings are what you get when you subtract expenses from sales.) Total dividends are to be paid out of £500,000, and the company has 1 million outstanding shares. Using those numbers, you know that CFN has earnings per share (EPS) of £1.00 (£1 million in earnings divided by 1 million shares) and that it pays an annual dividend of 50 pence per share (£500,000 divided by 1 million shares). The dividend cover is 2 (the £1 earnings per share is twice the dividend of 50 pence). This number is a healthy dividend cover because even if the company's earnings fall by 10 per cent or 20 per cent, it still has plenty of room to pay dividends. People concerned about the safety of their dividend income should regularly watch the dividend cover. Generally 2 or higher is considered safe because the company can well afford to pay its dividend. Around 1.5 would be on the risky side and less than 1 would be dangerous as the company is using the previous year's earnings (or worse still, debt) to pay its dividend.

When a company suffers significant financial difficulties, its ability to pay dividends is compromised. So if you need dividend income to help you pay your bills, you better be aware of the dividend cover. Generally, a dividend cover of 2 or more is safe. Obviously, the higher the number is, the safer the dividend.

Diversifying your shares

If most of your dividend income comes from shares in a single company or from a single industry, consider reallocating your investment to avoid having all your eggs in one basket. Concerns for diversification apply to income shares as well as growth shares. If all your income shares are in the electricity industry, then any problems in that industry are potential problems for your portfolio as well. See Chapter 4 for more on diversification.

Examining the company's bond rating

Bond rating? What's that got to do with dividend-paying shares? Actually, the company's bond rating is very important to income share investors. The bond rating offers insight into the company's financial strength. A *bond* is a type of share by which the authorised issuer owes the holders a debt, and is obliged to repay the capital and interest at a later date, when the bond is said to *mature*. Bonds get rated for quality for the same reasons that consumer agencies rate products such as cars or toasters. Standard & Poor's (S&P) is the major independent rating agency that looks into bond issuers. It looks at the issuer of a bond and asks the question 'Does the bond issuer have the financial strength to pay back the bond and the interest as stipulated in the bond indenture?' To understand why this rating is important, consider the following:

- ✔ If the bond rating is good, that means that the company is strong enough to pay its obligations. These obligations include expenses, payments on debts, and dividends that are declared. If a bond rating agency gives the company a high rating (or if it raises the rating), that's a great sign for anyone holding the company's debt or receiving dividends.

- ✔ If a bond rating agency lowers the rating of a bond, that means that the company's financial strength is deteriorating – a red flag for anyone who owns the company's bonds or shares. A lower bond rating today may mean trouble for the dividend later on.

- ✔ If the bond rating isn't good, that means that the company is having difficulty paying its obligations. If the company can't pay all its obligations, then it has to choose which ones to pay. More times than not, a financially troubled company chooses to cut dividends or (in a worst case scenario) not pay dividends at all.

The highest rating issued by S&P is AAA. The grades AAA, AA, and A are considered *investment grade*, or of high quality. Bs and Cs indicate a poor grade, while anything lower than that is considered very risky (the bonds are referred to as 'junk bonds'). The lowest ratings tend to be Ds, which usually mean that the company is in default.

Exploring Typical Income Shares

Although virtually every industry has companies that pay dividends, some industries have more dividend-paying companies than others. And some industries are likely to pay higher dividends than others. You won't find too many companies in the computer or biotech industry paying higher than average dividends! The reason is that when companies need a lot of money to finance expensive research and development (R&D) projects to create new products, they can't afford to pay dividends. Without R&D, the company can't create new products to fuel sales, growth, and future earnings. Computer, biotech, and other innovative industries are often better for growth investors.

Utilities

Utilities generate a large cash flow. (If you don't believe me, look at your gas and electric bills!) Cash flow includes money from income (sales of products and/or services) and other items (such as the selling of assets, for example). This cash flow is needed to cover things such as expenses, loan payments, and dividends. Utilities are considered the most common type of income shares, and many investors have at least one in their portfolios. Investing in your own local utility isn't a bad idea. At least it makes paying the utility bill less painful. Before you invest in a public utility, consider the following:

- **The utility company's financial condition:** Is the company making money, and are its sales and earnings growing from year to year? Make sure that the utility's bonds are rated A or higher. I cover bond ratings in the 'Examining the company's bond rating' section, earlier in this chapter.

- **The company's dividend cover:** Because utilities tend to have a good cash flow, don't be too concerned if the dividend cover reaches 1.5. Again, from a safety point of view, however, the higher the rate the better. See the 'Checking the company's dividend cover' section, earlier in this chapter, for more on dividend cover.

- **The company's geographic location:** If the utility covers an area that's doing well and offers an increasing population base and business expansion, that bodes well for your shares.

Real estate investment trusts (REITs)

Real estate investment trusts (REITs) were introduced to the UK market in January 2007. Although popular in many other countries, they are newcomers to the UK. A *REIT* is an investment that has the elements of both a share and *an investment trust* (a pool of money received from investors that's managed by an investment company). It's like a share in that it's a company whose shares are publicly traded on the stock market, and it has the usual features that you expect from a share – it can be bought and sold easily through a broker, income is given to investors as dividends, and so on. A REIT resembles an investment trust in that it doesn't make its money selling goods and services; it makes its money by buying, selling, and managing an investment portfolio – in the case of a REIT, the portfolio is full of real estate or property investments. It generates revenue from rents and property leases as any landlord does. In addition, some REITs own mortgages, and they gain income from the interest.

Because REITs are new to the UK, only a small number of property companies have converted to REIT status. They include major companies such as British Land, Great Portland Estates, and Hammerson. More companies are planning to make the switch but they have to pay 2 per cent of the market value of their property portfolios to convert. UK REITs have to distribute 90 per cent of their profit from tax-exempt property rental business to shareholders.

The main advantages to investing in REITs include the following:

- ✔ Unlike other types of property investment, REITs are easy to buy and sell. You can buy a REIT by making a phone call to a broker or visiting a broker's Web site, just as you can to purchase any share.

- ✔ REITs in the UK do not yet have the higher-than-average yields seen overseas. But they must distribute at least 90 per cent of their profit from tax-exempt property rental business to their shareholders, so their dividend yield, currently 2–4 per cent, is expected to rise.

- ✔ REITs involve a lower risk than the direct purchase of commercial property. Because you're investing in a company that buys the property, you don't have to worry about managing the properties – the company's management does that on a full-time basis. Usually, the REIT doesn't just manage one commercial property; it's diversified in a portfolio of different properties.

- ✔ Investing in a REIT is affordable for small investors. REIT shares are affordable and have tax advantages. They can be bought in tax-efficient wrappers such as ISAs, SIPPs, and even child trust funds.

REITs do have disadvantages. They have the same inherent risks as investing in commercial property directly. Property investment has reached manic record-high levels during the last few years, which means that a downturn may be around the corner. Whenever you invest in an asset (property and therefore REITs) that has already skyrocketed due to artificial stimulants (in the case of property, very low interest rates and too much credit and debt), the potential losses may offset any potential (unrealised) income.

When you're looking for a REIT to invest in, analyse it the way you'd analyse a property. Look at the location and type of the property. If shopping centres are booming in Essex and your REIT buys and sells shopping centres in Essex, then you should do well. However, if your REIT invests in office buildings across the country and the office building market is overbuilt and having tough times, so will you.

Banks

Banks may not always be popular with their customers but they tend to be looked upon more kindly by their shareholders. Every year as the annual results season for the banks comes around, you can expect a flood of headlines highlighting the 'exorbitant' profits of our high street institutions. But the good news for shareholders is that as profits jump so do their dividends.

Income investors may not always have been so keen on the UK banks precisely because of those banks' reliance on the UK. If the UK economy suffered, the banks may be hit hard as borrowers default on their mortgages and loans. In recent years, banks have become more astute at pricing their lending for such risks. They charge more for a loan to someone who is more likely to default. But they have also started to diversify outside of the UK with the biggest banks, such as HSBC and Barclays, now earning as much as half of their profit from overseas interests.

Although banks are paying high dividends at the moment they are heavily regulated and may be hit hard if consumer groups force through changes to the way that fees are charged.

Chapter 10

Using Basic Accounting to Choose Winning Shares

In This Chapter

▶ Determining a company's value

▶ Using accounting principles to understand a company's financial condition

Successful share picking sometimes seems like pulling a rabbit out of a hat. In other words, it seems like you need sleight of hand to choose shares. Perhaps picking shares is more art than science. The other bloke seems to always pick winners while you're stuck with losers. What does it take? A crystal ball or a system from a get-rich-quick-with-shares book? Well, with the book in your hands now and a little work on your part, we think you can succeed. This chapter takes the mystery out of the numbers behind the share. The most tried-and-trusted method for picking a good share starts with picking a good company. Picking the company means looking at its products, services, industry, and financial strength ('the numbers'). Doing research regarding the company's 'financials' is easier than ever before, thanks to the current information age.

Recognising Value When You See It

If you pick a share based on the value of the company that's issuing it, you're a *value investor* – an investor who looks at a company's value and judges whether he can purchase the share at a good price. Companies have values the same way many things have value, such as eggs or papier mâché umbrella stands. They also have such a thing as a fair price to buy them at, too. Eggs, for example, have value. You can eat them and have a tasty treat while getting nutrition as well. But would you buy an egg for £1,000 (and, no, you're not a starving millionaire on a desert island)? No, of course not. But what if you can buy an egg for 5 pence? At that point, it has value *and* a good price. This kind of deal is a value investor's dream.

Value investors analyse a company's fundamentals (earnings, assets, and so on) and see if the information justifies purchasing the shares. They see if the share price is low relative to these verifiable, quantifiable factors. Therefore, value investors use 'fundamental analysis', while other investors may use 'technical analysis'. *Technical analysis* looks at charts and statistical data, such as trading volume and historical share prices. Some investors use a combination of both.

History has shown us that the most successful long-term investors have typically been value investors using fundamental analysis as their primary investing approach.

When you look at a company from a value-oriented perspective, here are a few of the most important items to consider:

- ✔ **The balance sheet to work out the company's net worth:** A value investor doesn't buy a company's shares because they're cheap; the investor buys them because they're *undervalued* (the company is worth more than the price its shares reflect – its market value is as close as possible to its book value).

- ✔ **The P&L account to figure out the company's profitability:** A company may be undervalued from a simple comparison of the book value and the market value, but that doesn't make it a screaming buy. For example, what if you find out that a company is in trouble and losing money this year? Do you buy its shares then? No, you don't. Why invest in shares in a losing company? (If you do, you aren't investing – you're gambling or speculating.) The heart of a company's value, besides its net worth, is its ability to generate profit.

- ✔ **Ratios that let you analyse just how well (or not so well) the company is doing:** Value investors basically look for a bargain. That being the case, they generally don't look at companies that everyone is talking about, because by that point, the shares in those companies cease to be a bargain. The value investor searches for shares that will eventually be discovered by the market and then watches as the share price goes up. But before you bother digging into the fundamentals to find those bargain shares, first make sure that the company is making money.

See the section, 'Accounting for Value,' later in this chapter, for more on using balance sheets, profit and loss (or P&L) accounts, and ratios to help you analyse share values.

Value investors can find thousands of companies that have value, but they can probably buy only a handful at a truly good price. The number of shares that can be bought at a good price is relative to the market. In mature bull markets, a good price is hard to find because most shares have probably seen significant price increases, but in bear markets, good companies at bargain prices are easier to come by.

Understanding different types of value

Value may seem like a murky or subjective term, but value is the essence of good share picking. You can measure value in different ways, so you need to know the difference and understand the impact that value has on your investment decisions.

Market value

When you hear someone quoting a company at £47 per share, that price reflects the company's market value. The total market valuation of a company's shares is also referred to as its *market cap* or *market capitalisation.* How do you determine a company's market cap? With the following simple formula:

Market capitalisation = share price × the number of shares outstanding

If Bolshevik PLC's shares are £35 each and it has 10 million shares outstanding (or shares available for purchase), then its market cap is £350 million. Granted, £350 million dollars may sound like a lot of money, but Bolshevik PLC may still be considered a small-cap depending on the relative value of the rest of the market. For more information about small-cap shares, dip into Chapter 8.

Who sets the market value of shares? The market – millions of investors directly and through intermediaries such as fund managers – determines the market value of shares. If the market perceives that the company is desirable, investor demand for the company's shares pushes up the price.

The problem with market valuation is that it may not always be a good indicator of a good investment. In recent years, plenty of companies have had astronomical market values, yet they proved to be terrible companies and consequently terrible investments. For example, WorldCom was a multi-billion-dollar company, yet it eventually went bankrupt, and the shares became worthless. Investors (and analysts) misunderstood the difference between the fleeting market value of the company and its true, underlying value.

Book value

Book value (also referred to as *accounting value*) looks at a company from a balance sheet perspective (assets minus liabilities equal net worth or *share-holders' funds*). Book value is a way of judging a company by its net worth to see whether the company's market value is reasonable compared to the company's intrinsic value.

Generally, market value usually tends to be higher than book value. If market value is substantially higher than book value, the value investor becomes more reluctant to buy that particular share because the share is overvalued. The closer the company's market capitalisation is to the book value, the safer the investment.

We like to be cautious with a company whose market value is more than twice its book value. If the market value is £1 billion and the book value is £500 million or more, that's a good indicator that the company may be *overvalued*, or valued at a higher price than the company's book value and ability to generate a profit. Just understand that the further the market value is from the company's book value, the more you pay for the company's real potential value.

Earnings and sales value

A company's intrinsic value is directly tied to its ability to make money. In that case, many analysts like to value shares from the perspective of the company's P&L account. Two common barometers of value are expressed in ratios: the price to sale ratio and the price-to-earnings ratio. In both instances, the price is a reference to the company's market value (as reflected in its share price). Sales and earnings are references to the company's ability to make money. These two ratios are covered more fully in the section 'Playing around with ratios,' later in this chapter.

For investors, the general approach is clear. The closer the market value is to the company's intrinsic value, the better. And, of course, if the market value is lower than the company's intrinsic value, then you have a potential bargain worthy of a closer look. Part of looking closer means examining the company's *profit and loss statement,* also called the P&L account, or simply, the *P&L.*

Putting the pieces together

The more ways that you can look at a company and see value, the better. The first thing to look at is the *price to earnings ratio* (or P/E ratio). Does the company have one? (It sounds dumb, but if a company is losing money, it may not have one.) Does it look reasonable or is it in triple-digit, nosebleed territory? Is it reasonable or too high? Next, look at the company's debt load. Is it less than the company's equity? Are sales healthy and increasing from the previous year? Does the company compare favourably in these categories versus other companies in the same industry?

Simplicity is best. You may notice that the number '10' comes up frequently in measuring the company's performance, juxtaposing all the numbers that you need to be aware of. If net income is rising by 10 per cent or more, that's fine. If the company is in the top 10 per cent of its industry, that's great. If the industry is growing by 10 per cent or better (sales, and so on), that's great. If sales are up 10 per cent or more from the previous year, that's great. A great company doesn't have to have all these things going for it. But it should have as many of these things happening to ensure greater potential success.

Crash-test dummy candidate?

From 2001-2003, consumers were buying up people carriers faster than they were producing more people. Demand was high for those popular gas-guzzling vehicles and car giant General Motors (GM) was racking up record sales. Investors noticed GM's success, and its share price surpassed $76 in 2001. However, the numbers (and the times) were catching up with GM. Its zero-interest financing programme started to sputter. Debts and human resources liabilities (such as employee health and pension commitments) started accelerating. Energy costs rose, making people carriers less attractive. The red flags came out. GM's 2004 year-end balance sheet showed debt of over $451 billion while total shareholder equity was only $27.7 billion. GM's net income fell to just 1 per cent of net sales, and its price-to-earnings (P/E) ratio (see the 'Playing around with ratios' section, later in this chapter) ballooned to a lofty 39. The share price hit $25 by April 2005. Although the price rebounded to the mid-$30s by July 2005, investors had skid marks on their portfolio as the share lost nearly two thirds of its value during that time frame. By September 2005, GM reported a net loss (goodbye P/E ratio). GM has undergone a radical restructuring to try and hold on to its status as the World's largest car company and is investing $100 million on electric and biofuel cars to cash in on the new demand for environmentally friendly transport.

As a contrasting point, look at Exxon Mobil (XOM) during that same time frame. Its share price went from about $35 in early 2001 to $60 in July 2005 (its shares were doing so well in mid-2001 that investors were given two for every one they had – called a *2-for-1 share split* – to reduce the actual price of the share so new investors could afford to buy). XOM's net income was a healthy 8 per cent of sales and the P/E ratio was only 14. In its 2004 year-end balance sheet, total shareholder equity of $101.7 billion comfortably exceeded its total liabilities of $89.5 billion. A sound company with sound numbers. Early in 2007 it posted record annual profits of $39.5 billion – the highest annual profits ever for a US company.

The point here is that the share price ultimately reflects the financial health and vitality of the company, and you can easily find and evaluate that information. You don't need luck or a crystal ball. Again, just a little work in the form of fundamental analysis is sufficient.

Does every company or industry have to neatly fit these criteria? No. Of course not. But it won't hurt you to be as picky as possible. You only need to find a handful of shares from thousands of choices. (Hey, this approach has worked for Paul, his clients, and his students for over two decades.) Nuff said.

Accounting for Value

Profit is for a company what oxygen is for you and me. That's neither good nor bad; it just is. Without profit, a company can't survive, much less thrive. Without profit, it can't provide jobs, pay taxes, or invest in new products, equipment, or innovation. Without profit, the company eventually goes bankrupt, and the value of its shares evaporates.

In the heady days leading up to the bear market of 2000–2002, many investors lost a lot of money simply because they invested in shares in companies that weren't making a profit. Lots of public companies ended up like flies that just didn't see the windscreen coming their way. Global giants such as Enron and WorldCom entered the graveyard of rather-be-forgotten shares, and plenty of less well-known companies joined them. Investors around the world lost billions investing in glitzy companies that sounded good but weren't making money. When their brokers were saying, 'buy, buy, buy,' their hard-earned money was saying, 'bye, bye, bye!'

Investors in shares need to pick up a rudimentary knowledge of accounting to round out their share-picking prowess and to be sure that they're getting a good value for their investment cash. Accounting is the language of business. If you don't understand basic accounting, then you're going to have have difficulty being a successful investor. Investing without accounting knowledge is like travelling without a map. However, if you can run a household budget, using accounting analysis to evaluate shares is easier than you think.

Walking on a wire: The balance sheet

A company's balance sheet gives you a financial snapshot of what the company looks like in terms of the following equation:

Assets – liabilities = net worth

Analyse the following items that you find on the balance sheet:

- ✔ **Assets:** Have they increased from the previous year? If not, was the lack of increase due to the sale of an asset or a write-off (uncollectible accounts receivable, for example)?

- ✔ **Stock:** Is there more or less stock than last year? If sales are flat but the stock in the warehouse is growing, that may be a potential problem.

- ✔ **Debt:** Debt is the biggest weakness on the corporate balance sheet. Make sure that debt isn't a growing item and that any debt is under control. In recent years, debt has become a huge problem for many companies.

- ✔ **Derivatives:** A *derivative* is a speculative and complex financial instrument that doesn't constitute ownership of an asset (such as a share, bond, or commodity), but a promise to convey ownership. Some derivatives are quite acceptable because they are used as protective or hedging vehicles (such derivatives are not our primary concern). However, people frequently use them to generate income and they can then carry risks that can increase liabilities. Options and futures are examples of derivatives.

Find out whether the company dabbles in these complicated, dicey, leveraged financial instruments. Find out (from the company's annual report) whether it has derivatives and, if so, the total amount. If a company has derivatives that are valued higher than the company's net equity, it may cause tremendous problems. Derivatives problems sank many organisations ranging from the respected Barings Bank in the UK to the now infamous Enron.

✓ **Equity:** Equity is the company's net worth (what's left in the event that a company uses all the assets to pay off all its debts). Also known as shareholders' funds, equity should be increasing steadily by at least 10 per cent per year. If not, find out why.

By looking at a company's balance sheet, you can address the following questions:

✓ **What does the company own (assets)?** The company can own assets, which can be financial, tangible, and/or intangible. *Assets* can be anything that has value or that can be converted to or sold for cash. Financial assets can be cash, investments, or accounts receivable. Assets can be tangible things such as products and supplies, equipment, and/or buildings. They can also be intangible things such as licenses, trademarks, or copyrights.

✓ **What does the company owe (liabilities)?** *Liabilities* are anything of value that the company must ultimately pay to someone else. Liabilities can be invoices (accounts payable) or short-term or long-term debt.

✓ **What is the company's net equity (net worth)?** After you subtract the liabilities from the assets, the remainder is called *net worth, net equity,* or *net shareholders' funds.* This number is also critical when calculating a company's book value.

As you can see, a balance sheet isn't difficult to understand. A balance sheet is an important document that you should look at carefully to make sure that the company is in a strong financial position. Finding the relevant financial data on a company isn't difficult in the age of information. Most public companies publish their most recent financial documents including interim and annual results and annual reports on their Web sites.

The assets and liabilities relationship for a company has the same logic as the assets and liabilities in your own household. When you look at a snapshot of your own finances (your personal balance sheet), how can you tell if you're doing well? Odds are that you'd start by comparing numbers. If your net worth is 5,000, you may say, 'That's great!' But a more appropriate remark is something like, 'That's great compared to, say, a year ago.'

Compare a company's balance sheet at a recent point in time to a past time. You should do this comparative analysis with all the key items on the balance sheet. You do this analysis to see the company's progress. Is it growing its assets and/or shrinking its debt? Most importantly, is the company's net worth growing? Is it growing by at least 10 per cent from a year ago? All too often, investors stop doing their homework after they make an initial investment. You should continue to look at the company's numbers on a regular basis so that you can be ahead of the curve. If the company starts having problems, you can get out before the rest of the market starts getting out (which causes the share price to fall).

To judge the financial strength of a company, ask yourself the following questions:

- ✔ Are the company's assets greater in value than they were three months ago, a year ago, or two years ago? Compare current asset size to the most recent two years to make sure that the company is growing in size and financial strength.

- ✔ How do the individual items compare with previous periods? Some particular assets that you want to take note of are cash, stock, and accounts receivable.

- ✔ Are liabilities such as accounts payable and debt about the same, lower, or higher compared to previous periods? Are they growing at a similar, faster, or slower rate than the company's assets? Remember that debt that rises faster and higher than items on the other side of the balance sheet is a warning sign of impending financial problems.

- ✔ Is the company's net worth or equity greater than the previous year? And is that year's equity greater than the year before? In a healthy company, the net worth is constantly rising. As a general rule, in good economic times, net worth should be at least 10 per cent higher than the previous year. In tough economic times (such as a recession), 5 per cent is acceptable. Seeing the net worth growing at 15 per cent or higher is great news.

Looking at the P&L account

Where do you look if you want to find out what a company's profit is? Check out the company's P&L account. It reports, in detail, a simple accounting equation that you probably already know:

Sales – expenses = net profit (or net earnings or net income)

Look at the following figures on the P&L account:

- ✔ **Sales:** Are sales (often called turnover) increasing? If not, why not? By what percentage are they increasing? Preferably, they should be at 10 per cent higher than the year before. Sales are, after all, where the money is coming from to pay for the company's activities and subsequent profit.

- ✔ **Expenses:** Do you see any unusual items? Are total expenses reported higher than the previous year and by how much? If the item is significantly higher, why? A company with large, rising expenses is going to see profits suffer, which isn't good for the share price.

- ✔ **Research and development (R&D):** How much is the company spending on R&D? Companies that rely on new product development (such as pharmaceuticals or biotech firms) should spend an adequate amount because new products mean future earnings and growth.

- ✔ **Profit:** This figure reflects the bottom line. Is total profit (earnings) higher than the previous year? How about operating profit (leaving out expenses such as taxes and interest)? The profit section is the heart and soul of the P&L and of the company itself. Out of all the numbers in the financial statements, profit has the greatest single impact on the company's share price.

Looking at the P&L, an investor can try to answer the following questions:

- ✔ **What sales did the company make?** Companies sell products and services that generate revenue (known as *sales* or *turnover*). Sales are also referred to as the *top line*.

- ✔ **What expenses did the company incur?** In generating sales, companies pay expenses such as payroll, utilities, advertising, administration, and so on.

- ✔ **What is the net income?** Also called earnings or net profit, net income is the *bottom line*. After paying for all expenses, what profit did the company make?

The information you glean should give you a strong idea about the company's current financial strength and whether the management are successfully increasing sales, holding down expenses, and ultimately maintaining profitability. You can find out more about sales, expenses, and profits in the sections that follow.

Sales

Sales or turnover refers to the money that a company receives as customers buy its goods and/or services. Sales is a simple item on the P&L and a useful number to look at. Analysing a company by looking at its sales is called *top line analysis*.

As an investor, you should take into consideration the following points about sales:

✔ **Sales should be increasing.** A healthy, growing company has growing sales. They should grow at least 10 per cent from the previous year, and you should look at the most recent three years.

✔ **Core sales (sales of those products or services that the company specialises in) should be increasing.** Frequently, the sales figure has a lot of stuff lumped into it. Maybe the company sells widgets (what on earth is a widget, anyway?), but the core sales should not include other things, such as the sale of a building or other unusual items. Take a close look. Isolate the company's primary offerings and ask whether these sales are growing at a reasonable rate (such as 10 per cent).

✔ **Does the company have odd items or odd ways of calculating sales?** In the late 1990s, many companies boosted their sales by aggressively offering affordable financing with easy repayment terms. Say you find out that Suspicious Sales Ltd. (SSL) had annual sales of £50 million, reflecting a 25 per cent increase from the year before. Looks great! But what if you find out that £20 million of that sales number comes from sales made on credit that the company extended to buyers? Some companies that use this approach later have to write off losses as uncollectible debt because the customer ultimately can't pay for the goods.

If you want to get a good clue to whether a company is artificially boosting sales, check the company's *accounts receivable* (listed in the asset section of the company's balance sheet). Accounts receivable refers to money that is owed to the company for goods that customers have purchased on credit. If you find out that sales went up by £10 million (great!) but accounts receivable went up by £20 million (uh-oh), then something just isn't right. That may be a sign that the financing terms were too easy, and the company may have a problem collecting payment (especially in a recession).

Expenses

What a company spends has a direct relationship on its profitability. If spending isn't controlled or held at a sustainable level, it may spell trouble for a company.

When you look at a company's expense items, consider the following:

✔ **Compare expense items to the previous period.** Are expenses higher, lower, or about the same from the previous period? If the difference is significant, you should see commensurate benefits elsewhere. In other words, if overall expenses are 10 per cent higher compared to the previous period, are sales at least 10 per cent more during the same period?

✔ **Are some expenses too high?** Look at the individual expense items. Are they significantly higher than the year before? If so, why?

✔ **Have any unusual items been expensed?** Sometimes an unusual expense isn't necessarily a negative. Expenses may be higher than usual if a company writes off uncollectible accounts receivable as bad debt expense. Doing so inflates the total expenses and subsequently results in lower earnings. Pay attention to non-recurring charges that show up on the P&L and determine whether they make sense.

Profit

Earnings or profit is the single most important item on the P&L and also the one that receives the most attention in the financial media. When a company makes a profit, this profit is usually reported as earnings per share (EPS). So if you hear that XYZ Ltd beat last year's earnings by a penny, here's how to translate that news. Suppose that the company made £1 per share this year and 99 pence per share last year. If that company had 100 million shares outstanding, then its profit this quarter is £100 million (the EPS times the number of shares outstanding), which is £1 million more than it made in the previous year (£1 million is one pence per share times 100 million shares).

Don't simply look at current profit as an isolated figure. Always compare current profit to profit in past periods (usually a year). For example, if you're looking at a retailer's interim results, you can't compare that with the retailer's finals from the previous year. Doing so is like comparing apples to oranges. What if the company usually does well during the summer holidays but poorly in the winter? In that case, you don't get a fair comparison.

A strong company should show consistent earnings growth from the period (such as the year or the same quarter from the previous year) before, and you should check the period before that, too, so that you can determine whether earnings are consistently rising over time. Earnings growth is an important barometer of the company's potential growth and bodes well for the share price.

When you look at earnings, here are a few things to consider:

✔ **Total profit:** This item is the one to watch most closely. Total profit should grow year on year by at least 10 per cent.

✔ **Operating profit:** Break down the total earnings and look at a key subset – that portion of earnings derived from the company's core activity. Is the company continuing to make money from its primary goods and services?

✔ **Non-recurring items:** Is profit higher (or lower) than usual or than expected and why? Frequently, the difference results from items such as the sale of an asset or a large depreciation write-off.

We like to keep percentages as simple as possible. To reiterate, ten per cent is a good number – easy to calculate and a good benchmark. However, 5 per cent isn't unacceptable if you're talking about tough times, such as a recession. Obviously, if sales, earnings, and/or net worth are hitting or passing 15 per cent, that's great news.

Playing around with ratios

A ratio is a helpful numerical tool that you can use to find out the relationship between two or more figures found in the company's financial data. A ratio can add meaning to a number or put it in perspective. Ratios sound complicated, but they're easier to understand than you think.

Say that you're considering a share investment and the company you're looking at has earnings of £1 million this year. You may think that's a tidy sum, but in order for this amount to be meaningful, you have to compare it to something. What if you find out that the other companies in the industry (of similar size and scope) had earnings of £500 million? Does that change your thinking? Or what if you find out that the same company had earnings of £75 million in the previous period? Does that change your mind?

Two key ratios to be aware of are:

- ✔ Price-earnings ratio (P/E)
- ✔ Price-to-sales ratio (PSR or P/R)

 Every investor wants to find shares that have a 20 per cent average growth rate over the past five years and have a low P/E ratio (sounds like a dream). Use share-screening tools available for free on the Internet to do your research. Some brokers have them on their Web sites (such as The Share Centre at www.share.co.uk). Some excellent screening tools are also available from Proshare, the organisation that encourages share ownership (www.prosohareclubs.co.uk) and on the Financial Times Web site at www.ft.com. A *share-screening tool* lets you plug in numbers such as sales or earnings and ratios such as the P/E ratio or the dividend yield and then click! Up come shares that fit your criteria. This is a good starting point for serious investors. Check out Appendix B for even more on ratios.

Running into the P/E ratio

The price to earnings (P/E) ratio is important in analysing a potential share investment because this ratio is one of the most widely regarded barometers of a company's value, and is usually reported along with the company's share price in the financial pages. The major significance of the P/E ratio is that it establishes a direct relationship between the bottom line of a company's operations – the earnings – and the share price.

The *P* in P/E stands for the share's current price. The *E* is for earnings per share (typically the most recent 12 months of earnings). The P/E ratio is also referred to as the 'earnings multiple' or just 'multiple.'

You calculate the P/E ratio by dividing the price of the share by the earnings per share. If the price of a single share of a company is £10 and the earnings (on a per-share basis) are £1, then the P/E is 10. If the share price goes to £35 per share and the earnings are unchanged, then the P/E is 35. Basically, the higher the P/E, the more you pay for the company's earnings.

Why would you buy shares in one company with a relatively high P/E ratio instead of investing in another company with a lower P/E ratio? Keep in mind that investors buy shares based on expectations. They may bid up the price of the share (subsequently raising its P/E ratio) because they feel that the company's earnings are going to increase in the near future. Perhaps they feel that the company has great potential (a pending new invention or lucrative business deal) that will eventually make the company more profitable. More profitability in turn has a beneficial impact on the company's share price. The danger with a high P/E is that if the company doesn't achieve the hopeful results, the share price may fall.

You should look at two types of P/E ratios to get a balanced picture of the company's value:

- ✔ **Trailing P/E:** This P/E is the most frequently quoted because it deals with existing data. The trailing P/E uses the most recent 12 months of earnings in its calculation.

- ✔ **Forward P/E:** This P/E is based on projections or expectations of earnings in the coming 12-month period. Although this P/E may seem preferable because it looks into the near future, forward P/E is still considered an estimate that may or may not prove to be accurate.

The following example illustrates the importance of the P/E ratio. Say that you want to buy a business and we're selling a business. If you come to us and say, 'What do you have to offer?', we may say, 'Have we got a deal for you! We operate a retail business in the centre of town that sells spatulas. The business nets a cool £2,000 profit per year.' You reluctantly say, 'Uh, okay, what's the asking price for the business?' We reply, 'You can have it for only £1 million! What do you say?'

If you're sane, odds are that you politely turn down that offer. Even though the business is profitable (a cool £2,000 a year), you'd be crazy to pay a million quid for it. In other words, the business is way overvalued (too expensive for what you're getting in return for your investment cash). The million pounds would generate a better rate of return elsewhere and probably with less risk. As for the business, the P/E ratio (£1 million divided by £2,000 = a P/E of 500) is outrageous. This example is definitely a case of an overvalued company – and a lousy investment.

What if we offered the business for £12,000? Does that price make more sense? Yes. The P/E ratio is a more reasonable 6 (£12,000 divided by £2,000). In other words, the business pays for itself in about 6 years (versus 500 years in the prior example).

Looking at the P/E ratio offers a shortcut for investors asking the question, 'Is this company overvalued?' As a general rule, the lower the P/E, the safer (or more conservative) the shares are . The reverse is more noteworthy: The higher the P/E, the greater the risk.

When someone refers to a P/E as high or low, you have to ask the question, 'Compared to what?' A P/E of 30 is considered high for a large-cap electricity supplier but quite reasonable for a small-cap, technology firm. Keep in mind that phrases such as 'large-cap' and 'small-cap' are just a reference to the company's relative market value or size. 'Cap' is short for capitalisation (the total number of shares outstanding times the share price). See Chapter 3 for more on market cap.

The following basic points can help you evaluate P/E ratios:

- ✔ Compare a company's P/E ratio with its industry. Electricity industry shares generally have a P/E that hovers in the 9–14 range. Therefore, if you're considering an electricity supplier with a P/E of 45, then something is wrong with that company.

- ✔ Compare a company's P/E with the general market. If you're looking at a small-cap share on the Alternative Investment Market that has a P/E of 100 but the average P/E for established companies on the AIM is 40, find out why. You should also compare the share's P/E ratio with the P/E ratio for major indices such as the FTSE 100, the FTSE 250 and maybe even the Dow Jones Industrial Average (DJIA) (for more on market indices, see Chapter 5).

- ✔ Compare a company's current P/E with recent periods (such as this year versus last year). If it currently has a P/E ratio of 20 and it previously had a P/E ratio of 30, you know that the share price has declined or that earnings have risen. In the latter case, the share is less likely to fall. That bodes well for the company.

- ✔ Low P/E ratios aren't necessarily the sign of a bargain, but if you're look-ing at a company for many other reasons that seem positive (solid sales, strong industry, and so on) and it also has a low P/E, that's a good sign.

✔ High P/E ratios aren't necessarily bad, but they do mean that you should investigate further. If a company is weak and the industry is shaky, heed the high P/E as a warning sign. Frequently, a high P/E ratio means that investors have bid up a share price, anticipating future income. The problem is that if the anticipated income doesn't materialise, the share price may fall.

✔ Watch out for a share that doesn't have a P/E ratio. In other words, it may have a price (the P), but it doesn't have earnings (the E). No earnings means no P/E, meaning that you're better off avoiding it. Can you still make money buying a company with no earnings? You can, but you aren't investing; you're speculating.

Stock	P/E Ratio in 1999	Share Activity in 2000 and 2001	P/E Ratio in 2007
Cisco Systems	190	Share price fell from $80 to $15	25.59
eBay	3,980	Share price fell from $120 to $59	39.4
Yahoo!	896	Share price fell from $240 to $18	22.5

Discovering PSR

The *price to sales ratio* (PSR or P/S) is the company's share price divided by its sales. Because the sales number is rarely expressed as a per-share figure, it's easier to divide a company's total market value (see the section 'Market value,' earlier in this chapter, to find out what this term means) by its total sales for the last 12 months.

As a general rule, shares trading at a PSR of 1 or less are reasonably priced and worthy of your attention. For example, say that a company has sales of £1 billion and the stock has a total market value of £950 million. In that case, the PSR is 0.95. In other words, you can buy £1 of the company's sales for only 95 cents. All things being equal, that share may be a bargain.

Analysts frequently use the PSR as an evaluation tool in the following circumstances:

✔ In tandem with other ratios to get a more well-rounded picture of the company and its shares.

✔ When you want an alternate way to value a company that doesn't have earnings.

✔ By analysts who want a true picture of the company's financial health, because sales are tougher for companies to manipulate than earnings.

✔ When you're considering a company offering products (versus services). PSR is more suitable for companies that sell items that are easily counted (such as products). Companies that make their money through loans, such as banks, aren't usually valued with a PSR because deriving a usable PSR for them is more difficult.

Compare the company's PSR with other companies in the same industry, along with the industry average, so that you get a better idea of the company's relative value.

Part III
Picking Winners

'Your stock market investments, at this very moment, are being chosen with meticulous care by our team of approved experts.'

In this part . . .

*N*ow that you have the basics down, it's time to become a pro at picking individual shares. When you consider investing in a company, you need to know the key indications that a particular share's price is going to rise. And because the stock market doesn't operate in a vacuum, we introduce general economic and political factors that can have a huge effect on your shares. The chapters in this part steer you to key financial information and important company documents, and show you how to interpret the information you find.

Chapter 11

Decoding Company Documents

- -

In This Chapter

▶ Paging through an annual report

▶ Reviewing other sources of financial information

▶ Organising your own research library

- -

Good grief. Financial documents. Some people would rather suck a hospital mop than read a dry corporate or government report. Yet, if you're serious about choosing shares, you should be serious about your research. Fortunately, research is not as bad as you think (put away that disgusting mop!). When you see that basic research helps you build wealth, it gets easier.

In this chapter, we discuss the basic documents that you come across (or should come across) most often in your investing life. These documents include essential information that all investors need to know, not only at the time of the initial investment decision, but also for as long as those shares remain in their portfolio.

 If you plan to hold the shares for the long haul, reading the annual report and other reports covered in this chapter can only help you. If you intend to get rid of the shares soon or plan to hold them only for the short term, reading these reports diligently isn't that important.

Slices from the Big Cheeses: The Annual Report

When you're a regular shareholder, the company sends you its annual report. If you're not already a shareholder, contact the company's investor relations department for a hard copy.

 You can often view a company's annual report on its Web site. Any major search engine can help you find this site. Downloading or printing the annual report should be easy.

You need to carefully analyse an annual report to find out the following:

- ✔ **You want to know how well the company is doing.** Are earnings higher, lower, or the same as the year before? How are sales doing? These numbers should be clearly presented in the financial section of the annual report.

- ✔ **You want to find out whether the company is making more money than it's spending.** How does the balance sheet look? Are assets higher or lower than the year before? Is debt growing, shrinking, or about the same as the year before? For more details on balance sheets, see Chapter 10.

- ✔ **You want to get an idea of management's strategic plan for the coming year.** How are management planning to build on the company's success? This plan is usually covered in the beginning of the annual report – frequently in the letter from the chairman of the board.

Your task boils down to working out where the company has been, where the company is now, and where the company is going. As an investor, you don't need to read the annual report like a novel – from cover to cover. Instead, approach it like a newspaper and jump around to the relevant sections to get the answers you need in order to decide whether you should buy, or hold on to, the shares.

Analysing the annual report's anatomy

Not every company puts its annual report together in exactly the same way – the style of presentation varies. Some annual reports have gorgeous graphics or actual coupons for the company's products, while others are in a standard black-and-white typeface with no cosmetic frills at all. But every annual report does include common basic content, such as the profit and loss statement and the balance sheet. The following sections present typical components of an average annual report. Keep in mind that every annual report may not have the sections in the same order.

Letter from the chairman of the board

The first thing you see is usually the letter from the chairman of the board or the chairman's statement. This is the 'Dear Shareholder' letter that communicates views from the head big cheese. The chairman's letter is designed to put the best possible perspective on the company's operations during the past year. Be aware of this bias. If the company is doing well, the letter certainly points it out. If the company is having hard times, the letter probably tries to put a positive spin on the company's difficulties. If the Big Bad Wolf had an annual report, odds are that the letter would have reported, 'Our little pig capturing ventures are being upgraded to cope with the increased sophis-tication of building materials used by porcine targets. And we have decided to discontinue our Red Riding Hood subsidiary as the risks far outweigh the potential rewards'. You get the point.

To get a good idea of what issues the company's management team feels are important and what goals they want to accomplish, keep the following ques-tions in mind:

- ✔ What does the letter say about changing conditions in the company's business? How about changing conditions in the industry?

- ✔ If any difficulties exist, does the letter communicate a clear and logical action plan (cutting costs, closing loss-making plants, and so on) to get the company back on a positive track?

- ✔ What is being highlighted and why? For example, is the company focus-ing on research and development for new products or on a new deal with China?

- ✔ Does the letter offer apologies for anything the company did? If, for example, the company fell short of sales expectations, does it offer a reason for the shortcoming?

- ✔ Did the company make (or will it make) new acquisitions or major devel-opments (selling products to China or a new marketing agreement with a Fortune 500 company)?

The company's offerings

This section of an annual report can have various titles (such as 'Operating review'), but it covers what the company does to make its money. Whatever the company sells – products or services or both – understand what they are and why customers purchase them. If you don't understand what the com-pany offers, then understanding how the company earns money, which is the driving force behind the company's shares, is more difficult. Are the com-pany's core or primary offerings selling well? If the earnings of McDonalds are holding steady, but earnings strictly from burgers and fries are fizzling, that's a cause for concern. If a company ceases making money from its speciality, you should become cautious. Here are other questions to ask yourself:

- ✔ How does the company distribute its offerings? Through a Web site, shops, agents, or other means? Does it sell only to the UK market, or is its distribution international? The greater the distribution, the greater the sales and, ultimately, the higher the share price.

- ✔ Are most of the sales to a definable marketplace? If, for example, most of the company's sales are to a war-torn or politically unstable country, you should worry. If the company's customers aren't doing well, that has a direct impact on the company and, eventually, its shares.

✔ How are sales doing versus market standards? In other words, is the company doing better than the industry average? Is the company a market leader in what it offers? The company should be doing better than (or as well as) its peers in the industry. If the company is falling behind its competitors, that doesn't bode well for the shares in the long run.

✔ Does the report include information on the company's competitors and related matters? You should know who the company's competitors are because they have a direct effect on the company's success. If customers are choosing the competitor over your company, the slumping sales and earnings will ultimately hurt the share's price.

Financial statements

Look over the various financial statements and find the relevant numbers. Every annual report should have (at the least) a balance sheet and a profit and loss statement. Catching the important numbers on a financial statement isn't that difficult to do. However, it certainly helps when you pick up a little basic accounting knowledge. Chapter 10 can give you more details on evaluating financial statements.

First, review the *profit and loss statement* (called the P&L, but also known as the income statement). The P&L gives you the company's sales, expenses, and the result (net income or net loss).

Look at the balance sheet. The balance sheet provides a snapshot of a point in time (annual reports usually provide a year-end balance sheet) that tells you what the company owns (*assets*), what it owes (*liabilities*), and the end result (*net worth*). For a healthy company, assets should always be greater than liabilities.

Carefully read the footnotes to the financial statements. Sometimes big changes are communicated in small print.

Performance review

The performance review, which may also be called the summary of past financial figures, gives you a snapshot of the company's overall long-term progress. Most reports look at the company's performance over a five-year period and may even show a graph charting total shareholder return against the performance of the FTSE 100 Index (see Chapter 5 for more on indices).

Management issues

The management issues section of an annual report includes a reporting of current trends and issues, such as new things happening in the industry, that affect the company. This section may be called the Chief Executive's report or review or the Directors' statement. See whether you agree with management's assessment of economic and market conditions that affect the company's prospects. What significant developments in society does management perceive as affecting the company's operations? Does the report include information on current or pending legal action?

The auditor's report

Annual reports typically include comments from the company's auditors – qualified and certified accountants. It may be an opinion letter or a simple paragraph with the auditor's views regarding the financial statements that were prepared.

The report normally says that the accounts are true and fair – an opinion about the accuracy of the financial data presented and how the statements were prepared. Check to see whether the report qualifies this phrase in any way or includes any footnotes regarding changes in certain numbers or how they were reported. For example, a company that wants to report higher earnings may show depreciation more conservatively, rather than a more aggressive method of depreciating. In most cases, the auditor's reports in annual accounts are similar because they stick to accounting standard practice.

The 'About Us' section

Every annual report includes detailed information about the company and its subsidiaries (or lesser companies that it owns) and brands. Often each part of the business is given its own pages to explain who runs that part of the business and exactly what it does and where.

Directors' shareholdings

This section can usually be found as a table near the back of the report alongside details of directors' earnings (called remuneration). This gives a good picture of which directors are increasing their stakes in the business and how the share price has to perform to trigger their next long-term incentive plan share option target. See Chapter 19 for more on directors' share ownership.

Share data

The share data section may include a history of the share price – usually over the last five years – along with information such as what exchange the share is listed on, the share code, the company's dividend reinvestment plan (if any), and so on. It also includes information on shareholder services and whom to contact for further information.

Going through the proxy materials

As a shareholder (or investor – same thing), you're entitled to vote at the annual shareholders' meeting called the *Annual General Meeting* (AGM). If you ever get the opportunity to attend one, do so. You get to meet other shareholders and ask questions of management and other company representatives. Usually, the investor relations department provides you with complete details. At the meetings, shareholders vote on company matters, such as approving any new share options plans for senior executives or deciding whether the salaries for executives are acceptable.

Companies also have occasional special meetings called EGMs or Extraordinary General Meetings, which are held to vote on a particular issue such as whether a proposed merger with another company should go ahead.

If you can't attend (which is usually true for the majority of shareholders), you can vote by proxy. *Voting by proxy* means essentially that you vote by post. You indicate your votes on the proxy statement (or card) and authorise a representative to vote at the meeting on your behalf. The proxy statement is usually sent to all shareholders, along with the annual report, just before the meeting. If you hold your shares in a nominee account with your stockbroker, you may not get a vote automatically. Talk to your broker about this. See Chapter 7 for more on dealing with brokers.

Getting a Second Opinion

A wealth of valuable information is available for your investing pursuits. The resources in this section are just a representative few – a good representation, though. The information and research they provide can be expensive if you buy or subscribe on your own, but fortunately, most of the resources mentioned are usually available in the business reference section of a well-stocked public library or on the Internet. To get a more balanced view of the company and its prospects, take a look at several different sources of information for the shares you're researching.

Company documents filed with the RNS

The serious investor doesn't overlook the wealth of information that you can cull from documents filed with the regulated news services such as RNS (Regulatory News Service) or Pimswire. Take the time and effort to review these documents because they offer great insight regarding the company's activities. Here's how to obtain the main documents that investors should be aware of:

- ✔ **Drop by the company itself.** Shareholder service or investor relations departments keep these publicly available documents on hand and usually give them at no cost to interested parties. Most companies put them on their Web sites.

✔ **Ask the Financial Services Authority, the UK's listings authority, by phone or online.** If you can't find the documents you want or the company doesn't want to let you see them, you can always ask the FSA whether there should be public access. You can find out more by contacting the Financial Services Authority, 25 The North Colonnade, Canary Wharf, London E14 5HS.

✔ **Check out regulatory news services to search any public documents filed.** Companies in the UK have to publish their financial reports through authorised news services. Some are free to access and others charge a subscription. A list of the main ones is given in Chapter 6.

✔ **Check out the London Stock Exchange's (LSE) free Annual Report Service (`www.londonstockexchange.com`).** The LSE provides free information on more than 1,300 listed companies.

✔ **Review the Annual Report Service (`www.annualreportservice.com`).** This site maintains an extensive database of company annual reports.

✔ **Use *The Financial Times* free annual report service.** If you read this newspaper's financial pages and see a company with the club symbol (like the one you see on a playing card), then you can order that company's annual report by calling 0208 391 6000 or by visiting the Web site `www.ftannualreports.com`.

Trading updates

As the name suggests, the *trading update* gives you an update on current trading. Trading updates – sometimes called *trading statements* – tend to be issued every quarter. They give a brief overview of the company's progress since the last formal report – probably the annual or half-year results.

Unlike the annual report that you get from the company, a trading update tends not to provide very much detailed financial information. It covers the general progress of the company and a little bit of information on each of the company's main divisions. Retailers tend to publish these updates shortly after the major seasons – for example Christmas trading updates are common in the retail sector. The update may give an indication of how business is doing in terms of percentages, but is unlikely to give figures in pounds and pence. It may say that growth of 10 per cent has been seen in sales, or that a division has had its best quarter for five years, but not say how much profit has been made. The meat is kept for the next results.

You can find trading updates reported in the press and on financial Web sites such as:

✔ Motley Fool (`www.fool.co.uk`)

✔ Digital Look (`www.digitallook.com`)

Keep in mind that not every company has the same financial year or the same financial calendar. A company with a calendar year financial year (ending 31 December) will probably file a trading update for the first quarter (1 January to 31 March) in May. Half-year results may be in August followed by a third quarter trading update in November and final or full-year results in February.

Insider reports

Two types of insiders exist: those who work within the company and those outside the company who have a significant (10 per cent or more) ownership of company shares. Tracking insider activity is profitable for investors who want to follow in the footsteps of the people who are in the know. See Chapter 19 for information about monitoring and benefiting from insider activity.

Every time an insider (such as the CEO or financial director) buys or sells shares, the transaction has to be reported to the FSA. The insider has to report the trade soon after the transaction. These reports become publicly available documents – published on the regulated news services – that allow you to see what the insiders are doing. Hearing what they say in public is one thing, but seeing what they're actually doing with their share transactions can be more important.

MarketStars

MarketStars is one of many information products provided by Digital Look, the specialist investment Web site. It is popular with serious investors looking for help in refining their strategies for picking winning shares. At the time of writing, a 30-day free trial of the service is available. It provides lots of tips and guidance on picking shares and investment alerts by email.

Standard & Poor's

Probably the most ubiquitous and venerable publisher is Standard & Poor's (S&P). Although it has a number of quality information products and services for both individual and institutional investors, the three you should take a look at are the following:

  ✔ **The S&P Stock Guide:** Available at many libraries, this guide comes out monthly and reports on shares on the New York Share Exchange, American Stock Exchange, and the largest firms listed on Nasdaq. It gives a succinct, two-page summary on each share. It offers a snapshot of the company's current finances along with a brief history and commentary on the company's activities. This guide also rates the company based on its financial strength.

✔ ***The S&P Industry Survey:*** S&P gives detailed reports on the top industries, cramming a lot of information about a given industry into four to seven pages. This annual publication provides a nice summary of what's happened in the industry in the past 12 months, what the industry looks like today, and the prospects for the coming year. It also provides the important numbers (earnings, sales, and industry ranking) for the top 50 to 100 firms in the industry.

✔ ***The S&P Bond Guide:*** Yes, we know this book is about shares. But a company's bond rating is invaluable for share investors. S&P analyses the strength of the bond issuer and ranks the bond for creditworthiness. If S&P looks at the company and gives it a high rating, you have added assurance that the company is financially strong. You want the company to have a bond rating of AAA, AA, or A because these ratings tell you that the company is 'investment-grade'. Check out S&P's Web site at www.standardandpoors.com.

Moody's Investment Service

Another stalwart publisher, Moody's, offers vital research on shares and bonds.. It offers share and bond guides similar to S&P and also provides an independent bond rating service. A share rated highly by both Moody's and S&P is a great place for investors hunting for value investments. Check out www.moodys.com for more.

Brokerage reports: The good, the bad, and the ugly

Clint Eastwood, where are you? Traditionally, brokerage reports have been a good source of information for investors seeking informed opinions about shares. And they still are, but in recent years some brokers have been criticised for biased reports. Brokers should never be the sole source of information. Otherwise, Clint may ask them whether they're lucky punks.

The good

Research departments at brokerage firms provide share reports and make them available for their clients and investment publications. The firms' analysts and market strategists generally prepare these reports. Good research is critical, and brokerage reports can be valuable. What better source of guidance than full-time experts backed up by multi-million pound research departments? Brokerage reports have the following strong points:

✔ The analysts are professionals who should understand the value of a company and its shares. They analyse and compare company data every day.

✔ They have at their disposal tremendous information and historical data that they can sift through to make informed decisions.

✔ If you have an account with the firm, you can usually access the information at no cost.

✔ They have regular meetings with company insiders and the ability to ask probing questions about the company's fortunes.

The bad

Well, brokerage reports may not be bad in every case, but at their worst, they're quite bad. Brokers make their money from commissions and investment banking fees (nothing bad here). However, they can find themselves in the awkward position of issuing brokerage reports on companies that are (or may be) customers for the brokerage firm that employs them (hmmm – could be bad). Frequently, this relationship can result in a brokerage report that paints a more positive picture of a company than it really merits (yes, that's bad).

Sometimes, good research can be compromised by conflicts of interest.

During 1998-2000, an overwhelming number of brokerage reports issued glowing praise of companies that were mediocre or dubious. Investors bought up shares in tech and Internet companies. The sheer demand pushed up share prices, which gave the appearance of genius to analysts' forecasts, yet the prices rose essentially as a self-fulfilling prophecy. The shares were highly overvalued and were cruisin' for a bruisin'. Analysts and investors were feeling lucky.

The ugly

Investors lost a ton of money (sounds ugly). Money that people had painstakingly accumulated over many years of work vanished in a matter of months as the bear market of 2000 hit (uglier). Retirees who had trusted the analysts saw nest eggs lose 40 to 70 per cent in value (blimey, very ugly). Not all investors had been reading the brokers' notes on these shares. Many novice investors gambled their savings because of the buzz in the media about tech shares.

During that bear market, a record number of lawsuits and complaints were filed against brokerage firms. Brokers and investors discovered a few tough facts. Regarding research reports from brokerage firms, the following points can help you avoid getting a bad case of the uglies:

✔ Always ask yourself, 'Is the provider of the report a biased source?' In other words, is the broker getting business in any way from the company they're recommending?

✔ Never, never, NEVER rely on just one source of information, especially if this source is the same one that's selling you the shares or other investment.

✔ Do your research first before you rely on a brokerage report.

✔ Do your due diligence before you buy shares anyway. Look at the chapters in Part I and Part II to understand your need for diversification, risk tolerance, and so on.

✔ Verify the information provided to you with a trip to the library or Web sites (see Appendix A).

Although we generally do not rely on brokerage analysts, we do track a few independent investment analysts. You can find some of our favourites mentioned in Chapter 13.

Compiling Your Own Research Department

You don't need to spend an excessive amount of time or money, but you should maintain your own library of resources. You may only need one shelf (or a small amount of memory on your computer's hard drive). But why not have a few investment facts and resources at your fingertips? Paul maintains his own library loaded with books, magazines, newsletters, and tons of great stuff downloaded on his computer for easy search and reference. When you start your own collection, keep the following in mind:

✔ **Keep selected newspapers.** *The Financial Times* and *The Wall Street Journal* regularly have editions that are worth keeping.

✔ **Subscribe to financial magazines.** Publications such as *The Investors Chronicle* magazine and *The Business* offer great research and regularly review shares, brokers, and resources for investors.

✔ **Keep annual reports.** Regarding the shares that are the core holdings in your portfolio, keep all the annual reports (at the least, the most recent three).

✔ **Go to the library's business reference section.** Go periodically to stay updated. Hey, you pay the tax that maintains the public library – you may as well use it to stay informed.

✔ **Use the Internet.** The Web offers plenty of great sites to peruse, and we list some of the best in Appendix A.

Financial reports are important and easier to read than most people think. An investor can easily avoid a bad investment by simply noticing the data in what seems like a jumble of numbers. Figure out how to read them. For a great book to help you with reading financial reports (without needless technicality), check out *Interpreting Company Reports For Dummies* by Ken Langdon, Alan Bonham and John A. Tracy (Wiley).

Chapter 12

Analysing Industries

*S*uppose that you have to bet your entire nest egg on a one-mile race. All you need to do is select a winning group. Your choices are the following:

Group A: A group of thoroughbred race horses

Group B: A group of overweight Elvis impersonators

Group C: A group of lethargic snails

This isn't a trick question, and you have one minute to answer. Notice that I didn't ask you to pick a single winner out of a giant mush of horses, Elvis's, and snails; I only asked you to pick the winning group in the race. The obvious answer is the thoroughbred race horses (and, no, they weren't ridden by the overweight Elvis impersonators because that would take away from the eloquent point being made). In this example, even the slowest member of group A easily outdistances the fastest member of group B or C.

Industries aren't equal, and life isn't fair. After all, if life was fair, Elvis would be alive and the impersonators wouldn't exist. Fortunately, picking shares doesn't have to be as difficult as picking a winning racehorse. The basic point is that you can pick a successful company to invest in more easily from a group of winners (a growing, vibrant industry). Understanding industries only enhances your share-picking strategy.

A successful, long-term investor looks at the industry just as carefully as he or she looks at the individual company. Luckily, choosing a winning industry to invest in is easier than choosing individual company shares. We know investors who can pick a winning company in a losing industry, and I also know investors who have chosen a losing company in a winning industry (the former are far outnumbered by the latter). Just think how well you do when you choose a great company in a great industry! Of course, if you repeatedly choose bad companies in bad industries, then you may as well get out of the stock market altogether (maybe your calling is to instead be a celebrity impersonator!).

Interrogating the Industries

Your common sense is an important tool in choosing industries with winning shares. The following sections explore some of the most important questions to ask yourself when you're choosing an industry. Keep in mind that an industry isn't the same as a sector. Even some market pros use the two words almost interchangeably. A *sector* is basically a 'mega-industry' or a group of interrelated industries. For example, pharmaceuticals and private hospital providers each constitute separate industries, but both of them are part of the healthcare sector. An industry, on the other hand, is typically a category of business that performs a precise activity (such as computer chips or trucking). Not all industries in a sector perform equally in the same market conditions.

Is the industry growing?

The question may seem too obvious, but you still need to ask it before you purchase shares. The saying 'the trend is your friend' applies when choosing an industry in which to invest, as long as the trend is an upward one. If you look at three different shares that are equal in every significant way but you find that share A is in an industry growing 15 per cent per year while the other two shares are in industries that have little growth or are shrinking, which share would you choose?

Sometimes, shares in a financially unsound or poorly run company go up dramatically because the industry the company is in is exciting to the public. The most obvious example is dot.com shares from 1998 to 2000. Shares such as `Amazon.com` shot up to incredible heights because investors thought the Internet was the place to be. Sooner or later, the measure of a successful company is its ability to be profitable. Serious investors look at a company's fundamentals (see Chapter 10 to find out how to do this) and the prospects for the industry's growth before settling on a particular share.

To judge how well an industry is doing, various information sources monitor all the major industries and measure their progress. The more reliable sources include the following:

✔ Confederation of British Industry (www.cbi.org.uk)

✔ Standard & Poor's Industry Survey (www.standardpoor.com)

✔ Hoover's Industry Snapshots (www.hoovers.com)

✔ Yahoo! Finance News (uk.biz.yahoo.com/news)

✔ Financial Times (www.ft.com)

The preceding sources generally give you in-depth information about the major industries. Visit their Websites to read their current research and articles along with links to relevant sites for more details. The Financial Times (published by Pearson), for example, publishes indexes for all the major sectors and industries so that you can get a useful snapshot of how well an industry is doing (including information about whether shares are up or down and how they are performing year-to-date), and it updates its Web site regularly.

Are the industry's products or services in demand?

Look at the products and services that an industry provides. Do they look like things that society will continue to want? Are products and services on the horizon that may replace them? Does the industry face a danger of potential obsolescence?

When evaluating future demand, look for a *sunrise industry,* which is one that is new or emerging or has promising appeal for the future. Good examples in recent years have been biotech and Internet companies. In contrast, a *sunset industry* is one that is declining or has little potential for growth. For example, you probably shouldn't invest in the video cassette manufacturing industry as demand for DVDs increases. Owning shares in a strong, profitable company in a sunrise industry is obviously the most desirable choice.

Ranking the industries

Standard and Poor's (S&P) Industry Survey is an excellent source of information on America's industries. A good source of information on industries from a UK perspective is RBA (Rhodes-Blakeman Associates) on the Web site www.rba.co.uk. It provides links to other sites with information on various industries as well as sources for useful reports.

Current research unveils the following megatrends:

- ✔ **The ageing population:** More senior citizens than ever before will be living in the UK. Because of this, financial and healthcare services are set to prosper.

- ✔ **Advances in new technology:** Internet, telecoms, medical, and biotechnology innovations will continue.

- ✔ **Increasing need for basic materials:** As society advances here and in the rest of the world, building blocks such as metals and other precious commodities are sure to be in demand.

- ✔ **Security concerns:** Terrorism and other international tensions mean more attention for defence, national security, and related matters.

- ✔ **Energy challenges:** Traditional and non-traditional sources of energy (such as solar, biofuels, and so on) are sure to demand society's attention as it faces the prospect of life after oil.

What does the industry's growth rely on?

An industry doesn't exist in a vacuum. External factors weigh heavily on its ability to survive and thrive. Does the industry rely on an established megatrend, in which case it should be strong for a while, or on factors that are losing relevance? Technological and demographic changes are other factors that may contribute to an industry's growth.

Perhaps the industry offers great new medical products for senior citizens. What are the prospects for growth? Ageing population is an established megatrend. As more and more Britons live past the age of 60, profitable opportunities await companies that are prepared to cater for them.

Is this industry dependent on another industry?

This twist on the previous question is a reminder that industries frequently are intertwined and can become co-dependent. When one industry suffers, you may find it helpful to understand which industries will subsequently suffer. The reverse can also be true – when one industry is doing well, other industries may also reap the benefits.

In either case, if the shares you chose are in an industry that's highly dependent on other industries, you should know about it. If you're considering shares in holiday resort companies and you see the headlines blaring 'Airlines losing money as public stops flying,' what do you do? This type of question forces you to think logically and consider cause and effect. Logic and common sense are powerful tools that frequently trump all the number-crunching activity performed by analysts.

Who are the leading companies in the industry?

After you've chosen the industry, what types of companies do you want to invest in? You can choose from two basic types of companies:

- **Established leaders:** These companies are considered industry leaders or have a large share of the market. Investing in these companies is the safer way to go; what better investment for novice investors than companies that have already proven themselves?

- **Innovators:** If the industry is hot and you want to be more aggressive in your approach, investigate companies that offer new products, patents, or new technologies. These companies are probably smaller but have a greater potential for growth in a proven industry.

Is the industry a target of government action?

You need to know whether the government is targeting an industry because intervention by politicians and bureaucrats (rightly or wrongly) can have an impact on an industry's economic situation. For example, would you invest in a tobacco company now that smoking bans have been implemented at most restaurants, bars and workplaces across the country?

Investors need to take heed when political 'noise' starts coming out about a particular industry. An industry can be hurt by direct government intervention or by the threat of it. Intervention can take the form of lawsuits, investigations, taxes, regulations, or sometimes an outright ban. In any case, being on the wrong end of government intervention is the greatest external threat to a company's survival.

Sometimes, government action helps an industry. Generally, beneficial action takes two forms:

- **Deregulation and/or tax decreases:** Governments sometimes reduce burdens on an industry. In 1986, Margaret Thatcher deregulated the bus industry in the UK and spawned dozens of successful companies that made millions for their founders and healthy sums for their workers too. Companies such as Stagecoach, First Group, Arriva and Go-Ahead all had their origins in those initital changes to the restrictions on bus competition. Many of those bus firms started up by former bus drivers cut prices, increased passenger numbers and expanded routes into rural areas.

✔ **Direct funding:** Governments have the power to steer taxpayers' money toward business as well. Recent UK governments have steered away from directly bailing out failing industries, but they have encouraged foreign companies to the UK using government grants. The tonnage tax for instance has brought more than 800 ships into the UK shipping industry by allowing companies to pay a flat rate fee on their tonnage rather than paying corporation tax on their profits.

Which category does the industry fall into?

Most industries can neatly be placed in one of two categories: cyclical and defensive. In a rough way, these categories generally translate into what society wants and what it needs. Society buys what it *needs* in both good and bad times. It buys what it *wants* when times are good and holds off when times are bad. A need is a 'must have' while a want is a 'like to have'.

Cyclical industries

Cyclical industries are industries whose fortunes rise and fall with the economy's rise and fall. In other words, if the economy is doing well and the stock market is doing well, cyclical industries tend to do well. When the economy is doing well, consumers and investors are confident and tend to spend and invest more money than usual. Property and motoring are great examples of cyclical industries.

Your own situation offers you common-sense insight into the concept of cyclical industries. Think about your behaviour as a consumer, and you get a good idea about the thinking of millions of consumers. Think about the times you felt good about your career and your finances. When you (and millions of others) feel good about money and about the future, you have a greater tendency to buy more (and/or more expensive) stuff. When people feel financially strong, they're more likely to buy a new house or car or make another large financial commitment. Also, people take on more debt because they feel confident that they can pay it back. In light of this behaviour, which industries do you think would do well?

The same point also holds for business spending. When businesses think that economic times are good and foresee continuing good times, they tend to spend more money on large purchases such as new equipment or technology. They think that when they're doing well and flush with financial success, that they should reinvest that money to increase future success.

It takes money to spend money

The economic boom of the late 1990s was in many respects due to an explosion of spending financed by debt. Consumers and businesses felt great about the economy's expansion and spent money accordingly. Among the winning industries were motoring, property, and technology. Choosing strong shares in these categories meant tremendous profits for investors who did their homework.

Defensive industries

Defensive industries are industries that produce the goods and services needed no matter what's happening in the economy. Your common sense kicks in here. What do you still buy even when times are tough? Think about what millions of people buy no matter how bad the economy gets. A good example is food. People still need to eat regardless of good or bad times. Other examples of defensive industries are utilities.

In bad economic times, defensive shares tend to do better than cyclical shares. However, when times are good, cyclical shares tend to do better than defensive shares. Defensive shares don't do as well in good times because people don't eat twice as much or use up more electricity.

So how do defensive shares grow? Their growth generally relies on two factors:

- **Population growth:** As more and more consumers are born, more people become available to buy.

- **New markets:** A company can grow by seeking out new groups of consumers who can buy their products and services. Coca-Cola, for example, found new markets in Asia during the 1990s. As Communist regimes fell from power and more societies embraced a free market and consumer goods, the company sold more beverages, and its shares soared.

One way investors can invest in a particular industry is to take advantage of Exchange Traded Funds (ETFs), which have become popular in recent years. If you find a winning industry but you can't find a winning share (or don't want to bother with the necessary research), then ETFs are a great consideration.

Outlining Key Industries

Not all industries go up and down in tandem. Indeed, at any given time, some industries are successful no matter what's happening with the general economy. In fact, investors have made a lot of money simply by choosing an industry that benefits from economic trends.

For example, the economy was in bad shape during the 1970s. It was a period of *stagflation* – low growth, high unemployment, and high inflation. This decade was the worst time for the economy since the depression of the late 1920s; most industries (and therefore most shares) were having tough times. But some industries did well; in fact, they flourished. Property and precious metals, for example, performed well in this environment. Because the inflation rate soared into double digits, inflationary hedges such as gold and silver did well. During the '70s, gold skyrocketed from $35 an ounce to $850 an ounce by the end of the decade. Silver went from under $2 to more than $50 in the same period. What do you think happened to shares in gold and silver mining companies? That's right. They skyrocketed as well. Gold shares gave investors spectacular returns.

In the 1980s, the economy became rejuvenated when taxes were cut, some industry red tape decreased, and inflation fell. Most industries did well. But even in a growing economy, some industries struggle. Examples of industries that struggled during that time included precious metals and energy companies.

Now fast forward to 2007. Think about those industries that struggled and those that did well. Natural resources (energy, commodities, and so on) and property have done well in recent years. In the same time frame, industries such as airlines have had a rough time. Choosing the right industries (or avoiding the wrong ones) has always been a major factor in successful share picking.

For sale

I include property as a key industry because property is a cyclical *belwether industry* (one that has a great effect on many other industries that may be dependent on it). Property is looked at as a key component of economic health because so many other industries, including building materials, mortgages, household appliances, and contract labour services, are tied to it. When the property industry is booming, that bodes well for much of the economy.

Housing starts (new developments) are one way to measure property activity. This data is an important leading indicator of health in the industry. Housing starts indicate new construction, which means more business for related industries.

Keep an eye on the property industry for negative news that may be bearish for the economy and the stock market. Because property is purchased with mortgage money, investors and analysts watch the mortgage market for trouble signs such as rising *defaults* (missed debt payments) and *foreclosures* (when banks insist on repayment of a debt earlier than planned). These statistics serve as a warning for general economic weakness. Since 2002, the property industry has shown tremendous growth primarily driven by credit. Almost every month new records are being set for housing, but some investors are exercising caution because they say they're seeing growing evidence of a mania. A *mania* is typically the final part of a mature bull market. In a mania, the prices of the assets experiencing the bull market (such as shares or property) are skyrocketing to extreme levels, which excite more and more investors as they jump in. As more investors pile in, this causes the prices to rise even further. It gets to the point where seemingly everyone thinks that getting rich by buying this particular asset is easy and almost no one notices that the market has become unsustainable. After prices are exhausted and start to level off, investor excitement dies down and then investors try to exit by selling their holdings to realise at least some profit. As more and more sell off their holdings, demand decreases while supply increases. The mania disappears and the bear market has appeared. However, some investors have been expecting the property slump to appear any day since 2005 – at the time of writing, prices are still booming.

Baby, you can drive my car

The motor industry is another business that you want to watch carefully. When cars are selling well, you can generally interpret that as a positive indicator for the economy. People buy new cars when they're doing well. Cars are big-ticket items that are another barometer of people's economic well-being.

Conversely, trouble in the motor industry is a red flag for trouble in the general economy. If car repossessions and car loan defaults are rising, that's a warning about general economic weakness. In early 2005, weakness definitely showed up in the motor industry as MG Rover collapsed, putting more than 5,000 workers on the dole.

Thanking Mr. Roboto

In recent years, technology has become popular with investors. Indeed, technology is a great sector, and its impact on the economy's present and future success can't be underestimated. The price of shares of technology companies can rise substantially because investors buy them based on expectations – today's untested, unproven companies may become the Microsofts and IBMs of tomorrow. In spite of the sector's potential, companies can still fail if customers don't embrace their products. Even with technology shares, you must still apply the rules and guidelines that we discuss throughout this book for financially successful companies. Pick the best in a growing industry, and you are bound to succeed over the long haul. Because technology still hasn't recovered from its recent bear market, weakness in the industry means that investors need to be picky and cautious.

Banking on it

Banking and financial services are an intrinsic part of any economy. Debt is the most telling sign of this industry for investors. If a company's debt is growing faster than the economy, you need to watch to see how the debt affects the company's shares and bonds. If debt gets out of control, it can be disastrous for the economy. Debt and debt-related securities are currently at historic and, for many experts and investors, troublesome levels. This trend means that many financial shares may be at risk if a recession hits any time soon.

Chapter 13

Emerging Sector Opportunities

. . . .

In This Chapter

▶ Checking out bullish opportunities

▶ Understanding bearish opportunities

▶ Getting investment pointers for your unique situation

. . . .

*Y*es, you can do your own research (and you want to, don't you?), but we may as well make you privy to what our research tells us are the unfolding megatrends that offer the greatest potential rewards for investors in shares.

Making just a handful of changes in your portfolio over the past four decades would have made you tremendously rich. Had you put your money into natural resources (such as gold, silver, and oil) at the beginning of the 1970s and stayed put until the end of the decade, you would have made a fortune. Then had you cashed in and switched to Japanese shares in 1980 and held them for the rest of the decade, you would have made another fortune. Then had you switched in 1990 to US shares for the entire decade, you would have made yet another fortune. What if you had cashed in your shares in 2000? Well, for starters, you would have avoided huge losses in the bear market. How about being bullish? What looks like a strong bull market for this decade?

By and large, this decade seems to be a repeat of the '70s. The general realm of natural resources looks to be the primary bull market for this decade. Why? First, look at what this decade has in common with the '70s:

✔ Problems with energy (rising costs, supply disruptions, and so on)

✔ International conflict (Iraq, Afghanistan, Iran, and so on)

✔ Rising prices for natural resources (grain, metals, timber, and so on)

However, this decade has more to consider, including the following:

✔ Debt, debt, and more debt. Total UK personal debt at the end of January 2007 stood at **£1,300 billion**. Our debts are growing at 10.5 per cent a year.

✔ The UK as a major importer (versus being an exporter in the '70s)

✔ China and India as major economic competitors

✔ Terrorism affecting Europe and the US

✔ $372 trillion worth of derivatives (nine times larger than the world's total GDP! Many of these derivatives are arcane and risky.)

✔ Pension and health care liabilities (Rising costs start in 2008 as the oldest baby boomers start to retire)

This list isn't comprehensive (due to space limitations). The above points are enough to make you understand that this investing environment has changed dramatically and that you need to re-focus your overall game plan to keep your money growing.

By the way, you see two types of opportunities in this chapter: bullish and bearish. (See Chapter 15 for more information on bullish and bearish markets.) If I can't help you find the winning shares, at least I can show you the losers to stay away from.

Bullish Opportunities

Being bullish (or going *long*) is the natural inclination for most investors. It's an easy concept; buy low, sell high. No rocket science there. The following sections don't identify every bullish opportunity, but they do cover the most obvious ones (at least to me).

Commodities: Feeding and housing the world

What will have a mega-impact on the world can be boiled down to two words: China and India. In the past ten years, these two countries have put their economies on the fast track. Consider the following:

✔ They have generally turned away from socialism and a *command economy* in which the state dictates the supply and prices of goods, and have instead turned to a free market or more capitalistic system.

✔ Industrialisation, privatisation, and profit incentives have ignited tremendous booms in those countries.

✔ Both countries' populations have continued to grow. China has about 1.3 billion people while India recently surpassed 1.1 billion.

What do these facts mean for investors in shares?

Somebody's got to sell them what they need. China, for example, has a voracious appetite for natural resources such as building materials, energy, copper, grain, and so on. Companies that have provided the goods and services China needed do well. Tesco is one of the UK companies taking its business to China. It recently opened its first supermarket in Shanghai after signing a deal with local grocery chain Ting Hsin worth £140 million.

Of course, China and India are only a part of the world's emerging markets, but they're certainly the most important (in terms of economic impact). They are indeed 'megatrends' that help (or hurt) your portfolio. In the coming years, demand is likely to continue to be strong, and investors will see the obvious positive implications for solid companies that meet this demand.

To find out more, check out the resources in Appendix A, such as Jim Rogers's book entitled *Hot Commodities*. You can also conduct research at sites such as www.futuresource.com, the commodities section of www.marketwatch.com, and www.bloomberg.com.

Energy

Recent headlines tell us that the costs of energy are a major challenge for the economy. We are now realising that for decades, oil has been cheap – even if the taxation in the UK hides the fact from most users – but global supply and demand (among other things) is changing the situation. A barrel of oil has gone from $42 in January 2005 to about $72 by April 2006 (a 70 per cent increase!). A gallon of petrol has seen a similar meteoric rise. Scientists are talking about 'Peak Oil' (for more on this condition, check out the sidebar 'Taking a peek at Peak Oil', later in this chapter). Energy investors must become familiar with this because it has (and is going to) weigh heavily on the economy, because people are so dependent on oil for their modern lifestyle. The days of cheap oil are now history. Higher energy prices affect all shares. If you're going to pay more for energy, then you may as well benefit.

As energy prices have risen strongly over the past few years, how have shares fared? The general stock market (as represented by the FTSE 100 Index) did little, say from 2003 to mid-2005, although it has picked up since. But energy shares? Look at a major share such as BP. You may have invested in this company in 2003 for about £4.20 per share (and you'd get a nice fat dividend, too). By October 2005, the share hit nearly £6.75 (a gain of about 60 per cent, not including dividends).

Taking a peek at Peak Oil

In the late 1950s and early 1960s, geologist Marion King Hubbert conducted landmark studies related to the global supply of oil. His research indicated that the life of a particular underground reserve of oil goes through two phases. During the first phase, the oil can be easily and inexpensively extracted. However, after you get past the 50 per cent mark, the remaining oil is difficult (and hence expensive) to extract. That 50 per cent mark has come to be known as 'Hubbert's Peak' – the peak of production. Experts have come to use Peak Oil as a term for the peak of the entire planet's oil production. Hubbert made forecasts of when the world would hit this peak and so far his forecasts have been accurate. The United States hit Hubbert's Peak in the early 1970s (American dependence on foreign oil grew significantly after that). Current industry research suggests that all the major oil-producing countries have already reached their peak or will do so by the end of this decade. To find out more about Peak Oil, check out Web sites such as the Association for the Study of Peak Oil & Gas (www.peakoil.net).

Compare BP with a tech stock like Dell (a former high-flying growth share). In that same time frame, Dell shares experienced a modest gain of 16 per cent, and it had no dividends. Well, at least it grew.

The bottom line is that investors in shares have to consider energy in their investment strategies or risk having energy prices steamroll over their potential gains. Investment opportunities are plentiful in companies that provide, sell, distribute, or explore energy. But you may want to consider energy alternatives as well. The UK and the rest of the world will be forced to turn to alternative energy sources in the coming years. As conventional oil and gas become scarce, we are going to need energy from sources such as biofuels, hydro-electricity and other renewables 'such as wind, solar, and fuel cell technologies, among others.

As you read this chapter, you may not be sure about what particular company you should invest in. If that's the case, why not consider a convenient way to invest in an entire industry or sector? A good consideration is an *Exchange Traded Fund* (ETF). An ETF is like buying a whole portfolio of shares as if it was a single share. An example is an ETF with the symbol XLE. XLE has a cross section of the largest public oil and gas companies such as Exxon Mobil, Chevron Texaco, and others. In 2003, Paul bought this XLE for $18 per share. By August 2005, it hit $50. In the UK, ETFs are a fairly new offering and Barclays Wealth is the leading provider of ETFs, go to www.barclaysglobal.com or www.ishares.net for all the details.

Gold

Over the ages, gold has come to be synonymous with wealth. In modern times it has become known as an inflation hedge and 'investment insurance,' especially during times of inflation and geopolitical uncertainty. After being in a 20-year bear market (from its market top of $850 in 1980 to its low of $252 in 2000), conditions are ripe in the marketplace for a gold bull market that may reach or surpass its old high. Aggressive investors should be investigating gold shares. Why now?

According to many (if not most) gold market analysts, such as Bill Murphy of the Gold Anti-Trust Action Committee (www.gata.org), the fundamentals for gold are more bullish than ever. In recent years, demand has begun to significantly exceed supply. The shortfall has been filled from gold sales by central banks. Because of continued and growing demand both in the US and abroad (most notably India and China), total worldwide annual demand is outstripping supply by anywhere from 1,000-2,000 tons (depending on whose estimates you believe). Juxtapose this demand with current economic conditions (such as the declining value of the dollar and other paper currencies) and geopolitical instability, and it's easy to see that gold and gold-related investments (such as gold shares) show bullish potential.

Because gold does well in an inflationary environment, understanding inflation itself is important. Inflation isn't the price of things going up; it's the value of the currency itself going down. The reason it goes down in value is primarily due to the increase in the money supply. Add to that the incentive that gold is now a permitted investment in a Self Invested Personal Pension and you create a bullish environment for hard assets such as gold.

Gold analysts in the US, such as Bill Murphy, Doug Casey, Jay Taylor, James Sinclair, and many others, easily see the gold price hitting four figures in the not-too-distant future. In that case, gold mining shares would perform fantastically well (not unlike their heyday in the late 1970s). For conservative investors, consider the large, established mining firms such as Newmont Mining (NEM) or Gold Corp. (GG). For the more daring, consider junior mining shares. Do your research on the Web sites mentioned in this segment.

A common practice in the mining industry in recent years has been the practice of forward selling (also called 'hedging'). Forward selling is the process in which a company sells next year's production at a locked-in price today. The benefit for the company is that it makes money even if next year's gold price stays stable or goes down. However, if gold rises next year, the company loses out on the potential profit. From 2000, as gold went from $252 per ounce all the way to $439 in August 2005 (a 74 per cent rise), most un-hedged gold companies saw their shares double and triple in the same time frame. In comparison, hedged gold companies went up more modestly or not at all. Companies even went bankrupt because of hedging.

Silver

We may easily have lumped silver in with gold and just labelled the section 'precious metals', but we think that silver merits special attention. Out of all the precious metals (and base metals) that we've analysed, silver probably has the strongest potential. Why? Demand for silver is strong and growing stronger for various reasons (including investment, jewellery, industrial, and so on). Yet the above-ground supply of silver has been shrinking for more than two decades. In fact, silver has been experiencing a chronic deficit for more than a decade.

Although some point out that silver's primary use in industry (photography) is shrinking due to the growing popularity of digital photography, silver demand has been growing significantly in health care, electronics, and military equipment. For these reasons, the supply and demand fundamentals are outstanding. As a matter of fact, silver is more rare than gold. As the market catches on, silver's current modest bull market can easily become a 'raging bull'. Here are a couple of the bullish factors facing silver in 2007 and beyond:

✔ Only about 200 million ounces of above-ground silver are available.

✔ Major sources of supply are disappearing. (China is now an importer.)

What's the potential for share investors? One way to look at silver today is to take a look at the last great silver bull market and see how silver shares performed. In the late 1970s, silver soared from $2 per ounce all the way to $52 per ounce by 1980. In 1975, investors bought Lion Mines Co. for only 7 cents per share. As silver hit its high in 1980, Lion Mines stock hit an astounding $380 per share. That means that $184 worth of stock in 1975 was worth $1 million only five years later (talk about your silver lining!).

If silver and silver shares interest you, do your homework. The most widely followed silver analysts are Ted Butler and David Morgan. The most comprehensive Web sites on silver are www.silver-investor.com and www.silverstrategies.com. You can also invest in silver ETFs.

Health care

I'm sure that you've heard much about the 'grey pound'. This phrase obviously represents a firm megatrend in place. For investors, this megatrend is a purely demographic play and the 'numbers' are with you. The number of people who are over the age of 50, and especially those considered 'senior citizens', are the fastest growing segment of society. The same megatrend is in place in all corners of the world (especially Europe). As more and more people get into this category, the idea that companies that serve this segment also prosper becomes a no-brainer. Well-managed companies that run nursing homes and services caring for the elderly should see their shares rise.

Be careful which health care firms you select because this sector can include shares that are defensive and also shares that are cyclical. Companies that sell expensive equipment (such as CAT scans or MRI technology) may not do that well in an economic downturn because hospitals and other health care facilities may not want to upgrade or replace their equipment. Therefore, health care companies that sell big-ticket items can be considered cyclical. On the other hand, companies that sell medicine (pharmaceuticals) can be considered defensive. People who need medicine (such as aspirin or antacids) buy it no matter how bad the economy is. In fact, people probably buy even more aspirin and antacids in bad economic times.

Also be aware of political trends as they affect health care. Britain may be leaning further toward privatised medicine. If this possibility develops, grab your bullish expectations by the horns. History (and my experience) tells me that privatisations of an industry like health care mean big changes for investors (and patients, too).

To find out more about health care opportunities, check out the industry and main companies by using the resources in Appendix A.

National Security

The horrific terrorist attacks of recent years remind the world how vulnerable a free and open society can be. Bombings in Madrid and London show that terrorism is a global threat and countries have responded by increasing security at home while deploying forces across the world to combat terrorists and tangle with the countries that support them. Foes of the West aren't singular nations that are easily defined, fought, and defeated within a few months or a few years. Instead, they're implacable and virulent, and they're spread out over many countries.

Securing a nation becomes an unprecedented undertaking. Funding for security measures and for military needs is huge and 'getting huger' for the foreseeable future. Because British industry predominantly provides the goods and services necessary in this extensive national security effort, stock investors should take notice.

Bearish Outlook

Shares are versatile in that you can even make money when they go down in value. Techniques range from 'using put options' to 'going short'. (See Chapter 17 regarding 'going short', and find out more about put options at www.fool.co.uk.) For traditional investors, the more appropriate strategy is first and foremost to avoid or minimise losses. Making money betting that a stock is going to fall is closer to speculating than actual investing. So all we want is that investors see the pitfalls and act accordingly. The following sections offer cautionary alerts to keep you away from troubled areas in the economy (or find speculative opportunities to short investments).

Warning on housing

Property investment has been all the rage in recent years. Every other week in the weekend papers we see the promotions for adult education seminars on property investment. 'How to Get Rich through Property', 'Buy Property with No Money Down'. But I think 'Playing Property Poker' is more like it. Journalists who have attended free property investment seminars always find that a catch exists somewhere. Usually you have to shell out at the end of the seminar for another course, where the organisers' promise to reveal the 'secrets of success'.

In the old days, when asked the question about how to be successful investing in property, the answer was always 'location, location, location'. In this decade, that answer has morphed into 'credit, credit, credit', which is really 'debt, debt, debt'. You come to see that the housing bubble isn't really a problem but a symptom. If the bubble is a symptom, then what is the problem? The problem with property in recent years has really been too much debt, pretty lax lending standards, and rampant speculation. By the second quarter of 2007, the data shows a property market that many analysts insist is overheated, overpriced, and unsustainable.

More and more mortgages issued are interest-only mortgages for longer terms than normal – some lenders spread the mortgage over more than 40 years. Interest-only mortgages are cheaper than repayment mortgages as the buyers only pay interest and put no dent into the capital. In addition, many of these mortgages are being issued to buyers who are 'sub-prime', which means that their credit is less than strong, so to speak. These people have purchased a house and used 'creative' financing to lower the monthly payment. When interest rates (and other costs such as council tax, insurance, and maintenance costs) rise, millions of over-burdened property owners may have financial problems and this is bound to have a negative effect on the overall economy.

On top of that, many of these mortgages are issued at 100 per cent of the property's market value. When you add up these troublesome mortgages, they amount to billions. The value of all mortgages is now a sizeable proportion of the UK's GDP. Some analysts tell you that this isn't a problem because 'the economy is strong and job growth is good. But most of us remember the early 1990s when many people had their homes repossessed and struggled financially for years as a result.

Property is a major factor in the economy. Not only is it providing jobs in construction but property is fundamental to the mortgage businesses of banks and building societies. If housing and construction were to decline due to over-building (more supply) and fewer buyers (lower demand), that would mean a shrinking property market and fewer jobs – harming the economy. As the robot on the old TV show *Lost in Space* used to say, 'Warning Will Robinson! Danger! Danger!'

What should investors in shares be looking at? The most obvious thing to look at is housing shares. The stock market tends to be a leading indicator of how well (or how poorly) the economy is doing. Frequently, subsections of the stock market give you clues about a particular industry. Housing shares seem to be taking a gentle battering at the moment (May 2007), when they have been climbing steadily for years. Among the first things I ask myself about the direction of an industry is 'How are insiders behaving in the main companies of that industry?'

In recent years, as property was on a blazing hot streak, the home building shares were also bullish. A good example was British Land (BLND). That share has been on a meteoric rise since mid-2003. It has climbed from around £4 a share in 2003 to just over £17 at the start of 2007, a gain of 325 per cent! 'However, as the company embarked on a new journey – converting to one of the first UK real estate investment trusts – the shares started to slip a bit. But interestingly, most of the insiders have been buying more shares rather than selling. Homebuilders are among the first to see what's going on in their industry. So just when you may think the industry has probably hit its peak and sales are about to soften, the directors are showing that they believe the opposite is true. What's an investor to do?

First of all, be safe. Minimise exposure to any vulnerable sectors. I'm not just talking about directly investing in property , but also indirectly. Companies and industries that are reliant on the housing sector are also at risk, such as financial institutions, suppliers, and so on. For those of you who are aggressive, bearish strategies (like going short or, even better, buying put options) are a good speculation. To find out more about what's going on with this historic and gigantic housing bubble in the US and in the UK, check out the following great Web sites, www.housingbubble.com and www.housepricecrash.co.uk.

The great credit monster

Too much debt means that someone gets hurt. As the unprecedented explosion in debt gave a huge boost to the economy in the late 1990s, it now poses great dangers for the rest of this decade. This massive debt problem is obviously tied to the previous topic of property. However, it goes much further. Individuals, companies, and government agencies are carrying too much debt for comfort. It's not just mortgage debt; it's also consumer, business, government, and margin debt. With total UK personal debt including mortgages now in the vicinity of £1.3 trillion, saying that a lot of this debt won't be repaid is probably a safe bet. Individual and institutional defaults may rock the economy and the financial markets. Bankruptcy is bound to be a huge issue (in spite of bankruptcy reforms that came into force in April 2006).

Debt weighs heavily on shares directly or indirectly. Because every type of debt is now at record levels, no one is truly immune. Say the shares you have are in a retailer that has no debt whatsoever. Are you immune? Not really, because consumer debt (credit cards, personal loans, and so on) is at an all-time high. If consumer spending declines, then the retailer's sales go down, its profits shrink, and – ultimately – its share price goes down.

Debt is also a major political issue. Banks and other lenders are under huge pressure to be responsible lenders. Regulation of mortgages and advertising of loans has become tougher in recent years as the Financial Services Authority flexes its muscle. The Treating Customers Fairly initiative has forced many lenders to think carefully about how they market their products and about the consumers they target. Intense interest from the media and MPs – particularly on the influential Treasury Select Committee – is making it harder for lenders to make a killing on credit. So the credit monster can attack lenders in more ways than one.

What's an investor in shares to do? Well, remember that first commandment to 'avoid or minimise losses'. Make sure that you review your portfolio and sell shares that may get pulverised by the credit monster. Make sure that the companies themselves have no, low, or manageable debt. (Check their financial reports. See Chapter 11 for more details.) For the venturesome, seek shorting opportunities in those companies most exposed to the dangers of debt. (For more information on shorting, go to Chapter 17.)

Cyclical shares

Another group of shares that can be vulnerable to the current heavy debt environment are *cyclical* shares. Heavy equipment, cars, and technology tend to be cyclical and are highly susceptible to downturns in the general economy. Conversely, cyclical shares do well when the economy is growing or on an upswing (hence the label).

As individuals and corporations get squeezed with more debt and less disposable income, hard choices need to be made. Ultimately, the result is that people buy fewer 'big-ticket' items. That means that a company selling these items ends up selling less and earning less profit. This loss of profit, in turn, makes that company's share price go down.

Companies that experience lagging sales often turn to aggressive discounting. Retailers have been known to turn to heavy discounting to clear out stock when they have failed to buy the right products for their customers. Companies including Next, Marks & Spencer, and Selfridges have all turned to this tactic in the past when their buyers have failed to tempt consumers. The trouble is that even half-price tags do not make rails full of last season's fashions look appetising to discerning consumers.

In a struggling, recessionary economy, investing in cyclical shares is like sunbathing on an ant hill and using jam instead of sun block. Not a pretty picture.

The FTSE 100 hit its all-time high of 6,930.2 in December 1999. Almost eight years later, it's still stuck in the 6,000 to 7,000 range. In the last eight years, some share groups have grown well, and shares in general struggled for a period and bounced back. Other sectors have not done well. Choosing the right sector is critical for your share investing success.

Important for Bulls and Bears

We just want to reiterate a few of the points that apply here. We don't presume that shares go straight up or that they zig-zag upward indefinitely. Your due diligence is necessary for success. Make sure that you're investing appropriately for your situation. If you're 35 and heading into your peak earnings years and want to 'ride a rocket' all the way to retirement – and you understand the risks – then go ahead and speculate with those small-cap gold mining shares or the solar power technology shares.

But if you're more risk adverse or your situation is screaming out loud for you to be conservative, then don't speculate. Go instead with a more diversified portfolio of blue chip shares or get the ETF for that particular sector.

For those people who want to make money by 'going short' in those sectors that look bearish, again take a deep breath and remember what's appropriate. Conservative investors simply avoid the risky areas. Aggressive investors or speculators may want to deploy profitable bearish strategies (with a *portion* of their investible funds). Here are some highlights for all of you.

Conservative and bullish

After you choose a promising sector, just select large-cap companies that are financially strong, are earning a profit, have low debt, and are market leaders. This entire book shows you how to do just that. However, you may not like the idea of buying shares directly. Consider sector unit trusts or ETFs. That way you can choose the industry and be able to effectively buy a basket of the top shares in that area. ETFs have been a hot item lately, and I think that they're a great consideration for most investors because they offer some advantages over unit trusts. For example, you can put stop-loss orders on them or borrow against them in your share portfolio. Check with your financial advisor to see whether ETFs are appropriate for you.

Being conservative and bullish makes sense when you're in (or near) retirement, have a family to support, or live in a large shoe with so many kids that you don't know what to do.

Aggressive and bullish

If you're aggressive and bullish, you want to buy the shares directly. For real growth potential, look at mid-caps or small-caps. Remember that you're speculating, so you understand the risk that the price is going to fall but are willing to tolerate this risk because the potential reward may be handsome. Few things in the investment world give you a better gain than a super-charged share in a hot sector.

Conservative and bearish

For many (if not most) investors, making money on a falling market isn't generally a good idea. Doing so takes a lot of expertise and risk tolerance. Really, for conservative investors, the key word is 'safety'. Analyse your portfolio with an advisor you trust and sell the potentially troubled shares. If you're not sure what to do on a particular share, then (at the very least) put in stop-loss orders and make them GTC (good till cancelled). (See Chapter 17 for details.) As odd as it sounds, sometimes losing less than others makes you come out ahead if you play it right.

For example, look at the bear market that hit the stock markets in the mid-1970s. In 1973–74, the stock market fell 45 per cent. Stocks didn't recover until late 1982. If you had a share worth £10, that means it would have fallen to £5.50 and not returned to £10 until eight years later. Phew! Sometimes just stuffing your money in the mattress sounds like genius. What if you had a stop loss at £9? You would have got out with a minimal loss and may have reinvested the money elsewhere (such as bonds or CFDs) and looked much brighter than your neighbour struggling to sleep in a lumpy bed.

Aggressive and bearish

Being aggressive in a bearish market isn't for the faint of heart. However, it's where the quickest fortunes have been made by some of history's greatest investors. Going short can make you great money when the market is bearish but it can sink you if you're wrong. Paul doesn't usually tell his clients and students to 'short a share' because it can backfire. Yes, ways to go short with less risk are out there, but Paul prefers to buy put options.

Put options are a way to make money with limited risk when you essentially make a bet on an investment (such as shares) that will go down. Obviously, options go beyond the scope of this book, but at least let us give you some direction, because an appropriate options strategy exists for most share portfolios. You should be aware that trading options is more readily available in the US but you can trade US options if you open a dollar trading account in the UK. You can find great (free) tutorials on using options at Web sites such at www.incademy.com, an investor education site written by financial journalists.

Diversification

This point is self-explanatory, right? If you take a portfolio approach and spread your capital across three to five sectors, then you're making a safer bet. And don't forget the trailing stop-loss strategy (see Chapter 17 for more on this). That makes it safer still.

Chapter 14

Pounds, Prices, and Politics

In This Chapter

▶ Looking at the effects of politics on the economy

▶ Taking a crash course in general economics

*P*olitics can be infuriating, disruptive, meddlesome, corrupting, and harmful. But . . . enough positive spin! We can be negative too. Even if politics doesn't amuse or interest you, you can't ignore it. If you aren't careful, it can wreak great havoc on your portfolio. Politics wields great influence with the economic and social environment, which in turn affects how companies succeed or fail. This success or failure in turn either helps or hurts your shares' prices. Politics (manifested in taxes, regulations, and legislation) can make or break a company or industry faster than any other external force. *Economics* – how people spend, save, and invest their money in society – also does its share to drive share prices up and down.

What people must understand (especially government policy makers) is that a new tax, law, regulation, or government action has a *macro* effect on a company, an industry, or even an entire economic system, whereas a company has a *micro* effect on an economy. The following gives you a simple snapshot of these effects:

> Politics → policy → economy → industry → the company → the shares → the investor

Now, this chapter doesn't moralise about politics or advocate a political point of view; after all, this book is about investing in shares. In general, policies can be good or bad regardless of their effect on the economy – some policies are enacted for the greater good even if they kick you in the wallet. However, in the context of this chapter, politics is covered from a cause-and-effect perspective: How does politics affect prosperity in general and investing in shares in particular?

A proficient share investor cannot – must not – look at shares as though they exist in a vacuum. Our favourite example of this rule is the idea of fish in a lake. You can have a great fish (your share) among a whole school of fish (the stock market) in a wonderful lake (the economy). But what if the lake gets polluted (bad policy)? What happens to the fish? Politics controls the lake and can make it hospitable – or dangerous – for the participants. You get the point. The example may sound too simple, but isn't. So many people – political committees, corporate managers, bureaucrats, and politicians – still get it so wrong time and time again, to the detriment of the economy and investors in shares.

Although the two get inexorably intertwined, we try to treat politics and economics as separate issues.

Sorting the Sound Information from the Soundbites

The campaigns heat up. Labour, Conservative, Liberal Democrat, and smaller parties vie for your attention and subsequent votes. Socialists, moderates, and libertarians joust in the battlefield of ideas. But, after all is said and done, voters make their decisions. Election day brings a new slate of politicians into power, and they, in turn, joust and debate on new rules and programmes in the House of Commons or local council offices. Before and after election time, investors must keep a watchful eye.

For investors in shares, politics manifests itself as a major factor in investment-making decisions in ways shown in Table 14-1.

Table 14-1	Politics and Investing
Possible Legislation	*Effect on Investing*
Taxes	Will a new tax affect a particular share (industry or economy)? Generally, more or higher taxes ultimately have a negative impact on share investments. Income taxes and capital gains taxes are good examples.
Laws	Will the government pass a law that has a negative impact on a share, the industry, or the economy? Price controls – laws that set the price of a product, service, or commodity – are examples of negative laws.

Possible Legislation	Effect on Investing
Regulations	Will a new (or existing) regulation have a negative (or positive) effect on your choice of shares? Generally, more or tougher regulations have a negative impact on shares.
Government spending and debt	If government agencies spend too much or misallocate resources, they may create greater burdens on society, which in turn is bearish for the economy and the stock market. (For information on investing in bear or bull markets, see Chapter 15.)
Money supply	The UK money supply – the cash you use – is controlled by the Bank of England. People have different definitions of money supply but usually we mean M0, the cash in your wallet, in bank tills and on deposit in banks. You can find out how it affects shares in the 'Showing interest in the Old Lady' section, later in the chapter.
Interest rates	The Bank of England Monetary Policy Committee has crucial influence here. When it raises its base rate, the move is followed by every major UK bank and building society. This rise affects mortgage costs and savings, and in turn they affect the entire economy and the stock market. We cover this process in detail, later in this chapter.

When many of the items in Table 14-1 work in tandem, they can have a magnified effect that can have tremendous consequences for your share portfolio. Alert investors keep a constant vigil when the House of Commons is open for business, and they adjust their portfolios accordingly.

Understanding price controls

Share investors should be wary of *price controls* (they're a great example of regulation). A price control is a fixed price on a particular product, commodity, or service mandated by the government.

Politicians have tried price controls continuously throughout history, and they have continuously been removed because they ultimately do more harm than good. You can see why. Imagine that you run a business that sells chairs, and a law is passed that states, 'From this point onward, chairs can be sold only for £10.' If all your costs stay constant at £9 or less, the regulation isn't that bad. However, price controls put two dynamics in motion. First, the artificially lower price encourages consumption – more people buy chairs. Secondly, production is discouraged. Who wants to make chairs if they can't sell them for a decent profit?

What happens to the company with a fixed sales price (in this example, £10) and rising costs? Profits shrink, and depending on how long the price controls are in effect, the company eventually experiences losses. The chair producer is eventually driven out of business. The chair-building industry shrinks, and a chair shortage is the result. Profits (and jobs) soon vanish. So what happens if you own shares in a company that builds chairs? Just say that if we tell you which way the share price is going, you better be sitting down (if, of course, you have a chair).

Ascertaining the political climate

The bottom line is that you ignore political realities at your own (economic) risk. To be and stay aware, ask yourself the following questions about the shares of each company in which you invest:

- ✔ What laws directly affect my share investment adversely?
- ✔ Do any laws affect that company's industry?
- ✔ Do any current or prospective laws affect the company's sources of revenue?
- ✔ Do any current or prospective laws affect the company's expenses or supplies?
- ✔ Am I staying informed about political and economic issues that may possibly have a negative impact on my investment?
- ✔ Do such things as excessive regulations, price controls, or new taxes have a negative impact on my shares' industry?

Many shareholders benefited from increased share prices following the privatisation of major companies such as British Gas, British Telecom and BAA. The privatisations had been set in motion by Margaret Thatcher, the Conservative Prime Minister from 1979 to 1991. But when the Labour party returned to power in 1997, rather than re-nationalise all the companies, it exacted a windfall tax of nine times P/E ratio from the privatised companies. The move dramatically hit the share prices of the companies and raised £5 billion to pay for the New Deal – Labour's new policy to reduce unemployment.

Politics and economics are a double-edged sword. Understand them, and you can profit; misunderstand them, and you become a financial victim.

Discovering systemic and non-systemic effects

Politics can affect your investments in two basic ways: systemic and non-systemic.

Non-systemic means that the system isn't affected but a particular participant is affected. A *systemic effect* means that all the players in that system are affected. In this case, the 'system' is the economy at large. Politics imposes itself (through taxes, laws, regulations, and so on) and has an undue influence on all the members of that system.

Non-systemic

Say that you decide to buy shares in a company called Golf Carts Unlimited, PLC (GCU). You believe that the market for golf carts has great potential and that GCU stands to grow substantially. How can politics affect GCU?

What if politicians believe that GCU is too big and that it controls too much of the golf cart industry? Maybe they view GCU as a monopoly and want the government to step in to shrink GCU's reach and influence for the benefit of competition and consumers. Maybe the government believes that GCU engages in unfair or predatory business practices and is in violation of anti-trust (or anti-monopoly) laws. If the government acts against GCU, the action is a non-systemic issue: The action is directed toward the participant (in this case, GCU) and not the golf cart industry.

What happens if you're an investor in GCU? Does your share investment suffer as a result of government action directed against the company? Let's just say that the share price hooks left and ends up in the lake.

Systemic

Say that politicians want to target the golf industry for intervention because they maintain that golf should be free for all to participate in and that a law must be passed to make it accessible to all, especially those people who can't afford to play. So to remedy the situation, the following law is enacted: 'The Accessibility (Golf) Act declares that from this day forward, all golf courses that operate must charge only one pound for any golfer who chooses to participate.'

Playing monopoly

Government action against large companies for real (or alleged) abuses has happened many times. In the UK, former state monopolies such as BT – previously known as British Telecom – are often put under pressure from regulators to cut or limit prices and to make facilities available to open the market up to more competition. One statement or warning from a regulator can punch a small hole in BT's share price. Keep an eye on the share price the next time a regulator takes a swipe at BT. When government targets a company, regardless of the merits of the case, avoid investing in that company (until the trouble has passed). Investors should be wary when the government starts making noise about any company and potential legal actions against it.

That law sounds great to any golfer. But what are the unintended effects when such a law becomes reality? Many people agree with the sentiment of the law, but what about the cause-and-effect aspects of it? Obviously, all things being equal, golf courses may be forced to close. Staying in business is uneconomical if their costs are higher than their income. If they can't charge any more than a pound, how can they possibly stay open? Ultimately (and ironically), no one can play golf.

What happens to investors of Golf Carts Unlimited, PLC? If the world of golf shrinks, then demand for golf carts shrinks as well. The value of GCU's shares will certainly be 'triple-bogeyed'.

Examples of politics creating systemic problems are endless, but you get the point.

Poking into politics: Resources

To find out about new laws being passed or proposed, check out the government and what's going on at its primary Web portal: www.direct.gov.uk, which gives access to all government Web sites. For information about the Prime Minister, check the 10 Downing Street Web site at www.number-10.gov.uk

You may also want to check out www.theyworkforyou.com, a non-partisan Web site run by a charity that aims to make it easy for people to keep tabs on their elected representatives. This search engine can be used to find out whether an industry is being targeted for increased regulation or deregulation. You can also arrange to be emailed any mentions in Parliament of subjects you are interested in. In the late 1990s, utilities were hit hard when the government passed new regulations and tax rules (related shares went down). When the telecom industry was deregulated in the mid-1990s, the industry grew dramatically (related shares went up).

You can find more resources in Appendix A. The more knowledge you pick up about how politics and government actions can help (or harm) an investment, the better you're going to be at growing (and protecting) your wealth.

Easing into Economics

Economics sounds like a deadly dull pursuit. Actually, the wrong book on the topic or the wrong instructor can make the topic so boring that you feel like you're crawling backwards through the Slough of Despond. Economics really does matter, but do you have to really understand phrases such as 'inelasticity coefficient' and the 'Index of Leading Economic Indicators'? No, not really. But do you need to be familiar with phrases such as 'supply and demand' and 'price controls don't work' to operate in today's modern stock market? The answer is a resounding yes. Of course, you can invest without knowing much about economics. However, your chances for success are tremendously enhanced when you have a basic understanding of how economics works. Actually, economics explained in the proper way is fascinating. Knowing how the world ticks can be fun and profitable.

Understanding economic impact

When people comment about the economy, they make it sound like a giant, amorphous thing in the same way that they talk about the stock market and the weather. To put it into perspective, the economy is you and me and millions of others – producers, consumers, entrepreneurs, and workers all trading money for goods and services. The economy is millions of people and organisations voluntarily transacting with each other day in and day out. People and organisations buy, spend, save, and invest billions every hour of every day.

Looking at the economy is like seeing a huge picture and deciding where on the canvas are the greatest points of interest – investment opportunities. When you look at the economy, you look at the major numbers and trends and judge whether a particular company is well suited to profit from trends and opportunities. You simply rely on your common sense and apply it with the statistics that track the economy in general. If millions of consumers are buying product X and the market and demand for X are growing, then it stands to reason that the best company offering product X prospers as well. The reverse can also be true. If more and more people avoid, or just don't spend their money on, a particular product or industry, then the fortunes of those companies decline too.

Economic reports are important because sometimes just one report or statistic released is enough to move the stock market. The economic statistics and reports that are the most meaningful to you are the ones that have a direct bearing on your shares or industry. If you invest in property or construction shares, reports that cover housing starts and interest rates are critical to you. If you invest in retail shares, then information on consumer confidence and debt is important to you.

In table 14-2, we give examples of key industries and a statistic that's a relevant indicator:

Table 14-2	Some Economic Indicators by Industry	
Industry	*Statistic*	*Comments*
Property	New house building	This indicator tracks permits given for new housing to be built. Rising housing starts are desirable.
Car	Car sales	The industry's annual sales figure is a closely watched indicator. Rising sales are desirable.
Retail	Retail sales	The overall sales are watched, and you want them to be rising (especially in the fourth quarter of the year).

Industry trade publications and general financial publications, such as *The Financial Times* and other serious newspapers, regularly report this data. You can also find it (along with a tremendous database of economic data and statistics) at www.digitallook.com.

What are the important things in economic data that you need to be aware of? Keep reading. The following sections make this information clear.

Grossing you out with GDP

Gross domestic product (GDP), which measures the nation's total output of goods and services for the quarter, is considered the broadest measure of economic activity. Although GDP is measured in pounds (the UK GDP surpassed £305 billion by May 2007), GDP is usually quoted as a percentage. You typically hear a news report that says something like, 'The economy grew by

2.5 per cent last quarter'. Because the GDP is an important overall barometer for the economy, it should be a positive number. The report on GDP is released quarterly by the National Statistics Office (www.statistics.gov.uk).

You should regularly monitor the GDP along with economic data that relates directly to your share portfolio. The following list gives general guidelines for evaluating GDP:

- ✔ **Over 3 per cent:** This number indicates strong growth and bodes well for shares. At 5 per cent or higher, the economy is sizzling!

- ✔ **1 to 3 per cent:** This figure indicates moderate growth and can occur as the economy is rebounding from a recession or as the economy is slowing down from a previously strong period.

- ✔ **0 per cent or negative (as low as –3 per cent):** This number isn't good and indicates that the economy is either not growing or is actually shrinking a bit. A negative GDP is considered *recessionary* (meaning that the economy's growth is receding).

- ✔ **Under –3 per cent:** A GDP this low indicates a difficult period for the economy. A GDP under –3 per cent, especially for two or more quarters, indicates a serious recession or possibly a depression.

Looking at a single quarter isn't that useful. Track GDP over many quarters to see which way the general economy is trending. When you look at GDP for a particular quarter of a year, ask yourself whether the GDP is better (or worse) than the quarter before. If better (or worse), then ask yourself to what extent it has changed. Is it dramatically better (or worse) than the quarter before? Is the economy showing steady growth, or is it slowing? If several quarters show solid growth, the overall economy is generally bullish.

Traditionally, if two or more consecutive quarters show negative growth (economic output is shrinking), the economy is considered to be in a recession. A recession can be a painful necessity; it usually occurs when the economy can't absorb the total amount of goods being produced due to excess production. A bear market in shares usually accompanies a recession.

GDP is just a rough estimate at best. It can't possibly calculate all the factors that go into economic growth. For example, crime has a negative effect on economic growth, but crime is not reflected in GDP. Still, most economists agree that GDP provides a good snapshot of overall economic progress.

Showing interest in the Old Lady

The Bank of England, known as the Old Lady of Threadneedle Street (the street in the City of London where the Bank is based) is the UK's independent central bank. It plays a pivotal role in the economy and – because the City of London is an influential financial centre – in the global economy as well.

For more information about the Bank of England's money supply and interest rate policies, go to its Web site at www.bankofengland.co.uk. Also, the National Statistics Office (www.statistics.gov.uk) offers useful, readable research on the relationships between money growth, interest rates, and the stock market.

The Bank of England is one of the most closely watched institutions in the world, because it has such an impact on financial markets as well as the economy. Although it performs a number of functions, the Bank of England's fundamental roles are

- ✔ **Controlling the money supply:** The Bank of England monitors the actual quantity of banknotes that goes into circulation. It also has the responsibility for fighting or controlling inflation. People think that inflation is the cost of goods and services going up, when actually *inflation* refers to the value of money going down because too much money is circulating in the marketplace (the currency being *inflated*). In other words, too many pounds are chasing too few goods and services.

  The Bank of England tries to manage the difficult task of having just the right amount of money in the economy. Having too much money can create inflation, meaning that consumers see the purchasing power of their pounds shrink. Too little money means that not enough money is circulating in the economy. (In these financial conditions, some people use the terminology 'tight money', and others say that 'the economy lacks liquidity'.) Inflation, if not held in check, can have highly negative consequences. After all, how would you feel if the money in your pocket was rapidly shrinking in value? (The odds are that you'd feel like a parent with too many teenagers in the house!)

  Inflation is mainly reported as the Consumer Price Index (CPI) and the Retail Price Index (RPI). The *CPI* (sometimes called the cost-of-living index) and the RPI are calculated by the National Statistics Office (www.statistics.gov.uk) and measure changes in the price of a typical basket of consumer goods that reflect what the average consumer buys on a regular basis. The CPI is considered a warning of pending inflation. The *RPIX* is also closely watched by investors. It measures retail prices excluding mortgage costs.

- ✔ **Influencing interest rates:** Financial markets, such as the stock market and the bond market, closely monitor the Bank's influence on interest rates. Because the Bank of England can raise or lower interest rates at will, its actions become a powerful lever that can raise or lower many rates that literally millions of individuals and businesses pay primarily on their short-term debt.

You need to watch interest rates for several reasons:

- Interest rates affect corporate earnings. If companies pay more interest, that additional cost directly affects their profits. If profits shrink, then that puts downward pressure on share prices. Conversely, if the Bank of England cuts interest rates, companies typically see a positive impact on profits.

- Interest rates influence income investors. (See Chapter 9 for more on income investing.) When interest rates rise, investors looking for a higher return on their investments make decisions to pull their money out of shares and into other vehicles such as bonds or savings accounts. When interest rates continue to climb, more and more investors sell their shares, sending share prices down.

- Interest rates figure prominently in fighting inflation. Generally, interest rates have been a key weapon in the past 20 years in this fight. Because inflation means that the value of the pound shrinks, the Bank of England uses higher interest rates to offset this devaluation. When inflation hovers near double-digit rates, interest rates go through the roof. Conversely, lower interest rates coupled with an expanding money supply can ignite higher inflation.

On your marks, get debt . . .

Debt can be burdensome and have a negative impact on economic growth. As an investor, you need to know how much debt is in the economy and whether the debt is growing or shrinking. Whether the debt is consumer debt (credit cards, mortgages, and so on) or corporate debt (short-term borrowing, bonds, and so on), it harms the economy if not kept under control.

A major reason for the economy's (and stock market's) downturn in 2000–2002 was massive debt. In fact, during the 1990s, virtually every major category of debt hit record levels. People can only remove debt by paying it off or going bankrupt. Because so many individuals and businesses became overextended in debt during this time period, bankruptcies hit record levels as well. Those records are being beaten now.

Investors in shares must monitor debt levels for bear market potential (especially in this decade!). Too much debt slows the economy, which in turn can adversely affect the stock market. Overly indebted individuals don't have money to spend or invest. Overly indebted companies may face employee layoffs, cuts in spending, declining profits, and other negative actions. Watch also for corporate problems. If you have shares in a company that has too much debt or that sells to customers who are overburdened with debt, then that company is going to suffer. The Bank of England and other sources, including such publications as *The Financial Times,* report consumer and corporate debt levels.

Raising confident consumers

You may have heard that consumer spending accounts for two-thirds of the economy. Therefore, the consumer's behaviour is something that investors watch carefully. You can break down consumer activity into two categories:

- ✔ **Consumer income:** If consumer income meets or exceeds the CPI rate (see 'Showing interest in the Old Lady', earlier in this chapter), that bodes well for the economy.

- ✔ **Consumer confidence:** This index is measured by prominent surveys that essentially track how consumers feel about the economy in general and their personal situations in particular. The most widely followed survey is produced monthly by economists working for the Nationwide Building Society. If consumers feel good about the economy and their immediate futures, that bodes well for consumer spending.

Lumping together the data with economic indices

Because so much economic data is available, many investors prefer to look at indices that put the data in a nutshell. These indices try to summarise many economic indicators and put them into a neat, digestible format.

Economic indicators are grouped into categories that try to give a rough idea about the economy's upward and downward cycle. These cyclical indicators are put into three categories that try to time the various phases of the economy's movement:

- ✔ **Leading:** The leading indicators try to be predictive of the economy's path. Investors in shares are particularly interested in leading economic indicators because they usually don't invest because of past or present conditions – investors buy shares because of expectations for the future.

- ✔ **Coincident:** The coincident indicators essentially tell you where the economy is right now. (For stock investors, most coincident indicators are like the indicator on your car's dashboard blinking 'hot' when you see steam rising from your hood.) The most valuable coincident indicator is the GDP. (See the section 'Grossing you out with GDP', earlier in this chapter.)

- ✔ **Lagging:** This type of indicator tells you what just passed in the economy's path (which can be significant because some lagging indicators do precede leading indicators). The unemployment rate is a good example of a lagging indicator.

Of the three categories, the most widely followed is that of the Leading Indicators. A good example of an indicator that's included in the Leading Indicators is the statistic on new housing developments. If more new construction is being started, that's a positive harbinger of economic growth. Check out the National Statistics Web site for all the key economic indicators.

Predicting the economic weather

Excellent sources are available that make the arcane world of economics more readable and understandable. One is the About.com Web site (www.economics.about.com), which has a section for economics students that explains all the jargon and technical terms in simple language. More in depth information is available in the respected weekly magazine *The Economist* (www.economist.com). Most serious newspapers also carry reports on what is happening in the economy. By the way, as you navigate the world of economics, you come across various 'schools of thought'. Among the well-known ones are the Keynesian school and the Marx school. In my opinion and experience, the best is the Austrian school of economics (Mises is considered the 'dean' of this school). Austrian economists have been the most accurate in interpreting and forecasting economic events. Among the events they warned about were the Great Depression, the collapse of communism, and the dangers of America's current mammoth debt bubble.

Inquiring about economics: Resources

Keep in mind that, because of the scope of the topic and the finite number of pages in this book, this chapter can't do justice to the burgeoning world of economics. We encourage you to continue finding out about economics by conducting easy and interesting research with the resources listed here and in Appendix A.

Turn to the following sources for economic data:

- ✔ National Statistics, www.statistics.gov.uk
- ✔ Bank of England, www.bankofengland.co.uk
- ✔ Nationwide Building Society,
  www.nationwide.co.uk/consumer_confidence

Here are a few sources to help you understand economics:

- ✔ About.com, www.economics.about.com
- ✔ Motley Fool, www.fool.co.uk
- ✔ *The Financial Times*, www.ft.com
- ✔ *The Economist*, www.economist.com
- ✔ The Mises Institute, www.mises.org

Part IV
Investment Strategies and Tactics

'The taxmen never give up, do they?'

In this part . . .

Successful share investing is more than choosing a
particular share. It's also understanding the environment in which the market operates. Just as goldfish can
thrive in good water (or die in bad water), the stock
market reacts to the general economic climate. Successful
investors go beyond merely picking good shares and
watching the financial news. They implement techniques
and strategies that help them either minimise losses or
maximise gains (hopefully both). The chapters in this part
introduce some of the most effective investing techniques
to help you profit from shares in a bull or a bear market
and describe some smart ways to hold on to more of your
profits when tax time rolls around.

Chapter 15

Taking the Bull (Or Bear) by the Horns

. . . .

. . . .

*U*nderstanding the general markets and their major directional trend may even be more important to your wealth-building success than choosing the right shares. Recent years – and a century of stock market history – bear (no pun intended) witness to this point.

Bull and bear markets have a tremendous effect on your share choices. Generally, bull markets tend to precede economic uptrends (also called economic rebound, economic recovery, or economic growth), while bear markets tend to precede economic downtrends (also called recession, depression, or economic contraction).

The stock market's movement is based on the fact that share prices go up (or down) based on people's buying or selling behaviour. If more people are buying shares (versus selling), then share prices rise. If more people are selling shares, then share prices fall. Why do people buy or sell a share? It can be explained in one word: expectations. People generally buy (or sell) shares in expectation of economic events. If they feel that times are getting bad and the economic statistics back them up (in the form of rising unemployment, shrinking corporate profits, cutbacks in consumer spending, and so on), then they become more cautious, which can have a couple of results:

✔ They sell shares that they currently own.

✔ They don't buy shares because they feel that shares won't do well.

Of course, when the economy is doing well, the reverse is true.

Bulling Up

In the beginning, a bull market doesn't look like a bull market at all. It looks like anything but. Maybe that's why so few catch on early. Bull markets are marked by great optimism as the economy roars forward and shares go skyward. Everyone knows what a bull market should look like, and everyone can recognise it when the bull market has become a mature trend. The saying 'I don't know what it is, but I'll know it when I see it' is one that applies to a bull market. But if you can foresee it coming, you may be able to make a fortune by getting in just before the crowd sees it.

Just keep in mind that you personally want to behave like a contrarian. A *contrarian* is an investor who decides which securities to buy and sell by going against the crowd. To paraphrase the legendary billionaire J. Paul Getty, buy when people are selling and sell when people are buying. This is the essence of successful investing.

This contrarian attitude reminds me of the time I bought gold and silver mining shares in 2001 and made a 1000% gain when I sold them only a few years later. That group of shares was unpopular when I purchased it, but it benefited from the unfolding bull market in precious metals.

Because bull markets usually start in the depths of a bear market, do research regarding bear markets; read the section 'Identifying the beast,' later in this chapter.

Recognising the beast

In this book we concentrate on the modern era, starting in the early part of the twentieth century, but bull markets in shares have shown themselves many times throughout the past few hundred years – plenty of time to have established a few recognisable traits, such as the following:

✔ **Bull markets tend to start at the depths of pessimism – the same way that dawn starts at the edge of darkness.** People have probably just been beaten up by a bear market. The phrase 'I'm into investing in shares' is about as welcome in polite conversation as 'I have a contagious disease'. If investors are avoiding shares like the plague (or selling shares they already have), share prices drop to the point that much of the risk is wrung out of them. Value-oriented investors then can pick up solid companies at great prices. (See Chapter 10 for information on recognising a good share value.)

✔ **The major media mirrors this pessimism and amplifies it.** Usually, the mainstream media has greater value as a *counterindicator* because by the time the major publications find out about the economic trend and report it, the major trend has already played itself out and is probably ready to change course.

✔ **Economic statistics stabilise.** After the economy has hit rock bottom, the economic statistics start to improve. The most-watched set of economic indicators is compiled by National Statistics but Rhodes-Blakeman Associates also collects and publishes useful economic data. Investors want to make sure that the economy is getting back on its feet before it starts its next move upward. In 1982, the economy was just starting to recover from the 1981 recession. The economic expansion (and accompanying bull market) became the longest in history.

✔ **Economic conditions for individuals and companies are stable and strong.** You know that's true if profits are stable or growing for companies in general and if consumers are seeing strong and increasing income growth. The logic holds up well: More money being made means more money to eventually spend and invest.

✔ **Industries producing large-ticket items hit rock bottom and begin their climb.** After consumers and companies have been pummelled by a tough economy, they're not apt to make major financial commitments to items such as new cars, houses, equipment, and so on. Industries that produce these large, expensive items see sales fall to a low and slowly start to rebound as the economy picks up. In a growing economy, consumers and companies experience greater confidence (both psychologically and financially).

✔ **Demographics appear favourable.** Take a look at the census and government statistics on trends for population growth, as well as the growth in the number of business enterprises. The 1980s and 1990s, for example, saw the rise of the baby boomers, those born during the post-World War II period of 1946 to 1964. Baby boomers wielded much financial clout, much of it in the stock market. Their investment money played a major role in propelling the stock market to new highs.

✔ **General peace and stability prevail.** A major war or international conflict may have just ended. Beyond death and destruction, war is also bad for the economy and presents uncertainty and anxiety for investors.

Avoiding the horns of a bull market

Believe it or not, a mature bull market poses problems for investors and stock market experts. In a mature bull market, just about any share – good, bad, or indifferent – tends to go up. You can be a blind monkey throwing darts and pick a rising share. When everything goes up and everybody seems to be making a winning pick, human nature kicks in. Both beginners and serious investors believe that their good fortune can be chalked up to superior share-picking prowess and not simple luck or circumstance. Overconfidence is rampant at the top of the market and it becomes a prelude for disaster.

When investors become convinced that they have the newfound ability to consistently choose winning shares, they grow more daring in their investment approach; they make riskier choices, using less discipline and relying on less diligence and research. Then . . . wham! They get knocked out by the market. Overconfidence lures the unsuspecting investor to more dangerous territory, invariably resulting in an expensive lesson. Overconfidence and money don't mix.

Let us tell you about a common phenomenon of human behaviour that Paul refers to as the Wile E. Coyote effect. Do you remember Wile E. Coyote from those great Road Runner cartoons? Of course you do! You know the plot: Mr. Coyote is chasing the Road Runner and seems to be gaining on him. He's confidently ready to pounce on the seemingly unsuspecting bird, but the Road Runner makes a quick turn and watches as Mr. Coyote continues running over the cliff, ultimately plummeting down the ravine.

A mature bull market (also known as the 'mania' stage) does that to investors. Scores of true stories tell of investors lured to a game of easy riches (the dot-com fiasco, for example) only to watch their investments get pulverised. This phenomenon happened not only to beginners but also to experienced investors and many share investment experts. Crowd psychology, whether driven by fear or greed, is fascinating.

Toro! Approaching a bull market

Being fully invested in shares at the beginning of a bull market makes for spectacular success. But doing so takes courage. Then again, who says you have to go the whole hog? You can begin looking and get your first share now and slowly build your portfolio as the bull market emerges.

Choose the type of shares as well as the mix to fit into your unique situation and needs. So, when the bull market is in its infancy, start investing by using the following approach:

✔ **Be a bargain hunter.** Frequently, at the tail end of a bear market, share prices have been sufficiently battered after going through an extended period of low demand and/or disproportionately more selling of the shares by nervous investors. Let the shopping begin! At the bottom of the bear market, you have a good chance of acquiring shares at share

prices that are near (or in some cases below) the book value of the companies they represent. You also have less risk when you acquire the
shares of a company that is generating positive growth in sales and earnings. Chapter 10 can help you better understand concepts such as book
value.

✔ **Look for strong fundamentals.** Is the company you're choosing exhibit-
ing solid income and profit? Are income and profit rising compared to
the previous year? How about from the same quarter last year? Conduct
top line and bottom line analyses (which we discuss in Chapter 10).
Do the company's products and services make sense to you? In other
words, is it selling stuff that the public is starting to demand more of?

✔ **Consider the share's class.** Remember that some shares are more
aggressive choices than others. This choice reflects your risk tolerance
as well. Figure out whether you want to invest in a small-cap with phenomenal growth prospects (and commensurate risk) or a blue chip
that's a tried-and-true market leader.

All things being equal, small-cap shares exhibit the best growth performance in an emerging bull market. Small-caps are more appropriate for
investors who have a higher risk tolerance. Of course, most shares do
well in an emerging bull market (actually, that's what makes it a bull
market!), so even risk-adverse investors who put their money into larger
companies gain. (For more information on growth shares such as small-
caps, see Chapter 8.)

✔ **Choose appropriate industries.** Look at industries that are poised to
rebound as the economy picks up and individuals and organisations begin
to spend again. In a rising market, cyclical shares such as those in the car,
housing, industrial equipment, and technology industries resume growth.
When the economy is doing well, individuals and organisations begin to
spend more on items that meet their needs in an expanding economy.
Companies upgrade their technology. Families get a new car or move to
a bigger house. Construction firms need more and better equipment as
residential and commercial building increases.

✔ **Take stock of your portfolio.** As you start to add shares to your portfolio, first analyse your situation to make sure that you have diversification not only in different shares and/or unit trusts but also in non-share
investments, such as savings bonds and bank accounts. You don't have
to have 100 per cent of your investment in shares just because the
market is bullish. Instead, you should consider putting as much as 100
per cent of the growth component of your investment money in shares.

Say that you're investing for the long term. You're not that concerned
with risk, and you want maximum growth from your investments. After
setting aside money in an emergency fund, you decide that you want to
devote your remaining funds of £25,000 to growth shares. In this case,
100 per cent of that sum becomes the *growth component* of your investment portfolio. If you decide to play it safer and split it 50/50 between

bonds and shares, then £12,500 (or 50 per cent of your portfolio) is your growth component. The bonds are then your *income component*.

✔ **Evaluate your personal goals.** No matter how good the market and the foreseeable prospects for growth are, investing in shares is a personal matter that should serve your unique needs. For example, how old are you, and how many years away is your retirement? All things being equal, a 35-year-old should have predominately growth shares, while a 65-year-old requires a more proven, stable performance with blue chip market leaders. The information in Chapter 2 can help you identify appropriate investment goals.

Some investors in a bull market may have little money in shares. Why? Maybe they have already reached their financial goals, so wealth preservation is more appropriate than growth. Perhaps they have a million-pound portfolio and are 70 years old and no longer working. In that case, having, say, 80 per cent of their investments in stable, income-producing investments and 20 per cent in proven (yet modestly) growing shares may make more sense for them.

Bearing Down

Alas, shares go down as well as up. Some ferocious bear markets have hit shares on several occasions since the Great Depression. The bear markets of 1973–1975 and 2000–2002 rank as the toughest in modern times. A few brief, relatively minor ones occurred in the late 1980s and early 1990s. You don't need to worry about the occasional dips (referred to as *corrections*); however, be wary about *secular* (long-term) bear markets, which can last years. Discipline and a watchful eye can keep you and your money out of trouble.

History in the making

One of the worst bear markets since the Great Depression started in 1973. The stock market in the UK was pummelled as the Dow Jones Industrial Average (DJIA) fell 45 per cent during an 18-month period ending in 1975. However, the DJIA did not recover to its 1973 high until (you guessed it) 1982. The period from 1973 to 1982 had the hallmarks of tough times – high inflation, high unemployment, war (the Middle East conflict in 1973 and expansive Soviet aggression in Africa and Afghanistan), the energy crisis, and high taxes. The 1970s were a tough decade for most companies in the UK and the US. The 1980s and 1990s were great decades for stock investors. Alas, 2000–2002 were rough years for stocks as investors cumulatively lost billions.

Identifying the beast

Bear markets can be foreseen and they have been most often seen starting during apparently bullish, jubilant times. Bear markets come immediately on the heels of market peaks (when share buying reaches 'mania' levels). Anecdotal evidence about market peaks makes shrewd investors become cautious. Rumour has it that John D. Rockefeller (or was it Joe Kennedy?) got totally out of the stock market just before the 1929 crash when his shoeshine boy gave him a hot stock tip. Whether that story is true isn't the issue. The story is believable because you know similar moments have indeed happened in recent times. In 2000, investors and tabloid share tippers were appearing on television giving stock market advice. In 2005, football players, glamour models and taxi drivers were building buy-to-let property empires on the side. Long-time professional observers have come to realise that once everybody and their uncle (and their aunt and their parrot) starts telling you about easy riches in a market, it's time to get out!

Emerging bear markets have tell-tale signs, including the following:

- ✔ **Optimism abounds.** Everyone from London to Lerwick feels great. Financial reports declare that the business cycle has been conquered and a new economy or new paradigm has arrived. Good times are here for the foreseeable future! You start to see books with titles such as *The Footsie at 40,000* and *Easy Riches in the Stock Market* hit the bestseller lists. The *business cycle* refers to the economy's roller-coaster-like behaviour when it expands (growth) and contracts (recession).

  Sometimes, the financial experts believe that an economy is doing so well that it can continue to grow indefinitely. Examples of misguided exuberance abound in stock market history. In 1929, Irving Fisher, the best-known financial expert and share millionaire of his day, made the ill-fated declaration 'Stocks have reached a permanent plateau' as he predicted the bull market would continue for the foreseeable future. A few weeks later, the infamous stock market crash occurred. Everyone who had listened to Fisher got clobbered in the greatest bear market of the twentieth century. Even Irving Fisher himself filed for bankruptcy. Not even Irving Fisher should've listened to Irving Fisher. In stark contrast, Ludwig von Mises warned about the oncoming depression throughout the late 1920s and was ignored. Who needs a party-pooper, right? In 1999, one economist on TV boldly stated that the economy would continue growing forever and that 'recessions are a thing of the past.' Really? Today, that economist is probably in a new job saying, 'Would you like chips with that?'

- ✔ **Debt levels hit new highs.** When optimism is high, people buy things. In 1999, debt levels hit a record high in almost every category; corporate, consumer, mortgage, and margin debt ballooned during the late 1990s.

The financial press mostly ignored this massive debt, yet it was one of the major reasons for the subsequent bear market and recession. When people or companies accrue too much debt, it can be removed in only one of two ways: through repayment or by bankruptcy. Insolvencies in the UK are at record levels and look set to continue to climb. In Scotland, bankruptcies in 2006 were higher than at any time since records began. And in England and Wales, a total of 107,288 declared themselves insolvent through bankruptcy or Individual Voluntary Arrangements or IVAs. The equivalent figure in 1988 was 24,549.

✔ **Excessive speculation, credit, and money supply expand.** Whenever a country's money supply grows beyond the economy's needs, massive problems can result. When the money supply expands, more money is circulated into the banking system. (Go to www.bankofengland.co.uk to find out more about the money supply.) The banks then lend or invest this excess money. The oversupply of money flows into investment projects, such as new issues and bond offerings. When too much money is available for too few worthy projects, invariably a lot of money is invested unwisely. This situation causes massive imbalances in the economic system, ultimately resulting in economic downturns that can take years to rectify.

History proves the truth of this economic situation. It happened to the US economy in the late 1920s and to Japan in the late 1980s. Fortunately, statistics on credit and the money supply are easy to come by and readily available on the Internet. (See Appendix A for resources.)

✔ **Government intervention increases.** Government has the power to do much good, but when it uses its power improperly, it can do a great deal of harm. Throughout history, every economy that collapsed ultimately did so because of excessive government intervention. In progressive, free-market economies, this intervention usually occurs in the form of taxes, laws, and regulations. Keep a watchful eye on the Chancellor and parliament to monitor government intervention. Are they proposing policies that add burdens to the private economy? Are they advocating stringent new laws and regulations? I explain more about government's influence on the stock market and the general economy in Chapter 14.

✔ **National and/or international conflict arises.** Nothing can have a more negative impact on the economy than war or political or civil unrest. (Perhaps war is a good example of 'excessive government intervention'.) Keep your eye on the news. Ask yourself what effect a particular conflict may have on the economy and the stock market. Sometimes the conflict isn't a violent one; sometimes it takes the form of a trade war when competing countries aggressively implement tariffs and boycotts that can devastate companies or even industries in one or both of the countries.

Looking for Titanic tickets

In early 2000, the dapper pundits on TV told viewers to hang tight and hold on for the long haul. Shares then took a beating, prompting the pundits to say, 'It's a buying opportunity. Add to your portfolio'. Then what happened? The bear market took shares down again.

Investors would probably have avoided losing trillions during 2000–2002 if they had been more disciplined and if the pundits had been more careful in their pronouncements. When the economy is heading into treacherous waters, shares get the worst of it, yet experts continue to advise people to buy shares because shares are good for the long term. Hold on! Liking shares doesn't mean that you should always be in them. I mean, just because you like boating doesn't mean that you would take advantage of a free ticket on the *Titanic*.

Heading into the woods: Approaching a bear market

Sticking to a buy-and-hold strategy (where you buy shares and hold on to them for better or worse) at the onset of a bear market is financial suicide. People have a tough time selling, and financial advisors have an even tougher time telling them to cut their losses because that's tantamount to saying, 'Sorry, I was wrong'. Admitting failure is hard for most people to do.

Understand that investing should be a logical, practical, and unemotional pursuit. You can't be married to shares – until death do you part – especially because bear markets can divorce you from your money.

In an emerging bear market, keep the following points in mind to maximise your gains (or just to minimise your losses):

- ✔ **Review your situation.** Before you consider any move in or out of the market, review your overall financial situation to make sure that your money and financial condition are as secure as possible. Make sure that you have an emergency fund of three to six months' worth of gross living expenses. Keep your debt at a comfortably low level. Review your career, insurance, and so on. Schedule a financial checkup with your financial planner.

- ✔ **Remember that cash is king.** When the bear market is coming and economic storm clouds are rolling in, keep the bulk of your money in safe, interest-bearing vehicles such as bank and building society accounts, National Savings certificates, and/guaranteed income bonds. Doing so keeps your money safe. When shares are falling by 10 to 20 per cent or more, you're better off earning a low-percentage interest in a secure, stable investment. In addition, you can conduct research while your money is earning interest. Start shopping for undervalued shares with strong fundamentals.

✔ **Stick to necessities.** In an economic downturn, defensive shares generally outperform the market. *Defensive shares* are shares in companies that sell goods and services that people need no matter how good or bad the economy is doing. Good examples are food and drinks, energy, utilities, and certain health-care shares.

✔ **Use trailing stops.** Trailing stops are just the active use of stop-loss orders on a given share. (If a share is at £40, you have the stop loss at £36, if the stock moves to £46, then change the stop loss from £36 to £41, and so on. Chapter 17 provides a fuller explanation). In the case of a bear market, you *tighten the trail* – set your stop losses closer to the share's market price. Say, for example, that you once bought a share for £50 per share and this share is now at £110. Presume that you usually kept a trailing stop at 10 per cent below the current market price. If the bear market is becoming more evident to you, then change that 10 per cent to 5 per cent. Before, that trailing stop on the £110 stock was £99 (£110 minus 10 per cent, or £11), but now the trailing stop is at £104.50 (£110 minus 5 per cent, or £5.50). The trailing stop strategy is one of our favourite ways to protect our shares' gains.

Straddling Bear and Bull: Uncertain Markets

Uncertain markets are . . . well . . . uncertain. Markets aren't always up or down. The end of a bear market doesn't automatically mean the beginning of a bull market and vice versa. Sometimes markets move little way until investors and participants in the economy figure out what's what.

Pinpointing uncertainty is tough

Clashing points of view in the media tell you that even the experts aren't sure which way the market and the economy are going in the coming months. In uncertain markets, compelling evidence and loads of opinions evenly line up on both the pro and con sides of the economic debate – often in the same article. Bullish and bearish advisors and commentators may both seem persuasive, so you may be left scratching your head, wondering what to do. In this case, your patience and diligence should pay off.

Deciding whether you want to approach an uncertain market

The approach to take in uncertain markets is almost simplistic. If you think that a bull market is starting, you want to have 100 per cent of your growth portfolio invested in shares, and if a bear market is starting, you want the percentage to be 0. Therefore, in an uncertain market, 50 per cent in shares and 50 per cent in other investments is just right. Of course, these three scenarios need to be balanced by many non-share factors, such as your individual financial situation, age, debt level, career concerns, and so on. However, all things being equal, those allocations aren't far off the mark.

Treat uncertain markets as bear markets until your research starts to give you a clear idea of the market's direction. No matter how adventurous you are, the first rule of investing in shares is that you minimise or avoid losses. If no one can agree on the direction of the market, then you stand a 50 per cent chance of being wrong should you take the bullish stance. However, if you take a bearish stance and the market becomes decidedly bullish, no real harm is done except that you may miss an investment opportunity during a brief period of time. Just keep in mind that investing in shares is indeed a long-term pursuit. Jumping into a bullish market is easy, but recovering from losses may not be.

Chapter 16

Choosing a Strategy That's Just Right for You

....

In This Chapter

▶ Basing your strategy on your needs

▶ Deciding where to allocate your assets

▶ Recognising when to unload your shares

....

S hares are a means to an end. What end are you seeking? You should look at shares as tools for wealth building. Sometimes they're great tools, and sometimes they're awful. It depends on your approach. Some shares are appropriate for a conservative approach, while others are more suitable for an aggressive approach. Sometimes shares aren't a good idea at all. You what? A book about investing in shares that suggests that shares aren't always the answer! That's like a teenager saying, 'Dad, I respectfully decline your generous offer of money for my weekend trip, and I'd be glad to mow the lawn.'

Laying Out Your Plans

A senior citizen in one of Paul's investment seminars in 2000 wanted to be more aggressive with his portfolio; his broker was more than happy to cater to his desire for growth shares. Of course, shares got clobbered in the volatile bear market of 2000-2002, and yes, he did lose lots of money. However, Paul soon discovered that even after the losses, he still had a substantial shares portfolio valued at over £500,000. He had more than enough to ensure a comfortable retirement. He had sought aggressive growth even though it was really unnecessary for his situation. If anything, the aggressive strategy may have put his portfolio (and hence his retirement) in jeopardy.

Growth is desirable even in your twilight years because inflation can eat away at a fixed-income portfolio. But different rates of growth exist, and the type you choose should be commensurate with your unique situation and financial needs. Notice that we say 'needs', not 'wants'. These perspectives are entirely different. You may *want* to invest in aggressive shares regardless of their suitability (after all, it's your money), but your financial situation may dictate that you *need* to take another approach. Just understand the difference.

Shares can play a role in all sorts of investment strategies, but in this chapter, we discuss only a few well-known approaches. Keep in mind that a share investment strategy can change based on the major changes in your life and the lifestyle that you lead, such as the ones we present in the following sections.

Living the bachelor life: Young and single with no dependents

If you're young (age 20–40) and single, with no children or other dependents, being more aggressive with your shares selection is fine (as long as you don't use your rent money for investments). The reasoning is that if you do make riskier choices and they backfire, individuals dependent on you won't get hurt. In addition, if you're in this category, you can usually bounce back a lot easier over the long term even if you have financial challenges or if a bear market hits your shares. Chapter 15 can tell you more about bear and bull markets.

Consider a mix of small-cap, mid-cap, and large-cap (see Chapter 1 for an explanation of each of these shares) growth shares in growth industries. Invest some of your money in five to seven shares and the remainder in growth-shares and unit trusts. You can revise your investment allocations along the way as the general economy changes and/or your personal situation (like when you finally say 'I do' to the love of your life) changes.

Going together like a horse and carriage: Married with children

Married couples with children must follow a more conservative investing strategy, regardless of whether one spouse works or both spouses work. Children change the picture drastically (believe me, we have them and the baggy eyes to prove it). You need more stable growth in your portfolio (and unbreakable furniture in your home).

Safety first: Examining savings bonds

For the rest of this decade (this book is being written in 2007), fixed-interest bonds and other debt instruments (such as corporate bonds) generally aren't the right place to be because debt and interest rates are problematic for investors. A nice oasis in the valley of death known as Britain's debt load (currently ££1.3 trillion, which dwarfs our national GDP of about £305 billion!) is National Savings and Investment (NS&I) issued savings bonds and certificates. They come in several types – including fixed and variable rate bonds. NS&I savings bonds are bonds that are issued on behalf of the Treasury. They can be purchased for as little as £25 but normally the minimum investment is around £100. New interest rates for the various issues of certificates or bonds can change every few months as needed to reflect changing interest rates. If rates go up, Her Majesty's Treasury usually updates the interest rates on your savings bonds if you aren't locked in to a fixed rate. Savings bonds are ultrasafe, convenient, and inexpensive to buy, and they're usually tax free. Find out more at the NS&I Web site www.nsandi.com.

Consider a mix of large-cap growth shares and dividend-paying defensive shares. (See Chapter 9 for more on defensive shares.) Invest some of your money in five to seven shares and the remainder in growth and income unit trusts. Of course, you can tweak your allocations along the way according to changes in the general economic conditions or to your personal situation. Consider setting aside money for university in a growth-oriented unit trust and in other vehicles such as annual ISAs or savings bonds (as early as possible).

Getting ready for retirement: Over 40 and single or married

Whether you're over 40 and single, or you're over 40 and married (whether one or both of you work), you should start to slowly convert your portfolio from aggressive growth to conservative growth. Shift more of your money out of individual shares and into less-volatile investments, such as investment trusts, unit trusts, guaranteed income bonds and National Savings certificates.

Devote time and effort (with a financial planner if necessary) to calculating your potential financial needs at retirement time. This step is critical in helping you decide what age to target for financial independence. (What's that? I can stop working? Whoo-hoo!)

Consider five to seven large-cap shares that are predominantly dividend-paying defensive shares in stable and needed industries (such as utilities, food and drink, and so on). Put the remainder of your investment money in guaranteed equity bonds and National Savings certificates as well as unit trust or mutual funds. Have a large portion of your money in savings bonds and savings accounts. Remember that you can revise your allocations in the future as necessary.

Kicking back in the hammock: Already retired

If you're retired, you're probably in your 60s or older. Safe, reliable income and wealth preservation form the crux of your investment strategy. Growth-oriented investments are okay as long as they're conservative and don't jeopardise your need for income. At one time, financial planners told their retired clients to replace growth-oriented investments with safe income-oriented investments. However, times have changed as senior citizens live longer than ever before.

Issues such as longevity and inflation (steadily increasing costs of living) mean that today's (and tomorrow's) retirees need growth in their portfolios. To be safe, make sure that 5–20 per cent of retirement portfolios have a number of growth-oriented securities such as shares to make sure that you continue meeting your financial needs as the years pass. You should perform an annual review to see whether the shares allocation needs to be adjusted.

Consider a mix of large-cap shares dominated by dividend-paying defensive shares in stable industries. Spread your money over three to six shares and the remainder in mutual funds and short-term guaranteed equity bonds. Have a large portion of your money in savings bonds and savings accounts. You need to monitor and tweak your investment portfolio along the way to account for changes in the general economic environment or your lifestyle needs.

Allocating Your Assets

Asset allocation is really an attempt to properly implement the concept of diversification – the key to safety and stability. *Diversification* is the inclusion in your portfolio of different investments to shield your wealth from most types of current risk while planning for future growth. To achieve proper diversification, you need to analyse your entire portfolio to look for glaring weaknesses or vulnerable areas. I don't discuss your total investment plan here, only the shares portion.

Investors frequently believe that having different shares in different industries constitutes proper diversification. Well . . . not quite. Shares in closely related industries tend to be affected (in differing degrees) by the same economic events, government policies, and so on. It's best to invest in shares across different sectors. As we mention in Chapter 12, a sector is essentially a group of related industries. Water, gas, and electric services are industries, but together they (plus a few other industries) make up the utilities sector. For more on analysing industries in order to pick winning shares, see Chapter 12.

So far in this chapter, we talk about a few basics for investing, depending on your lifestyle, but how do you know how much you need to invest in order to meet your financial goals? In the following sections, we present typical amounts that most typical investors can (and should) devote to shares investing.

Investors with less than £5,000

If you have £5,000 or less to allocate to shares, you may want to consider a fund in a stocks and shares ISA rather than individual shares, because that sum of money may not be enough to properly diversify. But if you're going to invest a sum that small, consider allocating it equally into two to four shares in two different sectors that look strong for the foreseeable future. For small investors, consider sectors that are defensive in nature (such as food and utilities).

Because £5,000 or less is a small sum in the world of share investing, you may have to purchase fewer shares than you had hoped. This situation may be a particular problem in a new issue or flotation, when you have to say how much you want to invest before you know the price the share is going to start trading at. So you may find that instead of getting say 1,000 shares at £5 each, you get an uneven number of shares – say 936 shares at £5.34 each. Don't worry. You can build up the number of shares you own by reinvesting your dividends in the future. Find out whether the company has a dividend reinvestment plan (DRIP), and use the dividend money you earn to buy more shares. (We discuss DRIPs more fully in Chapter 18.)

New issues can be a good entry into the stock market but they are risky – so be sure to do your research before you invest. Penny shares, and other speculative issues are also a worry. Participation in them may cost little (penny shares often have penny prices), but the risk exposure is too high for inexperienced investors. (See Chapter 8 for more on new issue.)

Investors with £5,000–£25,000

If you have between £5,000 and £25,000 to invest, you have more breathing space for diversification. Consider buying four to six shares in two or three different sectors. If you're the cautious type, defensive shares should do. For growth investors, seek the industries in those sectors that have proven growth. This approach gets you off to a good start, and the section 'Knowing When to Sell', later in this chapter, can help you maintain your portfolio with changing strategy (if necessary).

Does diversification mean that you shouldn't in any circumstance have all your shares in one sector? It depends on you. For example, if you've worked all your life in a particular field and you're knowledgeable and comfortable with the sector, having a greater exposure is okay, because your greater personal expertise offsets the risk. If you worked in retail for 20 years and know the industry inside and out, you probably know more about the good, the bad, and the ugly of the retail sector than most City analysts. Use your insight for more profitability. You still shouldn't invest all your money in that single sector, however, because diversification is still vital.

Investors with £25,000 or more

If you have £25,000 or more to invest, have no more than five to ten shares in two or three different sectors. It's difficult to thoroughly track more than two or three sectors and do it successfully – best to keep it simple. For example, Warren Buffett, considered the greatest stock market investor of all time, didn't invest in Web site businesses when the were all the rage because he didn't understand them. He invests only in businesses that he understands. If that strategy works for billionaire investors, then, by golly, it can't be that bad for smaller investors.

We suggest investing in no more than seven shares, because you can get yourself into such a thing as over-diversification. The more shares you have, the tougher it is to keep track of them. Owning more shares means that you need to do more research, read more annual reports and news articles, and follow the business news of more companies. Even in the best of times, you need to regularly monitor your shares because successful investing requires diligent effort.

Consider whether to employ a wealth manager (a person that manages investment portfolios for a fee). If you have £25,000 or £50,000 or more, doing so may make sense. Get a referral from a financial adviser and carefully weigh the benefits against the costs. Here are a few points to consider:

✔ **Make sure that the wealth manager has a philosophy and an approach that you agree with.**

Ask the wealth manager to give you a copy of his or her written investment philosophy. How does he or she feel about small-cap shares versus large-caps? Income versus growth?

✔ **Find out whether you're comfortable with how the wealth manager selects shares.**

Is this wealth manager a value investor or a growth investor? Aggressive or conservative? Does he or she analyse a share because of its fundamentals (sales, earnings, book value, and so on), or use share price charts?

✔ **Ask the wealth manager to explain the strategy.**

A good way to evaluate the success (or failure) of the strategy is to ask the wealth manager for past recommendations. Did he or she pick more winners than losers?

Knowing When to Sell

The act of buying shares is relatively easy. However, the act of selling shares can be an agonising decision for investors. But it's agonising only in two instances: when you have made money with your shares and when you have lost it. That about covers it. It sounds like a bad joke, but it's not that far from the truth.

The idea of selling shares when they have appreciated (the share price has increased in value) comes with the following concerns:

✔ **Tax implications:** This concern is a good reason to consider selling. See Chapter 20 for information about how selling shares under given circumstances can affect your tax.

✔ **Emotional baggage:** 'Those shares were in our family for years.' Believe it or not, investors cite this personal reason (or one of a dozen other personal reasons) for agonising over the sale of an appreciated share.

The following is a list of issues that investors want to be aware of when they're selling shares that have lost money:

✔ **Tax benefits:** This issue is a good reason to consider selling shares. See Chapter 20 for more on timing your shares' sales to minimise your tax burden.

✔ **Pride:** 'If I sell, I'll have to admit I was wrong' (followed by silent sobbing). So what? The best investors in history have made bad investments (some that have been quite embarrassing, in fact). Losing a little pride is cheaper than losing your money.

✔ **Doubt:** 'If I sell my shares now, they may rebound later.' Frequently, when an investor buys shares at £5 and they go to £4, the investor believes that if he or she sells, the shares will make an immediate *rebound* – a recovery in value – and go to £6, and then the investor will be kicking him- or herself. That may happen, but usually the share price goes lower.

✔ **Separation anxiety:** 'But I've had this share so long that it's become a part of me.' People hang on to a losing share for all sorts of illogical reasons. Being married to a person is great; being married to a share is ludicrous. If a share isn't helping your goals, then it's hurting your goals.

People have plenty more reasons to agonise over the sale of a bad share. But you can find out how to handle the share sale in a disciplined manner.

You have only two reasons to consider selling a share regardless of whether the share price has gone up or down:

✔ **You need the money.** Obviously, if you need the money for a bona fide reason – such as paying off debt, wiping out a tax bill, or buying a home – then you need the money. This reason is easy to see. After all, regardless of investment or tax considerations, shares are there to serve you. We hope that you engage in financial planning so that you don't need to sell your shares for these types of expenses, but you can't avoid unexpected expenditures.

✔ **The shares ceased to perform as you desired.** If the share isn't serving your wealth-building goals or fulfilling your investment objectives, it's time to get rid of it and move on to the next share. Just as soon as you get a stiff upper lip and resolve to unload this losing share, a little voice saying, 'If I sell my share now, it may rebound later', starts to haunt you. So you hang on to the shares, but then – bam! – before you know it, you lose more money.

Selling a share shouldn't require a psychologist. This place is where discipline steps in. This belief is why we're big proponents of trailing stops. (See Chapter 17 for more on stop orders.) Trailing stops take the agony out of selling shares. All else being equal, you shouldn't sell a winning share. If it's doing well, why sell it? Keep it as long as possible. But if it stops being a winning share, sell it. If you don't know how or when to sell it, then apply a stop-loss order at 5 or 10 per cent below the market value and let the market action take its course.

Chapter 17

Using Your Broker and Trading Techniques

*I*nvestment success isn't just about picking rising shares; it's also about how you go about doing it. Frequently, investors think that good share picking means doing your homework and then making that buy (or sell). However, you can take it a step further to maximise profits (or minimise losses). As an investor in shares, you can take advantage of techniques and services available through your standard brokerage account. (Refer back to Chapter 7 for more on brokerage accounts.) This chapter presents a few of the best ways that you can use these powerful techniques – useful whether you're buying or selling shares. In fact, if you retain nothing more from this chapter than the concept of *trailing stops* (see the section 'Trailing stops'), you have had your money's worth.

Just before the share market bubble popped, Paul warned his students and readers that a bear market was on the way. All the data warned him about it, and undoubtedly, it seemed like a time for caution. (See Chapter 15 for information about bull and bear markets.) Investors didn't have to necessarily believe him, but they should have (at the least) used trailing stops and other techniques to ensure greater investing success. Investors who did use stop-loss orders avoided the carnage as the markets plunged. In this chapter, I show you how to use these techniques to maximise your investing profit.

Checking Out Brokerage Orders

Orders you place with your stockbroker neatly fit into two categories:

- ✔ Condition-related orders
- ✔ Time-related orders

Get familiar with both orders, because they're easy to implement and invaluable tools for wealth building and (more importantly) wealth saving!

Using a combination of orders helps you fine-tune your strategy so that you can maintain greater control over your investments. Speak to your broker about the different types of orders you can use to maximise the gains (or minimise the losses) from your share investment activities. If you want to use all these orders you need to find a broker who can accommodate you. Read the broker's policies on these orders on the brokerage Web site.

Condition-related orders

A *condition-related order* means that the order is executed only when a certain condition is met. Conditional orders enhance your ability to buy shares at a lower price, to sell at a better price, or to minimise potential losses. When stock markets become bearish or uncertain, conditional orders are highly recommended. A good example of a conditional order is a *limit order*. A limit order may say, 'Buy Mojeski PLC at £45'. But if Mojeski isn't at £45 (this price is the condition), then the order isn't executed.

Market orders

When you buy shares, the simplest type of order is a *market order* or *at best* – an order to buy or sell a share at the market's current best available price. It doesn't get any more basic than that.

Here's an example: Kowalski PLC is available at the market price of £10. When you call up your broker and give the instruction to buy 100 shares 'at the market', the broker implements the order for your account, and you pay £1,000 plus commission.

We say 'current best available price' because the share's price is constantly moving, and catching the best price can be a function of the broker's ability to process the share purchase. For very active shares, the price change can happen within seconds. It's not unheard of to have three brokers simultaneously place orders for the same shares and get three different prices because of differences in the broker's capability. (Some computers are faster than others.)

The advantage of a market order is that the transaction is processed immediately, and you get your share without worrying about whether it hits a particular price. For example, if you buy Kowalski shares with a market order, you know that by the end of that phone call (or Web site visit), you're assured of getting the share. The disadvantage of a market order is that you can't control the price that you pay for the share. Whether you're buying or selling your shares, you may not realise the exact price you expect (especially if you're buying a volatile share).

Market orders get finalised in the chronological order in which they're placed. Your price may change because the orders ahead of you in line caused the share price to rise or fall based on the latest news.

Stop orders (also known as stop-loss orders)

A *stop order* (or *stop-loss order* if you own the share) is a condition-related order that instructs the broker to sell a particular share only when the share reaches a particular price. It acts like a trigger, and the stop-loss order converts to a market order to sell the share immediately.

The stop-loss order isn't designed to take advantage of small, short-term moves in the share's price. It's meant to help you protect the bulk of your money when the market turns against your share investment in a sudden manner.

Say that your Kowalski share rises to £20 per share and you seek to protect your investment against a possible future market decline. A stop-loss order at £18 triggers your broker to sell the share immediately if it falls to the £18 mark. In this example, if the share suddenly drops to £17, it still triggers the stop-loss order, but the finalised sale price is £17. In a volatile market, you may not be able to sell at your precise stop-loss price. However, because the order automatically gets converted into a market order, the sale is done, and you prevent further declines in the share.

The main benefit of a stop-loss order is that it prevents a major decline in a share that you own. It's a form of discipline that's important in investing in order to minimise potential losses. Investors can find it agonising to sell a share that has fallen. If they don't sell, however, the share often continues to plummet as investors continue to hold on while hoping for a rebound in the price.

Practise discipline

Paul has a stack of several years' worth of investment newsletters in which investment experts made all sorts of calls regarding the prospects of a company, industry, or the economy in general. Some made forecasts that were spectacularly on target, but you should see the ones that were spectacularly wrong – ouch! However, even some of the winners suffered because of a lack of discipline. Those spectacular gains disappeared like football fans at a chess match.

One of the biggest recommendations by newsletter experts in 2000 was Cisco Systems (CSCO). In March 2000, CSCO was at $85 and its market value (share price times total shares outstanding) was a whopping $600 billion. Some share gurus even said that it would become the first trillion-dollar share. Other gurus said that

CSCO's earnings would grow 30–40 per cent per year, indefinitely. They were wrong.

From March 2000 to October 2003, CSCO painfully descended from $85 to just under $9 per share – a spectacular 90 per cent collapse. By June 2005, it had recovered to about $19 per share. It didn't recover its old glory. Had investors placed a stop-loss order at about 10 per cent below CSCO's then high ($85 less 10 per cent or about $77), they would have kept their wealth basically intact and would subsequently have had enough cash to buy four or five times more shares when they hit bottom.

Investing can be an emotional roller coaster. Keep your sanity and your profits by being disciplined. Use your stop-loss orders and fasten those seat belts.

Most investors set a stop-loss amount at about 10 per cent below the market value of a share. This percentage gives the share room to fluctuate, which most shares tend to do on a day-to-day basis.

Trailing stops

Trailing stops are an important technique in wealth preservation for seasoned share investors and can be one of your key strategies in using stop-loss orders. A *trailing stop* is a stop-loss order that the investor actively manages by moving it up along with the share's market price. The stop-loss order 'trails' the share price upward. As the stop-loss goes upward, it protects more and more of the share's value from declining.

A real-life example may be the best way to help you understand trailing stops. Say that in 1999 you bought Lucent Technologies (LU) at £25 per share. As soon as you finished buying it, you immediately told your broker to put a stop-loss order at £22 and make it a good-till-cancelled (GTC) order. Think of what you did. In effect, you placed an ongoing (GTC) safety net under your share. The share can go as high as the sky, but if it should fall, the share's price triggers a market order at £22. Your share is automatically sold, minimising your loss.

If Lucent goes to £50 per share in a few months, you can call your broker and cancel the former stop-loss order at £22 and replace it with a new (higher) stop-loss order. You simply say, 'Please put a new stop-loss order at £45 and make it a GTC order.' This higher stop-loss price protects not only your original investment of £20 but also a big chunk of your profit as well. As time goes by, and the share price climbs, you can continue to raise the stop-loss price and add a GTC provision. Now you know why it's called a trailing stop. It trails the share price upward like a giant tail. All along the way, it protects more and more of your growing investment without limiting its upward movement.

Michael Walters, tipster and former *Daily Mail* market columnist, advocates setting a trailing stop of 20 per cent below your purchase price. That's his preference. He suggests that investors in highly volatile shares may put in trailing stops of 10 per cent. Is a stop-loss order desirable or advisable in every situation? Michael thinks so. His faith in the stop-loss system protected many of his readers from serious losses in 2000 when the dot.com bubble burst. Stop-loss orders are appropriate in most cases, especially if the market seems uncertain (or you do!).

A trailing stop is a stop-loss order that you actively manage. The stop-loss order is good-till-cancelled (GTC), and it constantly trails the share's price as it moves up. To successfully implement trailing stops, keep the following points in mind:

- ✔ **Remember that brokers usually don't place trailing stops for you automatically.** In fact, they won't (or shouldn't) place any type of order without your consent. Deciding on the type of order to place is your responsibility. You can raise, lower, or cancel a trailing stop order at will, but you need to monitor your investment when substantial moves do occur to respond to the movement appropriately.

- ✔ **Change the stop-loss order when the share price moves significantly.** You have to decide when to change the stop-loss and this decision differs depending on the cost of the share. If you are buying shares at 20p then a 2p drop is significant. Say that you buy a share at £5 and place a stop-loss order at £4.50. Doing so shows that you are prepared to accept a loss of 50p and no more. So as the share climbs you need to change your order to match that wish. If the share hits £5.10 you want to set the stop-loss at £4.60 and so on. Some people set the stop based on percentages but that can be disappointing. If your share climbs to £10 and your stop-loss has trailed all the way up to sit at £9.50 you can still only lose 50p a share. If your stop-loss is set at 10 per cent you can lose a £1 a share. The decision is yours.

- ✔ **Understand your broker's policy on GTC orders.** If your broker usually has a GTC order expire after 30 days, you should be aware of it. You don't want to risk a sudden drop in your share's price without the stop-loss order protection. Make sure that you can renew the order for additional time.

If a share, or a market, goes into free fall the price of your shares may fall through the stop-loss. This event can happen if the share is falling too fast for the broker to find a buyer at your price. Your broker finds you the best price available which may be lower than you had hoped.

✔ **Monitor your share.** A trailing stop isn't a 'set it and forget it' technique. Monitoring your investment is critical. If shares fall, the stop-loss order you have prevents further loss. Should the share price rise substantially, remember to adjust your trailing stop accordingly. Part of monitoring the share is *knowing the beta*, which you can read more about in the next section.

Using beta measurement

To be a successful investor, you need to understand the volatility of the particular share you invest in. In share market parlance, this volatility is also called the *beta* of a share. *Beta* is a quantitative measure of the volatility of a given share (mutual funds and portfolios, too) relative to the overall market, usually the S&P 500 index. (For more information on the S&P 500, refer back to Chapter 5.) Beta specifically measures the performance movement of the share as the S&P moves 1 per cent up or down. A beta measurement above 1 is more volatile than the overall market, while a beta below 1 is less volatile. Some shares are relatively stable in the price movements; others jump around.

Because beta measures how volatile or unstable the share's price is, it tends to be uttered in the same breath as 'risk' – more volatility indicates more risk. Similarly, less volatility tends to mean less risk.

Table 17-1 shows sample betas of well-known companies (as of May 2007).

Table 17-1	Looking at Well-Known Betas	
Company (Market code)	*Beta*	*Comments*
Tesco (TSCO)	0.68	Less volatile than the market
Provident Financial (PFG)	1.11	More volatile than the market
Rentokil Initial (RTO)	0.79	Less volatile than the market

You can find a company's beta at Web sites providing a lot of financial information about companies, such as Yahoo!Finance (`finance.yahoo.com`) or Digital Look (`www.digitallook.com`).

The beta is useful to know because it gives you a general idea of the share's trading range. If a share is currently priced at £50 and it typically trades in the £48–£52 range, then a trailing stop at £49 doesn't make sense. Your share would probably be sold the same day you initiated the stop-loss order. If your share is a volatile growth share that can swing up and down by 10 per cent, you should more logically set your stop-loss at 15 per cent below that day's price.

The share of a large-cap company in a mature industry tends to have a low beta – one close to the overall market. Small and mid-cap shares in new or emerging industries tend to have greater volatility in their day-to-day price fluctuations; hence, they tend to have a high beta. (You can find out more about large, small, and mid-cap shares by referring back to Chapter 1.)

Limit orders

A *limit order* is a precise condition-related order, implying that a limit exists on the buy or the sell side of the transaction. You want to buy (or sell) only at a specified price or better. Limit orders work better for you if you're buying the share, but they may not be good for you if you're selling the share. Here's how it works in both instances:

- ✔ **When you're buying:** Just because you like a particular company and you want its share doesn't mean that you're willing to pay the current market price. Maybe you want to buy Kowalski but the current market price of £20 per share isn't acceptable to you. You prefer to buy it at £16 because you think that price reflects its true market value. What do you do? You tell your broker, 'Buy Kowalski with a limit order at £16.' You have to specify whether it's a day order (good for the day) or a GTC order, which I discuss in its own section earlier in this chapter.

  What happens if the share experiences great volatility? What if it drops to £16.01 and then suddenly drops to £15.95 on the next move? Actually, nothing, you may be dismayed to hear. Because your order was limited to £16, it can be transacted only at £16, no more or less. The only way for this particular trade to occur is if the share rises back to £16. However, if the price keeps dropping, then your limit order isn't transacted and may expire or be cancelled.

  When you're buying a share, many brokers interpret the limit order as 'buy at this specific price or better'. Presumably, if your limit order is to buy the share at £10, you are just as happy if your broker buys that share for you at £9.95. This way, if you don't get exactly £10, because the share's price was volatile, you still get the share at a lower price. Speak to your particular broker to be clear on what he or she means when talking about a limit order.

✔ **When you're selling:** Limit orders are activated only when a share hits a specific price. If you buy Kowalski at £20 and you worry about a decline in the share price, you may decide to put in a limit order at £18. If you watch the news and hear that Kowalski's price is dropping, you may sigh and say, 'I sure am glad that I put in that limit order at £18!' However, in a volatile market, the share price may leapfrog over your specified price. It may go from £18.01 to £17.99 and then continue its descent. Because the share price never hit £18 on the mark, the share isn't sold. You may be sitting at home satisfied (mistakenly) that you played it smart, while your share plummets to £15 or £10 or worse! Having a stop-loss order in place is best.

Time-related orders

Time-related orders mean just that; the order has a time limit. Typically, investors use these orders in conjunction with conditional orders. They are often used by day traders – and some UK brokers only offer these orders on specialist trades such as spread betting and derivatives. The two most common time-related orders are day orders and good-till-cancelled (or GTC) orders.

Day order

A *day order* is an order to buy a share that expires at the end of that particular trading day. If you tell your broker, 'Buy BYOB Ltd at £37.50 and make it a day order', you mean that you want to purchase the share at £37.50. But if the share doesn't hit that price, your order expires at the end of the trading day unfilled. Why would you place such an order? Maybe BYOB is trading at £39, but you don't want to buy it at that price because you don't believe the share is worth it. Consequently, you have no problem not getting the share that day.

When would you use day orders? It depends on your preferences and personal circumstances. Few events really cause you to say, 'I know, I'll just try to buy or sell between now and the end of today's trading action.' However, you may feel that you don't want a specified order to linger beyond today's market action. Perhaps you want to test a price. ('I want to get rid of share A at £39 to make a quick profit, but it's currently trading at £37.50. However, I may change my mind tomorrow.') A day order is the perfect strategy to use in this case.

Unless you know that your broker's policy is to treat every order as a day order if not told otherwise, you need to specify when you want a day order.

Good-till-cancelled (GTC)

A *good-till-cancelled* (GTC) order is the most commonly requested order by investors. Although GTC orders are time-related, they're always tied to a condition, such as when the share achieves a certain price. The GTC order means just what it says: The order stays in effect until it's transacted or until the investor cancels it. Although the order implies that it can run indefinitely, most brokers have a limit of 30 working days. By that time, the broker cancels the order or contacts you to see whether you want to extend it. Ask your brokers about their particular policy.

A GTC order is usually coupled with conditional or condition-related orders. For example, say that you want to buy ASAP PLC shares but you don't want to buy them at the current price of £48 per share. You've done your homework on the share, including looking at the share's price-to-earnings ratio, dividend cover, and so on (see Appendix B for more on ratios), and you say, 'Hey, this share isn't worth £48 a share. I'd only buy it at £36 per share'. You think the share would make a good addition to your portfolio but not at the current market price. (It's overpriced or overvalued according to your analysis.) How should you proceed? Your best bet is to ask your broker to do a 'GTC order at £36'. This request means that your broker buys the shares if and when they hit the £36 mark (or until you cancel the order). Just make sure that your account has the funds available to complete the transaction.

GTC orders are useful, so you should become familiar with your broker's policy on them. While you're at it, ask whether any fees apply. Many brokers don't charge for GTC orders because, if they happen to result in a buy (or sell) order, they generate a normal commission just as any share transaction does. Other brokers may charge a small fee.

To be successful with GTC orders, you need to know

✔ **When you want to buy:** In recent years, people have had a tendency to rush into buying a share without giving thought to what they should do to get more for their money. Some investors don't realise that the stock market can be a place for bargain-hunting consumers. If you're ready to buy a quality pair of socks for £16 in a department store but the sales assistant says that those same socks are going on sale tomorrow for only £8, what would you do – assuming that you're a cost-conscious consumer? Unless you're barefoot, you're probably better off waiting. The same point holds true with shares.

Say that you want to buy SOX PLC at £26, but it's currently trading at £30. You think that £30 is too expensive, but you're happy to buy the share at £26 or lower. However, you have no idea whether the share will move to your desired price today, tomorrow, next week, or even next month (maybe never). In this case, a GTC order is appropriate.

✔ **When you want to sell:** What if you bought a pair of socks at a department store, and you discovered that they have holes (darn it!)? Wouldn't you want to get rid of them? Of course you would. If a share's price starts to unravel, you want to be able to get rid of it as well.

Perhaps you already own SOX (at £25, for instance) but are concerned that market conditions may drive the price lower. You're not certain which way the share may move in the coming days and weeks. In this case, a GTC order to sell the share at a specified price is a suitable strategy. Because the share price is £25, you may want to place a GTC order to sell it if it falls to £22.50, to prevent further losses. Again, in this example, GTC is the time frame, and it accompanies a condition (sell when the share hits £22.50).

Buying on Margin

Buying on margin means buying securities, such as shares, by using funds you borrow from your broker. This type of service is not generally available through UK high street or online brokers. Specialist brokers who look after high net-worth clients should be able to offer the service, but don't expect your online broker to do the same. Buying share on margin is similar to buying a house with a mortgage. If you buy a house at a purchase price of £100,000 and put 10 per cent down as a deposit, your equity (the part you own) is £10,000, and you borrow the remaining £90,000 with a mortgage. If the value of the house rises to £120,000 and you sell (for the sake of simplicity, I don't include closing costs in this example), you make a profit of 200 per cent. How is that? The £20,000 gain on the property represents a gain of 20 per cent on the purchase price of £100,000, but because your real investment is £10,000 (the down payment), your gain works out to 200 per cent (a gain of £20,000 on your initial investment of £10,000).

Buying on margin is an example of using leverage to maximise your gain when prices rise. *Leverage* is simply using borrowed money when you make an asset purchase in order to increase your potential profit. This type of leverage is great in a favourable (bull) market, but it works against you in an unfavourable (bear) market. Say that a £100,000 house you purchase with a £90,000 mortgage falls in value to £80,000 (and property values can decrease during economic hard times). Your outstanding debt of £90,000 exceeds the value of the property. Because you owe more than you own, you're left with a negative net worth. Borrowing to buy shares is not recommended for inexperienced investors and although you may use other debt to fund your investments, reputable brokers caution against it.

Examining marginal outcomes

Suppose that you think that the share for the company Mergatroid PLC, currently at £40 per share, will go up in value. You want to buy 100 shares, but you have only £2,000. What can you do? If you're intent on buying 100 shares (versus simply buying the 50 shares that you have cash for), you can borrow the additional £2,000 from your bank. If you do that, what are the potential outcomes?

If the share price goes up

This outcome is obviously best for you. If Mergatroid goes to £50 per share, your investment is worth £5,000, and your outstanding loan is £2,000. If you sell, the total proceeds pay off the loan and leave you with £3,000. Because your initial investment was £2,000, your profit is a solid 50 per cent because ultimately your £2,000 principal amount generated a £1,000 profit. (For the sake of this example, I leave out any charges, such as commissions and interest paid on the loan.)

Leverage, when used properly, is profitable. However, it's still debt, so understand that you must pay it off eventually, regardless of the share's performance.

If the share price fails to rise

If the share goes nowhere, you still have to pay interest on the loan. If the share pays dividends, this money can offset some of the cost of the loan. In other words, dividends can help you pay off what you've borrowed from the bank.

Having the share neither rise nor fall may seem like a neutral situation, but you pay interest on your loan with each passing day. For conservative investors who invest in shares with high dividends, borrowing to buy shares may appear to make more sense, because the dividend can pay off the interest. But the dividend may not be enough to cover all the interest and the point of investing is to get the income (the dividend) not shell it out on interest.

The big problem with borrowing to buy shares becomes apparent when the share price goes down. What if Mergatroid goes to £38 per share? The market value of 100 shares is then £3,800, but your equity shrinks to only £1,800 because you have to pay your £2,000 loan. You're not exactly looking at a disaster at this point, but you'd better be careful, because the loan exceeds 50 per cent of your share investment. If it goes any lower, you would be considering selling. In fact you'd probably have a stop-loss (see earlier in this chapter) set at £45 or £40. Your broker would be selling your shares to cut your losses and you'd be left with a £2,000 loan to repay. See the next section, 'Contracts for Difference' for information about appropriate debt to equity ratios.

Contracts for Difference (CFDs)

One area of stockbroking where trading shares on margin is often encouraged is in *Contracts for Difference* (CFDs). A CFD is a contract between two parties (you and your stockbroker, for example) to exchange the difference between the opening and closing price of a share, an index, a fund, or just about anything that can be traded on a market. You can specify when the contract starts and ends and you never actually own the underlying investment you are (really) gambling on.

Some stockbrokers allow you to trade in CFDs with only 10 per cent of your investment paid up front. However you can lose much more than your original investment and may have to pay up at short notice. All reputable stockbrokers should warn you that trading in CFDs in this way is not an endeavour for novice investors.

With CFDs, you are predicting whether a share price or other tradable investment will go up (*go long*) or go down (*go short*). If you get it right you make a profit, if you get it wrong you can make substantial losses.

Say you wanted to buy a CFD for a rise in the price of Mergatroid, which is currently at £10 a share. You buy 1,000 shares at £10, paying just 10 per cent (£1,000) up front. When Mergatroid announces a big deal that day and the shares jump to £50 you are quick to close the contract, selling at £50. You've made £50,000 in a day – and you only had to pay £1,000 up front (plus a bit of commission on the purchase and sale). Sounds fab – so why aren't we all doing it?

Imagine that you thought that Mergatroid shares were expensive at £10 each and due for a correction. You buy a CFD for a fall in the share price (1,000 shares at £10 each, paying 10 per cent, £1,000, up front) and go on holiday for a couple of days. When Mergatroid announces its big deal and the shares jump to £50 you are whale watching in the Outer Hebrides and even your broker can't get hold of you on your mobile. Next day the shares climb again as the government announces restrictions that hit Mergatroid's competitors. The shares are £100 when you eventually check in with your (distraught) broker. Your broker insists that you close the contract and cover your losses and you have to sell your contract at £100 a share (100 × 1,000 = £100,000). You need to find £99,000 plus commission to pay off your debt. You also have to pay interest on the margin loan because (remember) you've been speculating with the broker's money. Sounds awful – that's why we are not all doing it.

In the UK, CFDs now account for more than 20 per cent of trading on the London Stock Exchange. You can typically trade CFDs in most larger UK companies as well as many European and American shares. You can also buy CFDs for the world's major indices (refer to Chapter 5 for more on indices).

Trading on margin, as you can see, can escalate your profits on the up side but magnify your losses on the down side. If your share plummets drastically, or your CFD heads in the wrong direction, you can end up with a margin loan that exceeds the market value of the share you used the loan to purchase.

It's not a good idea to borrow to buy shares. But if you do, whether on margin or with other loans, use a disciplined approach. Be extra careful when using leverage, such as a margin loan, because it can backfire. Keep the following points in mind:

- ✔ **Have ample reserves of cash or other liquid assets in your account.** Try not to invest more than you can actually afford to pay out.

- ✔ **If you're a beginner, you shouldn't be borrowing to buy shares at all. If you do, make sure that you invest in large companies with a relatively stable price and a good dividend record.** Some people buy income shares that have dividend yields that exceed the interest rate charged on their loans, meaning that the shares end up paying for the loan. Just remember those stop-loss orders.

- ✔ **Constantly monitor your shares.** If the market turns against you, the result is especially painful if you use debt to fund your investment.

- ✔ **Have a payback plan for your debt.** Loans are not free money, if you borrow to fund your investments, you have to pay interest. Your ultimate goal is to make money, and paying interest eats into your profit.

Going Short and Coming Out Ahead

The vast majority of investors are familiar with buying shares, holding onto them for a while, and hoping their value goes up. This kind of thinking is called *going long,* and investors who go long are considered to be *long on shares.* Going long essentially means that you're bullish and seeking your profit from rising prices. However, astute investors also profit in the market when share prices fall. *Going short* (also called *shorting a share, selling short,* or *doing a short sale*) on a share is a common technique for profiting from a share price decline. Investors have made big profits during bear markets by going short. A short sale is a bet that a particular share price is going to fall.

Going short is not generally available on ordinary share trades in the UK, but has become available on specialist trading such as spread betting and contracts for difference (see the earlier section 'Contracts for Difference' for more on CFDs).

Your broker has to be sure that you are credit worthy before agreeing to any shorting. Speak to your broker (or check for this information on the broker's Web site) about limitations in your account regarding going short.

Because going short on shares has greater risks than going long, we strongly advise new investors to avoid shorting shares until they become more experienced.

Most people easily understand making money by going long. It boils down to 'buy low and sell high'. Piece of cake. Going short means making money by selling high and then buying low. Eh? Thinking in reverse isn't a piece of cake. Although thinking of this share adage in reverse may be challenging, the mechanics of going short are really simple. Consider an example that uses a fictitious company called DOA PLC. As a share, DOA (£5 per share) is looking pretty sickly. It has lots of debt and plummeting sales and earnings, and the news is out that DOA's industry is facing hard times for the foreseeable future. This situation describes a share that's an ideal candidate for shorting. The future may be bleak for DOA, but promising for savvy investors.

You must understand brokerage rules before you conduct short selling. The broker must approve you for it (see Chapter 7 for information on working with brokers), and you must meet the minimum collateral requirement, which is typically an agreed percentage of the shorted share's market value. If the share generates dividends, those dividends are paid to the owner of the share, not to the person who is borrowing it to go short. (See the next section, 'Setting up a short sale', to see how this technique works.) Check with your broker for complete details and review the resources in Appendix A.

Setting up a short sale

This section explains how to go short. Say that you believe that DOA is the right share to short – you're pretty sure that its price is going to fall. With DOA at £5, you instruct your broker to 'go short 100 shares on DOA'. (This amount doesn't have to be 100 shares. We're just using that as an example.) Now, here's what happens next:

1. **Your broker borrows 100 shares of DOA, from his or her own account or from another client or broker.**

   That's right. The share can be borrowed from a client, no permission necessary. The broker guarantees the transaction, and the client, the owner of the share never has to be informed about it, because he or she never loses legal and beneficial rights to the share. You borrow 100 shares, and you return 100 shares when it's time to complete the transaction.

2. **Your broker then sells the share and puts the money in your account.**

   Your account is credited with £500 (100 shares at £5) in cash – the money gained from selling the borrowed share. This cash acts like a loan on which you're going to have to pay interest.

3. **You buy the share back and return it to its rightful owner.**

   When it's time to close the transaction (you want to close it, or the owner of the shares wants to sell them, so you have to give them back), you must return the number of shares you borrowed (in this case, 100 shares). If you buy back the 100 shares at £4 per share (remember that you shorted this particular share because you were sure that its price was going to fall) and these 100 shares are returned to their owner, you make a £100 profit. (To keep the example tidy, I don't include brokerage commissions.)

Oops! Going short when prices grow taller

You guessed it: The wonderful profitability of selling short has a flip side. Presume that you were wrong about DOA and that the share price rises from the ashes as it goes from £5 to £8.70. Now what? You still have to return the 100 shares you borrowed. With the share's price at £8.70, that means that you have to buy the shares for £870 (100 shares at the new, higher price of £8.70). Ouch! How do you pay for it? Well, you have that original £500 in your account from when you initially went short on the share. But where do you get the other £370 (£870 less the original £500)? You guessed it – your pocket! You have to cough up the difference. If the share continues to rise, that's a lot of coughing.

How much money do you lose if the share goes to £10 or more? A sack full! As a matter of fact, there's no limit to how much you can lose. That's why going short can be riskier than going long. With going long, the most you can lose is 100 per cent of your money. With going short, you can lose more than 100 per cent of the money you invest. Whoops!

Because the potential for loss is unlimited when you short a share, we suggest that you use a stop order (also called a *buy-stop order*) to minimise the damage. Better yet, make it a good-till-cancelled order, which we discuss earlier in this chapter. You can set the stop order at a given price, and if the share hits that price, you buy the share back so that you can return it to its owner before the price rises even higher. You still lose money, but you limit your losses.

Feeling the squeeze

If you go short on a share, remember that, sooner or later, you have to buy that share back so that you can return it to its owner. What happens when a lot of people are short on a particular share and its price starts to rise? All those short sellers are scrambling to buy the shares back so that they can close their transactions before they lose too much money. This mass buying quickens the pace of the share's ascent and puts a squeeze (called a *short squeeze*) on the investors who had been shorting the share.

Earlier in the chapter, I explain that your broker can borrow shares from another client so that you can go short on it. What happens when that client wants to sell the shares in his or her account – the shares that you borrowed and so are no longer in the account? When that happens, your broker asks you to return the borrowed shares. That's when you feel the squeeze – you have to buy the shares back at the current price. Contracts For Difference (see the section earlier in this chapter) give you more flexibility to decide when to sell if you are going short.

Going short can be a great manoeuvre in a declining (bear) market, but it can be brutal if the share price goes up. If you're a beginner, stay away from short selling until you have enough experience (and money) to risk it.

Chapter 18

Getting a Handle on DPPs, DRIPs, and PCA...ASAP

· ·

In This Chapter

▶ Buying shares directly from a company

▶ Looking at dividend reinvestment plans

▶ Using pound cost averaging

· ·

*W*ho says that you must buy 100 shares of a company to invest? Do you really have to go through a broker to buy shares, or can you buy direct? What if you only want to put your toe in the water and buy just one share for starters? Can you do that without paying through the nose for transaction costs, such as commissions? The answer to these questions is that you can buy shares directly (without a broker) and maybe save money in the process. That's what this chapter is about. In this chapter, we show you how direct purchase programmes (DPPs) and dividend reinvestment plans (DRIPs) make a lot of sense for long-term investors, and how you can do them on your own – no broker necessary – depending on the companies you choose to invest in. I also show you how to use the method of pound cost averaging (PCA) to acquire shares, a technique that works especially well with DRIPs.

The types of programmes are well-suited for people who like to invest small sums of money and plan on doing so on a consistent basis in the same shares (or stocks) over a long period of time.

Being Direct with DPPs

If you're going to buy a share anyway, why not buy it directly from the company and bypass the broker (and commissions) altogether? Several hundred companies now offer *direct purchase programmes* (DPPs), also called DIPs or DSPs (*direct investment programmes* or *direct stock purchase plans*), which give investors an opportunity to buy shares directly from these companies.

DPPs give investors the opportunity to get involved with little upfront money (usually enough to cover the purchase of one share) and usually no commissions. Why do companies give investors this opportunity? For their sake, they want to encourage more attention and participation from investors. These are SEC (Securities and Exchange Commission) regulated plans that are available for most large US companies and UK companies with a dual-listing in the US.

Investing in a DPP

If you have your sights set on a particular company and have only a few quid to start out with, a DPP is probably the best way to make your initial investment. The following steps can guide you toward your first shares purchase using a DPP:

1. **Decide what shares you want to invest in. (This whole book is about this topic.)**

   Say that you did your homework and you decide to invest in Yumpin Yimminy Ltd. (YY). Contact the company directly and request to speak to someone in the shareholder services or investor relations department. You can get YY's contact information through the stock exchange YY trades on – or its Web site. For example, if YY is traded on the New York Stock Exchange, you can call the NYSE or visit its Web site (www.nyse.com) and ask for the contact information for YY. So, you can contact NYSE to reach YY for its DPP ASAP. OK?

2. **Find out whether YY has a DPP (before you're an OAP! OK?)**

   Call YY's shareholder services department and ask whether it has a DPP. If it does, great; if it doesn't, ask whether it plans to start one. At the least, it may have a DRIP.

3. **Look into enrolling.**

   Ask the company to send you an application along with a prospectus – the programme document that serves as a brochure and, hopefully, answers your basic questions.

   The processing is typically handled by an organisation that the company designates (the plan administrator). From this point forward, you're in the dividend reinvestment plan. (See the section 'Dipping into DRIPs', later in this chapter.)

Finding DPP alternatives

Although several hundred companies offer DPPs, the majority of companies don't. What do you do if you want to invest in a company directly and it doesn't have a DPP? The following sections present alternatives.

Buy the first share through a broker to qualify for DRIPs

Yes, buying your first share through a broker costs you a commission; however, after you make that purchase, you can contact the company's shareholder services department and ask about its DRIP. (See the section 'Dipping into DRIPs', later in this chapter.) Once you're an existing shareholder, qualifying for the DRIP is a piece of cake.

To qualify for the DRIP, you must be on the shareholders register with the company's registrar. A *shareholders' register* is simply the database that the company uses to track every single outstanding share and the owner of those shares. The *registrar* is the person (usually a company) responsible for maintaining the database. Whenever shares are bought or sold, the registrar must implement the change and update the records on shares ownership. In the past, the broker would have issued a share certificate in your name once you owned the shares. Paper share certificates are slowly dying out and many investors hold their shares in nominee accounts (see Chapter 7 for more on different types of accounts). Having your name on a share certificate is still the most common way to get your name on the register, but you should still be able to qualify for the DRIP if your shares are held in a nominee account.

Your broker should be able to advise you on how to ensure that you can qualify for a company's DRIP – if your broker isn't helpful, find a new broker. Investor relations departments of the company involved should also help.

Get started in a DRIP directly through a broker

These days, more brokers are able to offer the features of the DRIP (like compounding interest) right in the brokerage account itself, making it more convenient than having to go to the trouble of setting up a DRIP with the company. This service is most likely a response to the growing number of long-term investors who are enjoying the benefits of direct investing that DPPs and DRIPs offer. The main drawback of a broker-run DRIP is that usually it doesn't allow you to make optional cash purchases (a big negative!). See the section 'Building wealth with *optional cash payments* (OCPs)', later in this chapter, for more on this topic.

Direct Purchase Plans are not a UK initiative, but many UK companies now offer DRIPs. Companies with dual listings on the London and New York Stock Exchanges usually make the same options available to their UK-based and US-based shareholders, but don't expect that generosity from all UK firms.

Recognising that every pro has a con

As beneficial as DPPs are, they do have minor drawbacks. (Doesn't everything?) Keep the following points in mind when considering DPPs as part of your share portfolio:

✔ Although more and more companies are starting to offer DPPs, still relatively few companies have them.

✔ Some DPPs require a high initial amount to invest (as much as £100 or more) or a commitment of monthly investments. In any case, ask the plan administrator about the investing requirements.

✔ A growing number of DPPs have some type of service charge. Usually this charge (if your DPP has a charge) is modest and lower than typical brokerage commissions. Ask about all the incidents, such as getting into the plan, getting out, and so on, that may trigger a service charge.

Don't invest in a company just because it has a DPP or DRIP. DPPs and DRIPs are simply a means for getting into a particular share with little money. They shouldn't be a substitute for doing diligent research and analysis on a particular share.

Dipping into DRIPs

Dividend reinvestment plans are called 'DRIPs,' which makes us scratch our heads. *Reinvestment* is one word, not two, so where does that *I* come from? But we digress. Whether you call them DRIPs or DRPs (as they are known in the US), they're great for small investors and for investors who are truly long-term investors in a particular share. A *DRIP* is a programme that a company may offer to allow investors to easily accumulate more of its shares. Sometimes the company does not charge commission, but increasingly companies are asking their registrars (who are also large stockbrokers) to handle the DRIPs, and the brokers do charge dealing fees.

A DRIP has two primary advantages:

✔ **Compounding:** The dividends get reinvested and give you the opportunity to buy more shares.

✔ **Optional cash purchases:** Some DRIPs give participants the ability to invest through the plan to purchase more shares, occasionally with no commission.

To be in a dividend reinvestment plan, here are the requirements:

✔ You must already be a shareholder for that particular company.

✔ You must already have a dividend reinvestment plan set up.

✔ The shares must be paying dividends. (You had to guess this one!)

Getting a clue about compounding

Dividends are reinvested, offering a form of *compounding* for the small investor. Dividends buy more of the shares, in turn generating more dividends. Sometimes the dividends generated don't buy entire shares, so they are carried over in the DRIP account until you have enough to buy whole shares.

Say, for example, that you own 20 shares of Fraction PLC. at £10 per share for a total value of £200. Fraction's annual dividend is £1, and it pays this dividend as a quarterly dividend of 25 pence every three months. What happens if you have a DRIP with Fraction? The 20 shares generate a £5 dividend payout in the first quarter, and this amount is applied to the shares purchase as soon as the amount is credited to the DRIP account. If you presume for this example that the shares price hasn't changed, the dividend payout wasn't enough to buy an entire share, so it stays credited to the account until the next payment.

Say that, in the preceding example, three months have passed and that you have acquired no other shares since your previous dividend payout. Fraction issues another quarterly dividend for 25 pence per share. Now what?

- ✔ The original 20 shares of Fraction PLCgenerate a £5 dividend payout.

- ✔ You have £5 credited to your DRIP account from the previous dividend.

- ✔ The two dividend payouts are added together to make £10 and this amount is used to buy one new share in Fraction PLC. This means you now have 21 shares and get dividends from 21 shares at the next dividend payout.

To illustrate our point, the preceding example uses a price that doesn't fluctuate. Shares in a DRIP act like any other shares; the price changes constantly. Every time the DRIP makes a share purchase, whether this purchase is monthly or quarterly, the purchase price is probably going to change each time.

Building wealth with optional cash payments (OCPs)

Some DRIPs give the participant the opportunity to make *optional cash payments* (OCPs). DRIPs usually establish a minimum and a maximum payment. The minimum is typically modest, such as £25 or £50. A few plans even have no minimum. This feature makes it affordable to regularly invest modest amounts and build up a sizeable portfolio of shares in a shorter period of time, often unencumbered by commissions.

DRIPs also have a maximum investment limitation, such as specifying that 'DRIP participants cannot invest any more than £10,000 per year'. For most investors, the maximum isn't a showstopper. However, consult with the administrator of the plan because all plans are a little different.

OCPs are probably the most advantageous aspect of a DRIP. If you can invest £25 to £50 per month consistently, year after year, at no (or little) cost, you may find that doing so is a superb way to build wealth.

Checking out the cost advantages

In spite of the fact that more and more DRIPs are charging service fees, DRIPs are still an economical way to invest, especially for small investors. The big savings come from not paying commissions. Although many DPPs and DRIPs do have charges, they tend to be relatively small (but keep track of them, because the costs can add up).

Some DRIPs actually offer a discount of between 2 per cent and 5 per cent (a few are higher) when buying shares through the plan. Still others offer special programmes and discounts on the company's products and services. Some companies offer the service of debiting your current account or salary to invest in the DRIP. One company offered its shareholders significant discounts to its restaurant subsidiary. In any case, ask the plan administrator because any plus is . . . well . . . a plus.

Weighing the pros with the cons

When you're in a DRIP, you reap all the benefits of shares investing (along with the risks and responsibilities). You get an annual report, and you qualify for share splits, dividend increases, and so on.

Before you start to salivate over all the goodies that come with DRIPs, be clear-eyed about some of the negative aspects to them as well. Negative aspects include the following:

✔ You need to get that first share. But you knew that.

✔ Even small fees cut into your profits.

✔ Many DRIPs may not be eligible to be wrapped in tax-efficient savings, such as Individual Savings Accounts (ISAs). (See Chapter 20 for more information on ISAs.)

✔ DRIPs are designed for long-term investing. Although getting in and out of the plan is easy, the transactions may take weeks to process because share purchases and sales are typically done all at once on a certain day during the month (or quarter).

✔ Read the prospectus. You may not consider doing so a negative point, but for some people, reading a prospectus is not unlike giving blood by using leeches. Even if that is your opinion, you need to read the prospectus to avoid any surprises, such as hidden fees or unreasonable terms.

✔ Understand the tax issues. There, you see? We knew that we'd ruin it for you. The point is that you should understand the tax consequences. Chapter 20 goes into greater detail. Just know that dividends, whether or not they occur in a DRIP, are usually taxable (unless the DRIP is in an ISA, which is a different matter).

✔ Perhaps the biggest headache of DRIPs is the need to keep good records. Keep all your statements together and use a good spreadsheet or accounting programme if you plan on doing a lot of DRIP investing. These records become especially important at self-assessment time, when you have to report any subsequent gains or losses from share sales. Because capital gains tax can be complicated as you sort out short term versus long term, DRIP calculations can be a nightmare without good record keeping.

DRIPs offer a great way to accumulate a large shareholding over an extended period of time. However, think about what you can do with these shares. Say that you accumulate 110 company shares, valued at £50 per share, in your DRIP. You can, for example, take out £5,000 worth of shares (100 shares at £50 per share) and place those 100 shares in your brokerage account. The remaining 10 shares can stay in your account to keep the DRIP and continue with dividend reinvestment to keep your wealth growing. Why remove those shares?

All things being equal, you are better off keeping the shares in the DRIP, but what if you have £2,500 in credit card debt and don't have extra cash to pay off that debt? Brokerage accounts still have plenty of advantages, such as, in this example, the use of margin (a topic we discuss in detail in Chapter 17). One way to reduce your debt would be to borrow per cent against the £5,000, as a margin loan and use this amount, for example, to pay off £2,500 worth of credit card debt. Replacing unsecured debt (credit card debt that may be charging 15 per cent, 18 per cent, or more) with secured debt, you can save money. However, think about moving your credit card debt to a cheaper card – some charge 0 per cent interest for up to a year on balance transfers. Or if you are getting less than 15 per cent on your investment, but paying that in interest it makes sense to pay off the debt rather than keep your money invested.

The One-Two Punch: Pound Cost Averaging and DRIPs

Whoa! Have we veered away from DRIPs into a brand new topic? Actually, no. Pound cost averaging (PCA) is a splendid technique for buying shares and lowering your cost for doing so. The example illustrated in Table 18-1 shows that investors don't find it uncommon to see a total cost that reflects a discount off the market value. PCA works especially well with DRIPs.

PCA is a simple method for acquiring shares. It rests on the idea that you invest a fixed amount of money at regular intervals (monthly, usually) over a long period of time in that particular share. Because a fixed amount (say, £50 per month) is going into a fluctuating investment, you end up buying less of that investment when it goes up in price and more of it when it goes down in price. As Table 18-1 illustrates, your average cost per share is usually lower than if you buy all the shares at once.

PCA is best presented with an example. Presume that you decide to get into the DRIP of the company Acme Lifts Ltd. (AL). On your first day in the DRIP, AL's shares are at £2.50, and the plan allows you to invest a minimum of £25 through its optional cash purchase programme. You decide to invest £25 per month and assess how well (hopefully) you're doing six months from now. Table 18-1 shows how this technique works. (Note: cash left over after purchasing shares each month is added to the next month's investment).

Table 18-1	Pound Cost Averaging (AL)			
Months	*Investment Amount*	*Purchase Price*	*Shares Bought*	*Accumulated Shares*
1	£25	250p	10	10
2	£25	200p	12	22
3	£25	175p	14	36
4	£25	150p	16	52
5	£25	175p	14	66

Months	Investment Amount	Purchase Price	Shares Bought	Accumulated Shares
6	£25	200p	13	79
Totals	£150	N/A	79	79

To assess the wisdom of your decision to invest in the DRIP, ask yourself questions:

✔ **How much did you invest over the entire six months?**

Your total investment is £150. So far, so good.

✔ **What is the first share price for AL, and what is the last share price?**

The first share price is £2.50, but the last share price is £2.

✔ **What is the market value of your investment at the end of six months?**

You can easily calculate the value of your investment. Just multiply the number of shares you now own (79 shares) by the most recent share price (£2). The total value of your investment is £158. (And you have about 66p left in your account for next month.)

✔ **What is the average share price you bought at?**

The average share price is also easy to calculate. Take the total amount of your purchases (£150) and divide it by the number of shares that you acquired (79 shares). Your average cost per share price becomes £1.89.

✔ **Is that your final answer?** (Do your best Chris Tarrant voice.)

Yes, these are my final answers (no need to ask the audience!), but you should take note of the following:

- Even though the last share price (£2) is lower than the original share price (£2.50), your total investment's market value is still higher than your purchase amount (£158 compared to £150)! How can that be?! Pound cost averaging is the culprit here. Your disciplined approach (using PCA) was able to overcome the fluctuations in the shares' price to help you gain more shares at the lower prices of £1.75 and £1.50.

- Your average cost per share is only £1.89. The PCA method helped you buy more shares at a lower cost, which ultimately helped you make money when the share price made a modest rebound.

- PCA works in helping you invest with small sums, all the while helping you smooth out the volatility in share prices. This process helps you make more money in your wealth-building programme over the long haul. Can you visualise that retirement hammock yet?

The bottom line for long-term investors is that PCA is a solid investing technique and DRIPs are a great share investment vehicle for building wealth.

Pound cost averaging is a fantastic technique in a bull market and an 'OK' technique in a flat or sideways market, but you probably shouldn't consider it during bear markets because the shares you are buying are going down in price and the market value can easily be lower than your total investment. If you plan on holding onto the shares long term, then simply cease your pound cost averaging approach until times improve for the shares (and its industry and the economy). Discover more about bear markets in Chapter 15.

Chapter 19

Looking at What the Insiders Do: Corporate Capers

In This Chapter

▶ Figuring out how to track insider trading

▶ Examining insider buying and selling

▶ Understanding the reasons for corporate buybacks

▶ Splitting shares

*I*magine that you're boarding a cruise ship, ready to enjoy a hard-earned holiday. As you merrily walk up the plank, you notice that the ship's captain and crew are charging out of the vessel, flailing their arms, and screaming at the top of their lungs – some are even jumping into the water below. Quiz: Would you get on that ship? You get double credit if you can also explain why (or why not). What does this scenario have to do with investing in shares? Plenty, actually. The behaviour of the people running the boat gives you important clues about the near-term prospects for the boat. Similarly, the actions of company insiders can provide important clues into the near-term prospects for their company.

Company *insiders* are individuals who are key managers or investors in the company. Insiders may be the chairman of the company, the treasurer, or another managing officer. An insider can be someone who owns a large stake in the company or someone on the board of directors. In any case, insiders usually have a bird's-eye view of what's going on with the company. They have a good idea of how well (or how poorly) the company is doing.

Keep tabs on what insiders are doing, because their buy/sell transactions do have a strong correlation to the near-term movement of their company's shares. However, don't buy or sell shares only because you heard that an insider did it. Use the information on insider trading to confirm your own good sense in buying or selling shares. Insider trading sometimes can be a great precursor to a significant move that you can profit from if you know what to look for. Many shrewd investors have made their profits (or avoided losses) by tracking the activity of the insiders.

Tracking Insider Trading

Fortunately, we live in an age of disclosure. Any trading by insiders has to be reported to the UK Listing Authority (UKLA), which is now part of the Financial Services Authority (FSA). Insiders who buy or sell shares must also file reports that document their trading activity with a *regulated information service* (RIS). Typically, companies make these reports on the London Stock Exchange's own RIS – the *Regulatory News Service* (RNS), which makes the documents available to the public. A number of other similar services publish these documents too – companies can choose which one to use. These services include PimsWire, Newslink Financial and PR Newswire. You have to subscribe to most of the services available if you want to see these announcements as soon as they are made. But you can access the information through media reports too. Every Saturday the Financial Times publishes a list of 'directors' dealings' which list the sales or purchases by company, sector, and the number of shares bought or sold.

Some of the most useful documents you can view on RNS include the following:

- ✔ **Transactions in shares:** When companies buy or sell their own shares they have to inform the various stock exchanges on which their shares are listed. Companies do this by issuing a *Transaction in shares* announcement. This announcement gives the details of the transaction, including how many shares were bought and at what price. It also states the total shareholding following the transaction.

- ✔ **Director/PDMR shareholding:** This is the document that shows the insider's activity. It has to be published whenever a director or a 'person discharging managerial responsibilities' – a PDMR – buys or sells company shares. It gives the name of the person involved, the date, and type of transaction, the number of shares involved and the price that was paid for them. Any purchase or sale must be reported as soon as possible and no later than the end of the business day on which the insider informed the company of the transaction. Insiders are required to inform their companies of transactions within four days.

- ✔ **Major interest in shares:** These statements are published when a large shareholding changes. Changes involving 3 per cent or more of the company's shares need to be notified. So if a fund manager buys or sells 3 per cent or more of a company's shares, the company has to make an announcement about it.

✔ **Grant of options:** Most company directors are given shares in the company as a part of a long-term incentive plan. In most cases, the bonus scheme is set up as a series of options to buy shares at a certain fixed price. So a director joining a company with shares priced at £1 each could be given 100,000 options at 90p which he or she can exercise after three years. The directors have an interest in working to push the share price higher so that when they do take up their options to buy at 90p, they are buying shares that are worth much more. If the shares climb to £1.90, they pocket £100,000. When directors are given options or exercise them, the company has to publish the details.

Companies are required to make public the documents that track their trading activity. The LSE's Web site offers limited access to these documents, but for greater access, check out www.uk-wire.com which offers free access to all RNS announcements.

The part of a company that looks after all the regulatory stuff is called *Investor Relations* (IR). The financial governance of a company is tightly controlled from the IR department. Well-run companies never issue any figures that have not first been agreed with their IR director. And the best run companies are now setting up their own IR Web sites to explain the financial figures that have been made public to shareholders. Even if Investor Relations don't have a Web site of their own, you usually find a telephone number for them on the company's main Web site or in the annual report. You can always try calling if you don't understand the figures.

The Sarbanes-Oxley Act

Often, a market that reaches a mania stage sees abuse reach extreme conditions as well. Abuse by insiders is a good example. In the share market mania of 1997–2000, this abuse wasn't just limited to insider buying and selling of shares; it also covered the related abuse of accounting fraud. Because insiders were primarily the top management, when they deceived investors about the financial conditions of the company they subsequently were able to increase the perceived value of the company's shares. The shares could then be sold at a price that was higher than market value. In the US, Congress took notice of these activities and, in 2002, passed the Sarbanes-Oxley Act (SOXA). Congress designed this act to protect investors from fraudulent accounting activities by corporations. SOX established a public accounting oversight board and also tightened the rules on corporate financial reporting. Its reach is not restricted to the US as any UK company with listings in the US must comply. And similar accounting governance, at least for banks and financial companies, is coming to the UK from Europe as the second of the Basel Accords approaches.

Looking at Insider Transactions

The classic phrase 'Actions speak louder than words' was probably coined for insider trading. Insiders are in the know, and keeping a watchful eye on their transactions – both buying and selling their company's shares – can provide you with useful investing information. Analysing insider buying versus insider selling can be as different as day and night. Insider buying is simple, while insider selling can be complicated. In the following sections, we present both sides of insider trading.

Getting info from insider buying

Insider buying is usually an unambiguous signal about how an insider feels about the company. After all, the primary reason that all investors buy shares is that they expect it to do well. If one insider is buying shares, that's generally not a monumental event. But if several or more insiders are buying, those purchases should certainly catch your attention.

Insider buying is generally a positive omen and beneficial for the share's price. Also, when insiders buy shares, fewer shares are available to the public. If the investing public meets this decreased supply with increased demand, then the share price rises. Keep these factors in mind when analysing insider buying:

✔ **Identify who's buying the share.** The CEO is buying 5,000 shares. Is that reason enough for you to jump in? Maybe. After all, the CEO certainly knows how well the company is doing. But what if that CEO is just starting positioning the job? What if before this purchase he or she had no shares in the company at all? Maybe the shares are part of the employment package.

The fact that a new company executive is making a first share purchase isn't as strong a signal urging you to buy as the fact that a long-time CEO is doubling holdings. Also, if large numbers of insiders are buying, that sends a stronger signal than if a single insider is buying.

✔ **See how much is being bought.** In the example in the previous section, the CEO bought 5,000 shares, which is a lot of shares no matter how you count it. But is it enough for you to base an investment decision on? Maybe, but a closer look may reveal more. If the CEO already owned 1 million shares at the time of the purchase, then buying 5,000 additional shares wouldn't be such an exciting indicator of a pending share rise. In this case, 5,000 shares is a small incremental move and doesn't offer much to get excited about.

However, what if this particular insider has owned only 5,000 shares for the past three years and is now buying 1 million shares? Now that should arouse your interest! Usually, a massive purchase tells you that particular insider has strong feelings about the company's prospects and is making a huge increase in share ownership. Still, a purchase of 1 million shares by the CEO isn't as strong a signal as ten insiders buying 100,000 shares each. Again, if only one person is buying, that may or may not be a strong indication of an impending rise. However, if lots of people are buying, consider it a fantastic indication.

An insider purchase of any kind is a positive sign. But the sign is always more significant when a greater number of insiders are making purchases. 'The more the merrier!' is a good rule for judging insider buying. All these individuals have their own, unique perspectives on the company and its prospects for the foreseeable future. Mass buying indicates mass optimism for the company's future. If the treasurer, the chairman, the sales director, and several other key players are putting their wealth on the line and investing it in a company that they know intimately, that's a good sign for your share investment as well.

✔ **Insiders are acting on information that is out there.** Directors, and other people in the know, cashing in on 'insider information' is illegal. Strict rules exist about when directors can and can't trade in their company's shares. If directors are buying, or selling, their decision is based on information that has already been made public. You just have to look for it.

Picking up tips from insider selling

Insider buying bodes well for the company or is a neutral event at worst. Insider share buying is rarely a negative event. But how about insider selling? When an insider sells shares, the event can be neutral or negative. Insider selling is usually a little tougher to figure out because insiders may have many different motivations to sell shares that have nothing to do with the company's future prospects. (See the next paragraph for a list of common reasons.) Just because the chairman of the company is selling 5,000 shares from a personal portfolio, that doesn't necessarily mean that you should sell, too.

Insiders may sell their shares for a couple reasons: They may think that the company won't be doing well in the near future – a negative sign for you – or they may simply need the money for a variety of personal reasons that have nothing to do with the company's potential. Some typical reasons why insiders may sell shares include the following:

- ✔ **To diversify their holdings.** If an insider's portfolio is heavily weighted with one company's shares, a financial advisor may suggest balancing the portfolio by selling some of that company's shares and purchasing other securities.

- ✔ **To finance personal emergencies.** Sometimes an insider needs money for medical, legal, or family reasons.

- ✔ **To buy a home or make another major purchase.** An insider may need the money to make a deposit on a house or perhaps to buy something outright without having to take out a loan.

How do you find out about the details regarding insider share selling? Although insiders must report their pertinent share sales and purchases to the UKLA, the information isn't always revealing. As a general rule, consider the following questions when analysing insider selling:

- ✔ **How many insiders are selling?** If only one insider is selling, that single transaction doesn't give you enough information to act on. However, if many insiders are selling, you should see a red flag. Check out any news or information that is currently available. Web sites such as www.ft.com, www.fool.co.uk, and www.bloomberg.com can help you get that information (along with other sources in Appendix A).

- ✔ **Are the sales showing a pattern or unusual activity?** If one insider sold shares last month, that sale alone isn't that significant an event. However, if ten insiders have each made multiple sales in the past few months, those sales are cause for concern. See whether any new developments at the company are potentially negative. If massive insider selling has recently occurred and you don't know why, consider putting a stop-loss order on your shares immediately. (Refer to Chapter 17 where we cover stop-loss orders more fully.

- ✔ **How many shares are being sold?** If a CEO sells 5,000 shares but still retains 100,000 shares, that's not a big deal. But if the CEO sells all or most of his or her holdings, that's a possible negative. Check to see whether other company executives have also sold shares.

- ✔ **Do outside events or analyst reports seem coincidental with the sale of the share?** Sometimes, an influential analyst may issue a report warning about a company's prospects. If the company's management pooh-poohs the report but most of them are bailing out anyway (selling their shares), you may want to do the same.

Some insider dealing is illegal. Insiders who know damaging information is coming before it is in the public domain, and sell their shares in advance of the information being made public, can expect a call from the Serious Fraud Office.

Similarly, if the company's management issues positive public statements or reports that are contradictory to their own behaviour (they're selling their share holdings), the FSA may investigate to see whether the company is doing anything that may require a penalty. The FSA regularly tracks insider sales.

Considering Corporate Share Buybacks

When you read the financial pages or watch the financial shows on television, you sometimes hear that a company is buying its own shares. The announcement may be something like, 'SuperQuids PLC has announced that it is spending £2 billion pounds to buy back its own shares.' Why would a company do that, and what does that mean to you if you own the share or are considering buying it?

When companies buy back their own shares, they're generally indicating that they believe their shares are undervalued and that they have the potential to rise. If a company shows strong fundamentals (for example, good financial condition and increasing sales and earnings) and is buying more of its own shares, investigate – it may make a great addition to your portfolio.

Just because a company announces a share buyback doesn't always mean that one will happen. The announcement itself is meant to stir interest in the shares and cause the price to rise. The share buyback may be only an opportunity for insiders to sell shares, or it may be needed for executive compensation – recruiting and retaining competent management is a positive use of money.

If you see that a company is buying back its shares while most of the insiders are selling their personal shares, this is not a good sign. It may not necessarily be a bad sign, but is not a positive sign. Play it safe and invest elsewhere.

The following sections present common reasons why a company may buy back its shares from investors as well as ideas on the negative effects of share buybacks.

Boosting earnings per share

By simply buying back its own shares from shareholders, a company can increase its earnings per share (refer back to Chapter 10 and see Appendix B for more on earnings per share) without actually earning extra money. Sound like a magician's trick? Well, yes, kind of. A corporate share buyback is a financial sleight of hand that investors should be aware of. Here's how it works: Nomore Earnings Ltd (NEL) has 10 million shares outstanding, and is expected to net earnings of £10 million for the fourth quarter. NEL's earnings per share (EPS) would be £1 per share. So far, so good. But what happens if NEL buys 2 million of its own shares? Total shares outstanding shrink to 8 million. The new EPS becomes £1.25 – the share buyback artificially boosts the earnings per share by 25 per cent!

The important point to remember about share buybacks is that actual company earnings don't change – no fundamental changes occur in company management or operations – so the increase in EPS can be misleading. But the marketplace can be obsessive about earnings, and because earnings are the lifeblood of any company, an earnings boost, even if cosmetic, can also boost the share price.

If you watch a company's price-to-earnings ratio (refer to Chapter 10), you know that increased earnings usually mean an eventual increase in the share price. Additionally, a share buyback affects supply and demand. With fewer available shares in the market, demand necessarily sends the share price upward.

Whenever a company makes a major purchase, such as buying back its own shares, think about how the company is paying for it and whether it seems like a good use of the company's purchasing power. In general, companies buy their shares for the same reasons that any investor buys shares – they believe that the share is a good investment and will appreciate in time. Companies generally pay for a share buyback in one of two basic ways, funds from operations or borrowed money. Both methods have a downside. For more details, see the section 'Exploring the downside of buybacks' later in this chapter.

Beating back a takeover bid

Suppose that you read in the financial pages that Company X is attempting a hostile takeover of Company Z. A hostile takeover doesn't mean that Company X sent storm troopers armed with pepper spray to Company Z's headquarters to trounce its management. All a *hostile takeover* means is that X wants to buy enough shares of Z to effectively control Z (and Z is unhappy about being owned or controlled by X). Because buying and selling shares are done in a public market or exchange, companies can buy each other's shares. Sometimes the target company prefers not to be acquired, in which case it may buy back some of its own shares to give it a measure of protection against unwanted moves by interested companies.

In some cases, the company attempting the takeover already owns some of the target company's shares. In this case, the targeted company may offer to buy those shares back from the aggressor at a premium to thwart the takeover bid.

Takeover concerns generally prompt interest in the investing public, driving the share price upward and benefiting current shareholders.

Exploring the downside of buybacks

As beneficial as share buybacks can be, they have to be paid for, and this expense has consequences. If a company pays for the shares with funds from operations, it may have a negative effect on the company's ability to finance current and prospective operations. When a company uses funds from operations for the share buyback, less money is available for other activities, such as upgrading technology or research and development. In general, any misuse of money, such as using debt to buy back shares, affects a company's ability to grow its sales and earnings – two measures that need to maintain upward mobility in order to keep share prices rising.

A company faces even greater dangers when it uses debt to finance a share buyback. If the company uses borrowed funds, it has less borrowing power for other uses (such as upgrading technology or making other improvements). In addition, the company has to pay back the borrowed funds with interest, thus lowering earnings figures.

Say that NEL (a fictional company introduced in the 'Boosting earnings per share' section, earlier in this chapter) typically pays an annual dividend of 25 pence per share and wants to buy back shares with borrowed money with a 9 per cent interest rate. If NEL buys back 2 million shares, it won't have to pay out £500,000 in dividends. That's money saved. However, NEL is going to have to pay interest on the £20 million it borrowed to buy back the shares over that same time frame to the tune of £1,800,000 (9 per cent of £20,000,000). The net result from this rudimentary example is that NEL sees an outflow of £1,300,000 (the difference between the interest paid out and the dividends savings). Using debt to finance a share buyback needs to make economic sense – it needs to strengthen the company's financial position. Perhaps NEL could have used the share buyback money toward a better purpose, such as modernising equipment or paying for a new marketing campaign. Because debt interest ultimately decreases earnings, companies must be careful when using debt to buy back their shares.

Share Scrips: Staging a Comeback

Frequently, management teams decide to do a *share scrip*. A share scrip is the exchange of existing shares for new shares from the same company. Share scrips don't increase or decrease the capitalisation of the company. They just change the number of shares available in the market and the per-share price.

In a typical share scrip, a company may announce that it is doing a 2-for-1 share scrip. For example, a company may have 10 million shares outstanding, with a market price of £40 each. In a 2-for-1 scrip, the company then has 20 million shares (the share total doubles), but the market price is adjusted to £20 (the share price is halved). Companies do other scrips, such as a 3-for-2 or 4-for-1, but 2-for-1 is the most common scrip. This is known as a *share split* in the US and is sometimes called a *capitalisation issue* or *bonus issue* in the UK.

Why do companies carry out share scrips? Usually, management believes that the share's price is too high, thus possibly discouraging investors from purchasing it. The share scrip is a strategy to stir interest in the share, and this increased interest frequently results in a rise in the share's price.

Qualifying for a share scrip is similar to qualifying to receive a dividend – you must be listed as a shareholder as of the date of record. (For information on the date of record, see Chapter 6.)

A share scrip is technically a neutral event because the ultimate market value of the company's shares doesn't change as a result of it. The following sections present the two most basic types of scrips: ordinary and reverse share scrips.

Ordinary share scrips

Ordinary share scrips – when the number of shares increase – are the ones we usually hear about. (For example, a 2-for-1 share scrip doubles the number of shares.) If you own 100 shares of Dublin Ltd (at £60 per share), and the company announces a share scrip, what happens? If you own the shares in certificate form, you receive a new share certificate for 200 shares of Dublin Ltd. Now, before you cheer over how your money just doubled, check the share's new price. Each share is adjusted to a £30 value.

Not all shares are in certificate form. Shares held in a brokerage account are recorded by registrars. Most shares, in fact, are held in nominee accounts. A company only issues share certificates when necessary or when the investor requests it. If you keep the shares in your broker account – called a nominee account – check with your broker for the new share total to make sure that you're credited with the new number of shares after the scrip issue.

A scrip issue is primarily a neutral event, so why does a company bother to do it? The most common reason is that management believes that the shares are too expensive, so it wants to lower the share price to make individual shares more affordable and therefore more attractive to new investors. Studies have shown that share scrips frequently precede a rise in the share price. Although share scrips are considered a non-event in and of themselves, many share experts see them as bullish signals because of the interest they generate among the investing public.

Reverse share scrips

A *reverse share scrip* or *consolidation* usually occurs when a company's management wants to raise the price of its shares. Just as ordinary scrips can occur when management believes that the price is too expensive, a reverse share scrip means that the company feels that the share's price is too cheap. If a share's price looks too low, that may discourage interest by individual or institutional investors (such as mutual funds). Management wants to drum up more interest in the share for the benefit of shareholders (some of whom are probably insiders).

A reverse split can best be explained with an example. TuCheep Ltd (TCL) is selling at 2p per share on AIM. At that rock-bottom price, the investing public may ignore it. So TCL announces a 10-for-1 reverse share scrip. Now what? If an existing shareholder had 100 shares at 2p (the old shares), the shareholder now owns 10 shares at 20p.

Technically, a reverse scrip is considered a neutral event. However, just as investors may infer positive expectations from an ordinary share scrip, they may have negative expectations from a reverse scrip, because a reverse scrip tends to occur for negative reasons.

If, in the event of a share scrip, you have an odd number of shares, the company doesn't produce a 'fractional share'. Instead, you get a cheque for the cash equivalent or the company gets the money. For example, if you have 51 shares and the company announces a 2-for-1 reverse scrip, the odds are that they'll give you 25 shares and a cash payout for the odd share (or fractional share). Some companies ask you to donate the money to charity rather than ask for a cheque to be issued.

Keep good records regarding your share scrips in case you need to calculate capital gains for tax purposes. (See Chapter 20 for more information on tax issues.)

Chapter 20

Tax Benefits and Liabilities

*A*fter conquering the world of making money with shares, now you have another hurdle – keeping your money. Some people may tell you that tax is brutal, complicated, and counterproductive. Other people may tell you that it's a form of legalised theft, while others still say that they're a necessary evil. And then there are pessimists. In any case, this chapter shows you how to keep more of the fruits of your hard-earned labour.

Keep in mind that this chapter isn't meant to be comprehensive. For a fuller treatment of personal taxation, refer to the latest edition of *Paying Less Tax For Dummies,* by Tony Levene (Wiley). However, in this chapter, I cover the most relevant points for share market investors. As a share market investor, you need to know the tax treatment for dividends and capital gains and losses, along with common tax deductions for investors and some simple tax-reducing strategies.

You must take tax planning seriously because tax can be the single biggest expense during your lifetime. The average taxpayer pays more in tax than in food, clothing, and shelter combined!

Paying through the Nose

This section tells you what you need to know about the tax implications you'll face when you start investing in shares. It's good to know the basics in advance it will matter to your investing strategy. If you're the type of investor who likes to cash in on a profitable share quickly, then realise that you will probably pay more in tax than if you are more patient. Sometimes the difference can be just a matter of days. What if you are about to sell a share that you've held for 35 months and 28 days? Well waiting just a few more days could mean less tax which means more money in your pocket.

Understanding income and capital gains tax

Profit you make from your share investments can be taxed in one of two ways, depending on the type of profit. If you are a taxpayer, because you earn more than your personal tax allowance, you will either pay income tax or capital gains tax.

✔ **Income tax:** For the purposes of tax, dividends are treated as income. All UK dividends are paid *net of* 10 per cent tax – even if you do not normally pay tax. This means that if you get a dividend cheque for £9, you have actually earned a dividend of £10 and paid £1 in tax before it even gets to you. If you normally pay income tax at the lower 10 per cent rate or at basic rate you don't have to pay any more tax on the dividend. But if you are a higher rate taxpayer you have to pay the extra – 22.5 per cent – when you complete your tax return. Two types of investment profits get taxed as ordinary income: Dividends and short-term capital gains.

- **Dividends:** When you receive dividends from your shares (either in cash or shares), these dividends get taxed as ordinary income. This is also true if those dividends are in a dividend reinvestment plan. (See Chapter 18 if you want to know more about dividend reinvestment plans, or DRIPs.) If, however, those dividends occur in a tax-sheltered savings scheme, such as an ISA then they're exempt from tax for as long as they're in the scheme. Retirement plans are covered in the section 'Taking Advantage of Tax-Advantaged Retirement Investing,' later in this chapter. At the end of March each year, investors who have joined DRIPs will be sent a *consolidated tax voucher* (CTV) from the issuer of the dividends that includes information on the amount of dividends earned in the tax year.

- **Short-term capital gains:** If you sell share for a gain and you've owned the share for fewer than three years, you may have to pay capital gains tax at the full rate. To calculate the time you have owned the share, you use the trade date (or date of execution). (For more on important dates, see Chapter 6.) However, if these gains occur in a tax-sheltered savings scheme, such as an ISA, no tax payment is triggered.

✔ **Capital Gains Tax:** In 1998 the government introduced the concept of *taper relief* for capital gains. This means that gains on shares owned for more than three years are not hit with the full Capital Gains Tax whack. After three years you pay tax on 95 per cent of the gain falling to 60 per cent of the gain after 10 years. The tax rules – which change again in April 2008 – currently reward patient investors. Holding the shares for an extra day (what a difference a day makes!), can take you into the next year of ownership and reduce your tax rate. Get more information on capital gains in HMRC publication Help Sheet IR279.

Because the tax on capital gains is the most relevant tax for share investors, don't forget to read the section 'Minimising the tax on your capital gains,' later in this chapter.

Managing the tax burden from your investment profits is something that you can control. Gains are taxable only if the gain is *realised* – in other words, only if a sale actually takes place. If your share in GazillionBucks, PLC, goes from £5 per share to £87, that £82 appreciation isn't subject to taxation unless you actually sell the share. Until you sell, that gain is 'unrealised.' Time your share sales carefully – the longer you hold them – the lower your tax liability will be.

When you buy shares, record the date of purchase and the *cost basis* (the purchase price of the share plus any ancillary charges, such as commissions). This information is very important when you have to fill in your tax return – especially if you have sold some shares. The date of purchase helps to establish the *holding period* (how long you've owned the shares) that determines whether your gains are subject to taper relief.

Say that you buy 100 shares of GazillionBucks, PLC, at £5 each and pay a commission of £18. Your cost basis is £518 (100 shares times £5 plus £18 commission). If you sell the share at £87 per share and pay a £24 commission, the total sale amount is £8,676 (100 shares times £87 less £24 commission). If this sale occurred less than three years after the purchase, it's a short-term gain You get no taper relief and have to pay up to 40 per cent tax (the capital gains tax rate for a higher rate taxpayer). Of course, I'm assuming that you have already used up your annual capital gains allowance of £9,200 for the 2007/ 2008 tax year on a previous sale. Read the following section to see the tax implications if your gain is a long-term gain.

Every individual has an annual *capital gains allowance* – an amount up to which profits can be made on the sales of assets, including shares, without triggering a tax charge. The allowance is set once a year by the Chancellor of the Exchequer in his Budget Speech.

Taper relief on Capital Gains Tax may be abolished in April 2008. At the time of publication of this book, however, you can still get taper relief on shares.

Taper relief: Another angle

Taper relief was only introduced in the UK in 1998, and there are two distinct threads to the rules that govern it. The gain that you pay tax on reduces slightly if the asset being sold is a non-business asset. After one and two years you still pay tax on 100 per cent of your gain. After three years you pay it on 95 per cent and, after four years, on 90 per cent of your gain. Each further year the chargeable gain falls by five per cent until you have owned the share for 10 years or more when you would only pay tax on 60 per cent of your gain. However, if the shares you are selling are considered a business asset, you get taper relief at a much more generous rate. Your shares will be classed as a business asset if you are entitled to exercise at least 25 per cent or more of the voting rights, or if the company involved is one you work for most of your time, and you are entitled to exercise at least five per cent of the voting rights.

Minimising the tax on your capital gains

Long-term capital gains are taxed at a more favourable rate than short-term gains. To qualify for long-term capital gains treatment, you must hold the investment for more than three years (in other words, for at least three years and one day).

Recall the example in the previous section with GazillionBucks, PLC. As a short-term transaction at the 40 per cent tax rate, the tax would have been £3,470 (£8,676 × 40 per cent). After you revive, you say, 'Gasp! What a chunk of dough. I better hold off a while longer.' You hold on to the share for at least three years to qualify for capital gains taper relief. How does that change the tax? You still pay 40 per cent tax but on a smaller proportion of your gain – 95 per cent of it. So you'd pay 40 per cent of 95 per cent of £8,676. A total of 3,297. This means waiting a few years has saved you £173 (£3470 less £3,297). Okay, it's not a fortune, but it is much better off in your pocket than paid over in tax. And the longer you hold on to your shares the more taper relief you will earn.

Because every taxpayer's circumstances are different, it is a good idea to check with your personal tax advisor if you have one. Even the documents published by HMRC are only for guidance.

Don't sell a share just because it qualifies for taper relief, even if the sale would ease your tax burden. If the share is doing well and meeting your investing criteria, then hold on to it.

Capital Gains Tax *can* be lower than the ordinary income tax, but not higher. If you pay tax at the starting rate of 10 per cent that is how much you will pay on capital gains. A basic rate taxpayer, paying 22 per cent on income will pay 20 per cent on capital gains and a higher rate taxpayer paying 40 per cent on income pays the same on capital gains – unless he gets a break with some taper relief. Don't forget you have an annual capital gains allowance to use which is currently £9,200 for the 2007–2008 tax year.

Coping with capital losses

Ever think that having the value of your shares fall could be a good thing? Perhaps the only real positive regarding losses in your portfolio is that they can reduce your tax. A *capital loss* means that you lose money on your investments. This amount is generally deductible on your tax return, and you can claim a loss on either long-term or short-term share holdings. This loss can go against your other income and lower your overall tax bill.

Say that you bought Worth Zilch Co. shares for a total purchase price of £3,500 and sold it later at a sale price of £800. Your capital loss would be £2,700. This loss is tax deductible.

You don't always have to realise the loss to claim it as a capital gains loss. If the asset has fallen to a negligible value it can be counted for this purpose. And, any excess loss isn't really lost – you can carry it forward to the next year. However most of the time you need to realise a loss to claim it and there are times when investors sell up to do just that. Sort of cutting your losses to get the benefit of your losses – if that makes sense. See the section on bed and breakfasting later in this chapter..

Gains and losses scenarios

Of course, any investor can come up with hundreds of possible scenarios. For example, you may wonder what happens if you sell part of your holdings now as a short-term capital loss and the remainder later as a long-term capital gain. You must look at each sale of shares (or potential sale) methodically to calculate the gain or loss you would realise from it. Figuring out your gain or loss isn't that complicated. Here are some general rules to help you wade through the morass:

✔ If you add up all your gains and losses and *the net result is a short-term gain*, it's taxed at your highest tax bracket (usually the same as income tax).

✔ If you add up all your gains and losses and *the net result is a long-term gain*, you will qualify for some taper relief which can be used to minimise your tax bill.

✔ If you add up all your gains and losses and *the net result is a loss*, it's deductible as a loss either this year or it can be carried forward to next year.

Before you can deduct losses, you will be expected to use capital losses from your investments to offset any capital gains. If you realise long-term capital gains of £7,000 in share A and £6,000 of realised long-term capital losses in share B, then you have a net long-term capital gain of £1,000 (£7,000 gain less the offset of £6,000 loss). Whenever possible, see whether losses in your portfolio can be realised to offset any capital gains to reduce any potential tax.

Here's your optimum strategy: Where possible, keep losses on a short-term basis and push your gains into long-term capital gains status to qualify for taper relief. If a transaction can't be tax free, then at the very least try to defer the tax to keep your money working for you.

Sharing Your Gains with the Taxman

Of course, you don't want to pay more tax than you have to, but as the old cliché goes, 'Don't let the tax tail wag the investment dog.' You should buy or sell a share because it makes economic sense first, and consider the tax implications as secondary issues. After all, tax consumes a relatively small portion of your gain. As long as you experience a *net gain* (gain after all transaction costs, including tax, broker's fees, and other related fees), consider yourself a successful investor – even if you have to give away some of your gain in tax.

Hold on to shares over the long term to keep transaction costs and tax down. Remember that you don't pay tax on a share profit until you sell the share.

Try to make tax planning second nature in your day-to-day activities. No, you don't have to consume yourself with a blizzard of paperwork and tax projections. I simply mean that when you make a share transaction, keep the receipt and maintain good records. When you make a large purchase or sale, pause for a moment and ask yourself whether you'll have to face any tax consequences. (Refer to the section 'Paying through the Nose,' earlier in this chapter, to review various tax scenarios.) Speak to a tax consultant beforehand to discuss the ramifications.

Filling out forms

Most investors report their investment-related activities on their individual tax returns (Self-assessment Form). The reports that you will probably receive from brokers and other investment sources include the following:

- ✔ **Brokerage and bank statements:** Monthly statements that you receive
- ✔ **Trade confirmations:** Documents to confirm that you bought or sold shares

✔ **Dividend vouchers:** Reporting dividends paid to you

✔ **Consolidated tax voucher:** Reporting the total tax deducted on income paid to you including interest and dividends.

You may receive other, more obscure forms that aren't listed here, but you should retain all documents related to your share investments.

The supplementary self-assessment pages that most share investors need to be aware of and/or attach to their Tax Return (SA 100) include the following:

✔ **SA 150:** Guide to your Tax Return

✔ **SA 108:** Capital gains supplementary pages

✔ **SA 108 Notes:** Notes on capital gains

✔ **IR279:** Guide to taper relief

You can get these publications directly from the HMRC at 0845 9000 404, or you can download them from the Web site www.hmrc.gov.uk.

If you plan to do your own tax, consider using the latest tax software products, which have become inexpensive and are easy to use. These programmes usually have a question-and-answer feature to help you do your tax step-by-step, and they include all the necessary forms. Consider getting either TaxCalc 2007 (www.taxcalc.com) or Digita Personal Tax (www.digita.com) both have been successfully tested by HMRC's online service and can support all tax return supplementary pages.

Playing by the rules

Some people get the smart idea of 'Hey! Why not sell my losing shares by April 5 and just buy back the shares on April 6 in the new tax year so that I can say I haven't really made a change to my investment?' Not so fast. The HMRC (at the time it was still called the Inland Revenue) put the kibosh on manoeuvres such as that when a practice called *bed-and-breakfasting* (B&B) was outlawed in the 1998 Budget. Thank you Gordon Brown. B&B allowed investors to sell a share one day and buy it back the next. Their investment portfolio didn't change but they were able to crystallise a gain or loss which could be offset against other gains or losses that had already been made in that tax year. You can still use bed and breakfasting but not as an overnight ploy. You have to wait 30 days to repurchase the share or the taxman will not view the sale as having taken place and you lose the tax advantage.

Some people use spread betting to cover 'missing' shares for the 30 day period. This is a risky tactic as spread betting is just that – gambling or speculation. Not only can you lose all your money but it can cost you extra cash.

No Such Thing as a Free Share

Every so often investors find themselves getting a little bonus – some extra shares free from one of the companies they have invested in. This is not generosity on the part of the company it is usually the result of a particular corporate action. Now you might think, and a lot of people do – or did, until the taxman put them right – that if a share if free it has no value and therefore cannot be taxed. Wrong! Some people say that if you can count it, that makes it taxable. But that doesn't mean that the taxation of free shares is always the same, as we explain. There are three main categories of 'free shares':

✔ **Loyalty bonus shares**: In most privatisations – when the government sells off a state-owned business – shareholders who buy shares from the government and hold them for a specific time, may be entitled to an issue of extra shares. For taxation purposes, these shares are treated as if they were purchased at their market value. So if you get 50 free shares from an electricity company when the company's shares are worth £3 each and you sell them later at £5 each you will be taxed on a gain of £2 a share – even though you appear to have walked away with a £5 a share profit. This type of bonus may also be paid in the case of a conversion – when a mutually-owned business (one owned by its customers) converts to a public listed company owned by shareholders. Standard Life's conversion last year offered bonus shares to those who had held their shares for more than 12 months. For more on conversions see the section later in this list.

✔ **Scrips**: A share scrip or split is not really free shares – but to some investors it does seem like it. This is an exchange of shares usually to make a share more saleable. So if the share price of Dodo Holding PLC has hit £10 a share and the company wants to encourage more shareholders to invest, it might prefer to have a share price of £1 a share. To do this it would exchange current shareholdings in a 10 for 1 scrip. If you had one share worth £10 before, you now have 10 shares worth £1 each, still a total holding of £10. As far as tax is concerned, you may have more shares but the value of your holding has not changed – although it might if more shareholders pile in. You shouldn't pay any more tax from selling these shares than if you'd sold the £10 ones. But it is important that you keep all the paperwork about any scrips that come along so you accountant can work out the real profit or loss when you do sell.

✔ **Conversion shares**: Firms that are mutually owned are still a big feature of UK corporate life, but they are getting fewer. Building societies, co-operative societies, friendly societies and some life and pension companies are owned by their customers or members rather than by shareholders. In recent years there have been a number of big demutual-isations where mutually-owned companies (or mutuals) have converted to companies listed on the stock market. Examples include Halifax Building Society (now part of HBOS group), Standard Life and Woolwich (now part of Barclays). When these companies changed status from mutual to PLC they paid their members compensation for loss of membership rights. These demutualisation shares – also called windfall shares – are issued to members who qualify under certain criteria. Members do not have to pay for their shares and are issued varying amounts depending on the conversion rules. Some mutuals give all members the same amount; others dish out more shares to members with larger interests – such as bigger savings balances in the building society. However the shares are issued, the taxation is pretty clear. If you get free shares worth £1,000 and sell them immediately you have realised a capital gain of £1,000 and could be taxed on it if you have already used your capital gains allowance for the year. The shares are considered to have zero value when you were issued with them, so when you do sell you will have to pay tax on the total sale price – that will be the profit. Of course, if you hold on to the shares for three years you will qualify for taper relief. See the section 'Understanding income and capital gains tax' earlier in this chapter.

There are millions of unclaimed conversion shares waiting to be collected. Many have been allocated to customers who failed to reply to letters telling them about the proposed demutualisation. Most can still be claimed but for some of the oldest only the cash equivalent can now be retrieved. Contact the Unclaimed Assets Register or the company itself if you think any of the unclaimed shares might be rightfully yours.

✔ **Incentive shares:** If you work for a company that is listed on a stock market, there is a chance you will be offered shares as part of a savings scheme or incentive plan. For senior executives, these plans (sometimes called *long term incentive plans*, or L-TIPs) can get very complex, involving the award of share options over several years. Share options are just that, the option to buy a share at a given price but on a future date. For instance you may work for a young company which has a low share price of 10p. To encourage you to work hard and boost the companies fortunes, you could be offered options to buy a certain number of shares at 20p in two year's time, 30p in three year's time and 50p in five year's time. These are pretty tough targets. But say the company discovers a blockbuster product and the shares hit £1 within two years, £2 in three years and £10 in five years. When your options mature on those dates you can buy £1 shares for 20p (hurray!), £2 shares for 30p (double hurray!), and £10 shares for 50p (someone crack open the bubbly!). Of course you will have to pay tax on any gains when you finally dispose of the shares.

Although it may seem strange to discuss 'free' shares in a book about investing in shares, you would be mad to dismiss these ways of boosting your shares portfolio. Many privatisation and conversion shares are now blue chip companies and the bedrock of thousands of share portfolios. Don't ignore them and don't turn them down – especially if you are getting them for free.

Keep all your paperwork to do with buying, selling or being awarded shares or dividends. You will need it when it comes to calculate how much tax you owe.

Givin' it away

What happens if you donate shares to your favourite (registered) charity? The donation does not give rise to a capital gain or loss but you can claim income tax relief on the value of any shares donated to charity.

Say that last year you bought shares for £2,000 and they are worth £4,000 this year. If you donate them this year, you can deduct the market value from your income tax liability at the time of the contribution. In this case, you have a £4,000 deduction against your income tax liability. You can also deduct the cost of selling the shares if there are any, such as broker's fees.

To get more guidance from HMRC on this matter, get its free Publication ''IR 178 on giving shares to charity by calling 0845 3020203.

Don't bank on tax deductions

In some countries you can offset some of the costs of investing against your gains to save on tax. Can you do that in the UK? Fat chance. You will only save tax by:

- ✔ Keeping excellent records of all your share dealings
- ✔ Using tax-efficient investment vehicles where possible
- ✔ Timing your sales to realise capital gains and losses at the optimal time

Are you having fun yet? You're probably saying 'Why read the rest of the chapter? Can't I just wait for the movie?' Yeah, I know, tax can be intimidating. So, write to your MP and complain. After all, it's your money!

Taking Advantage of Tax Advantages

If you're going to invest for the long term (such as your retirement or to pay for your toddler's school and university fees), then you may as well maximise your usage of tax-sheltered savings plans. More than one way exists to skin the tax-efficient cat and here I touch on the most popular ones. Although savings plans may not seem relevant for investors who buy and sell shares directly (as opposed to a unit trust or investment trust), some plans, such as self select ISAs and Self Invested Personal Pensions, allow you to invest directly.

ISAs

Individual Savings Accounts (ISAs) are accounts that you can open with a financial institution, such as a bank, building society or fund management company. An ISA is available to almost anyone over the age of 16 who has earned income, and it allows you to set aside and invest money for short or long term savings. Opening an ISA is easy, and virtually any bank, building society or fund manager can guide you through the process. The two basic types of ISAs are the cash mini ISA and the stocks and shares maxi ISA.

Cash Individual Savings Account (ISA)

The cash Individual Savings Account (also called the mini ISA) was introduced in 1997 to encourage long term savings. The basic point of the cash ISA is that you can save up to £3,000 in any tax year and pay no tax on the interest. The money can continue to grow tax free for as long as it stays in the ISA.

You don't have to pay tax on the money when you do withdraw it. You would only pay tax on any interest you earned on it if you invested it in another type of account.

If you take money out of an ISA you can top it up again to the £3,000 as long as you do it before the end of the tax year. So if you invest the full £3,000 and then withdraw £500 for an emergency you can put the £500 back into the ISA at any time up to April 5 and still get the tax benefit. ''

Everyone is entitled to have an ISA whether they are working and or earning or not. But ISAs are only available for those aged over 16. Then they were first introduced the minimum age limit was 18 but this was lowered to 16 to encourage school leavers in their first jobs to save. .

Wait a minute! You may be thinking that ISAs usually are started up with fund managers or bank investments. How does the share investor take advantage of a cash ISA? Well apart from saving up some initial capital to invest with, you can't. But Share investors can open a stocks and shares ISA with a brokerage firm. This means that you can buy and sell shares in the account with no tax on dividends or capital gains. The account is tax free, so you don't have to worry about tax on your gains or your withdrawals. Also, many dividend reinvestment plans (DRIPs) are ISA-able as well. See Chapter 18 for more about DRIPs.

Stocks and Shares ISA

The stocks and shares ISA is a great way to invest in the stock market and escape tax on your successes. We wish it had existed a long time ago. Here are some ways to distinguish the stocks and shares ISA from the cash ISA:

- ✔ You can invest £7,000 in the stocks and shares ISA but only £3,000 in the cash ISA.
- ✔ There is no tax to pay on dividends or capital gains in a stocks and shares ISA.
- ✔ Many brokers offer ISA facilities.

You can opt for a range of shares in a fund to be held in an ISA or you can use the £7,000 investment to chose your own shares to be held in the account. This option is called a self select ISA. You can decide to hold one share or several shares in the one account.

You can't invest more than £7,000 in ISAs in one tax year so if you have £3,000 in a cash ISA you can only invest a further £4,000 in a stocks and shares ISA.

Pensions

Pension plans are investment vehicles which are designed to build a capital sum for an individual, payable on retirement. There are significant tax advantages to investing in a pension plan.

Company pension plans

Company-sponsored pension plans are widely used and are very popular. In a company pension, employees set aside money from their monthly salary that is invested in a group fund for employees' retirement. In many cases the employer at least matches the amount invested each month. There is no tax to pay on the growth of the fund but the pension paid from it is taxable. The big advantage is that investing in a pension attracts tax relief from the government, which adds a serious sum to your investment. For instance for a basic rate taxpayer, the government will top every £78 you invest in your pension up to £100.

SIPPs

Self invested personal pensions are the latest big noise on the pension stage. Thousands of them are now being sold and they have become mainstream. You can invest up to 100 per cent of your annual pre-tax earnings (most of us need some of our earnings to live on, but the option is there!) up to a limit of

£225,000 (we wish!) in the 2007-8 tax year and still get tax relief. The limit will increase by £10,000 a year until 2010-11.

Non-earners can also invest up to £3,600 a year and still get tax relief. In this case you'd only have to invest £2,808 and the taxman would provide the other £782.

But there is more to SIPPs than just stuffing money away for the future. As the name suggests, you get to choose the investments yourself. You can get a manager to help you but you have more choice of the types of investments you can pick from. You can invest in individual shares, stock market and property funds and bonds, real estate investment trusts, unquoted shares, gilts, cash, and commercial property.

There had been plans to allow investments in residential property but the government backtracked on that offer before it got off the ground. However you can invest in commercial property – even investing in your own business by buying the premises in your SIPP. And you can even borrow half of the value of your SIPP to fund the purchase.

Part V
The Part of Tens

In this part . . .

This wouldn't be a *For Dummies* book if we didn't include a Part of Tens. Here you find quick reference lists to many of the most basic share investing concepts and practices. Check the information in this part when you don't have time to read the denser parts of the book or when you just need a quick refresher on what to do before, after, and even during your stock investing pursuits.

Chapter 21

Ten Warning Signs of a Share's Decline

In This Chapter

▶ Slowdown in earnings and sales

▶ Reduced dividends

▶ Industry or political troubles

▶ Questionable accounting practices

*H*ave you ever watched a film and noticed that one of the characters coughs excessively throughout? To us, that's a dead giveaway that the character is a goner. Or maybe you've seen a film in which a bit-part character annoys a crime boss, so right away you know that it's time for him to 'sleep with the fishes.' Shares aren't that different. If you're alert, you can recognise some definite signs that your investment may be ready to kick the bucket.

Let the tips in this chapter serve as a 'symptoms checklist' on your share investments. This chapter will help you catch your share as it starts to 'cough,' so that you can get out before it 'sleeps with the fishes.' (We just can't help you with mixed metaphors.)

Earnings Slow Down or Head South

Profit is the lifeblood of a company, so lack of profit is a sign of a company's poor financial health. Watch the earnings. Are they increasing or not? If they aren't, find out why. If the general economy is experiencing a recession, stagnant earnings are still better than hefty losses – everything is relative. Earnings slowdowns for a company may very well be a temporary phenomenon. If a company's earnings are holding up better than its competitors and/or the market in general, you don't need to be alarmed.

Nonetheless, a company's earnings are its most important measure of success. Keep an eye on the company's P/E ratio. It could change negatively (go up) because of one of two basic scenarios:

- ✔ The share price goes up as earnings barely budge.
- ✔ The share price doesn't move, yet earnings drop.

Both of these scenarios result in a rising P/E ratio that ultimately has a negative effect on the share price.

A P/E ratio that is lower than industry competitors' P/E ratios makes a company's shares favourable investments.

Don't buy the argument 'Although the company has losses, its sales are exploding.' This argument is a variation of 'The company may be losing money, but it'll make it up on volume.' For example, say that R.U.B. Bish PLC(RUBB) had sales of £1 billion in 2005 and that sales expect to be £1.5 billion in 2006, projecting an increase at RUB by 50 per cent. But what if RUB's earnings were £200 million in 2005 and the company was actually expecting a loss for 2006? The company wouldn't succeed, because sales without earnings isn't enough – the company needs to make a profit. Remember that if you put your money in the shares of a company that has losses, you're not investing, you're speculating.

Sales Slow Down

Sales figures may not give you the whole picture on a company's health, but you can't generate profit without them. Before you invest in a company, make sure that sales are strong and rising. If sales start to decline, that downward motion ultimately affects earnings. (See the previous section, 'Earnings Slow Down or Head South.') Although the earnings of a company may go safely up and down, sales should consistently rise. If they cease to rise, a variety of reasons may be to blame. First, it may be temporary because the economy in general is having tough times. However, it may be more serious. Perhaps the company is having marketing problems, or a competitor is eating away at its market share. Maybe a new technology is replacing its products and services. In any case, falling sales raise a red flag you shouldn't ignore.

By the way, when we talk sales, we're talking about the sales of what the company usually offers (its products or services). Sometimes a company may sell something other than what it normally offers (such as equipment, property, or a subdivision of its business) and this sale may make the total sales number temporarily blip upward. Watch for this because it can fool you regarding the company's financial strength. Maybe the unusual sale is due to financial or cash flow problems that the company is experiencing. The bottom line is to simply keep an eye on it.

Exuberant Analysts Despite Logic

Sometimes, analysts give glowing praise to companies that any logical person with some modest financial acumen would avoid like the plague. Why is this? In some cases, the reasons are murky (or you could argue that plain stupidity is to blame). In any case, remember that analysts are employed by companies that earn hefty investment banking fees from the very companies that these analysts tout. So you can see why some analysts might feel the pressure to modify their opinions.

Conflict of interest was cited as a primary factor in a survey taken in the USA in 2000 showing that brokers overwhelmingly gave glowing recommendations on shares ('strong buy,' 'buy,' and 'market outperform'). The survey noticed only an outright 'sell' recommendation in less than 1 per cent of all the recommendations that it reviewed, even though 2000 witnessed crashing prices in most of the popular shares that were analysed. Analysts, no matter how objective they may sound, are still employees of companies that make money from the same companies that the analysts analyse.

In fact, you should be wary of analysts' views, especially the analysts who make positive recommendations even when the company in question has worrisome features, such as no income and tremendous debt. It seems like a paradox: Sell a share when all the pros say to buy it? How can that be? Remember, the merits of any share should speak for themselves. When a company is losing money, all the great recommendations in the world can't reverse its fortunes. Also, keep in mind that if everybody is buying a particular share – the current analysts' favourite – who's left to buy it? When it turns out to be a dud, you aren't able to sell it because all the other suckers already own it (thanks to analysts' recommendations). And, if they already own it, they're probably already aware of the company's flaws. What happens then? You got it: More and more people end up selling it. When more people are selling than buying a share, its price declines.

Insider Selling

Heavy insider selling is to a company's shares what garlic, sunrises, and crosses are to vampires: an almost certain sign of doom! If you notice that increasing numbers of insiders (such as the chairman of the company, the finance director, and the chief executive, for instance) are selling their holdings, you can consider it a red flag. In recent years, massive insider selling has become a telltale sign of a company's imminent fall from grace. After all, who better to know the company's prospects for success (or lack of) than the company's high-level management? What management does (selling shares, for example) speaks louder than what management says. (Do you hear that loud and persistent coughing again?) For more information on insider trading, see Chapter 19.

Dividend Cuts

For investors who own income shares, dividends are the primary consideration. But, income shares or not, dividend cuts are a negative sign. Of course, if a company is having modest financial difficulty, perhaps a dividend cut is a good thing for the overall health of the company. However, usually analysts see a dividend cut as a sign that a company is having trouble with its earnings or cash flow. In either case, a dividend cut is a warning sign that trouble may be brewing for the firm as it becomes . . . uh . . . less firm.

If the company you own shares in announces a dividend cut, find out why. The cut may be simply a temporary measure to help the company out of some minor financial difficulty, or it may be a sign of deeper trouble. Check the company's fundamentals and then decide. (Refer to Chapter 11 to find out how to read and interpret company financial documents.)

Increased Negative Coverage

You may easily recognise unfavourable reports of a company's shares as a sign to unload them. Or you may be a contrarian and see bad press as an opportunity to scoop up some shares in a company victimised by negative reporting. In any case, take the negative reports as a signal to further investigate the merits of holding on to the shares or as a sign for selling it so that you can make room in your portfolio for a more promising choice of shares.

Industry Problems

Sometimes being a strong company doesn't matter if that company's industry is having problems; if the industry is in trouble, the company's decline probably isn't that far behind. Tighten up those trailing stops. (See Chapter 17 to find out how.) Also, try to be aware of industries that are intimately related to your industry. Very often, problems in one industry can affect or spread to a related industry. If car sales are plummeting (for example), then that's likely to have a negative effect on prospects for car parts or car servicing companies.

Political Problems

Political considerations are always a factor in investing. Be it taxes, regulations, or other government actions, politics can easily break a company and send its shares plummeting. If your company's shares are sensitive to political developments, be aware of potential political pitfalls for your choice of company(or industry). Reading *The Financial Times* and regularly viewing major financial Web sites can help you stay informed. (We give you lists of sources in Appendix A.) In recent years, drug and tobacco shares in general suffered because of prevailing political attitudes. Also, certain shares in particular (Microsoft in the late 1990s comes to mind) have seen their share prices drop drastically because they were targets of government actions for reasons ranging from antitrust concerns to public safety issues.

Debt Is Too High or Unsustainable

Excessive debt is the kiss of death for a struggling company. Record numbers of companies are going bankrupt through debt, including companies that experts thought were invincible.

The most obvious example is Enron. Many analysts and investment advisory publications actually touted Enron as a strong buy – even though the amount of problematic data could have made Godzilla gag. Not many investors get a kick out of reading old issues of financial magazines that listed the defunct company the year before its demise as one of ten shares 'for the long haul!' Blimey. Writers like that end up getting hobbies like hang-gliding during hurricane season. Chapter 11 and Appendix B can help you read and understand a company's financial data clearly so that you can make an informed decision about buying or selling its shares.

Funny Accounting: No Laughing Here!

Throughout this book, we discuss the topic of accounting as an important way to see how well (or how poorly) a company is doing. Understanding a company's balance sheet and income statement, and making a simple comparison of these documents over a period of several years, can give you great insights into the company's prospects. You don't have to be an accountant to grasp key concepts. Enron is a perfect example of how you can avoid an investing disaster with some rudimentary knowledge of accounting.

Despite the fact that Enron hid many of its financial problems from public view, the information that was available made the message clear: 'Houston, we have a problem!' If investors had done some simple homework, they would have plainly seen the following revealing points in 2000, over a year and a half before the collapse:

- ✔ **Enron's price to earnings (P/E) ratio hit 90 in 2000.** This stratospheric P/E kept most value investors (including Paul) away. (See Chapter 10 for more information on P/E ratios.)

- ✔ **Its price to book (P/B) ratio hit 12.** For investors, this ratio meant that the market value of the company, compared to the company's book value (also called ''accounting value''), was 12 to 1 – for every $12 of market value, investors were getting only $1 in book value. When you consider that a P/B ratio of 3 or 4 is considered nosebleed territory for value investors, you can see that Enron's P/B ratio was screaming, 'Watch out below!'

- ✔ **The price to sales (P/S) ratio hit an incredible 22.** This ratio means that investors paid $22 in market value for every $1 of sales the company generated. When a P/S of 5 or 10 is considered too high, 22 is nosebleed territory!

Paul found this information in public filings that anyone could have seen. To understand these points more fully (along with other equally incisive and lucid accounting and financial points), and to know how to use the information to avoid similar mistakes in the future, see Chapters 10 and 11 and Appendix B.

For more info on understanding the detail of company documents, check out *Interpreting Company Reports For Dummies*, by Ken Langdon, Alan Bonham and Lita Epstein (Wiley).

Chapter 22

Ten Signals of a Share Price Increase

*I*f you find a share that has all ten signals listed in this chapter, back up the truck and load up. The odds are that you won't need all ten to indicate that it's a share worth a closer look. Probably five or more signals are enough to merit further consideration. In any case, the more signals, the better your chances of choosing a winning share.

Regardless of market conditions and investor sentiment (how investors 'feel' about shares and the economy), remember the three rules of investment success: profits, profits, profits, also known as earnings, earnings, earnings. This advice is as important as property's location, location, location. It's that important . . .uh . . . important, important.

Rise in Earnings

If a company earned £1 per share for the past three years and its earnings are now £1.20 per share (a 20 per cent increase), consider this increase a positive harbinger. As the saying goes, 'Earnings drive the market,' so you need to pay attention to the company's profitability. The more a company makes, the greater the chance that its share price will increase.

Some people wonder whether to invest in a company that was losing money and then finally turns a profit. Perhaps you're considering shares in a company involved in new, untested technology. Our advice is that you need to be careful in this situation. In such a case, predicting whether a second year of profits will show up is hard, but of course, that's what investors are hoping.

For the serious investor, a track record of positive earnings is important. Several years of earnings (especially growing earnings) are crucial in the decision-making process. As earnings rise, make sure that the growth is at a rate of 10 per cent or higher.

Say that you're looking at the company Buckets-o-Money, . (BOM). BOM had earnings of £1 per share in 2004, £1.10 in 2005, and £1.21 in 2006. First, you can see that the company is a profitable enterprise. Second (and more importantly), you can see that the earnings grew 10 per cent each year. The fact that earnings grew consistently year after year is important because it indicates that the company is being managed well. Effective company management has a very positive effect on the share price as the market notices the company's progress.

Growing earnings are important for another reason – inflation. If a company earns £1 per share in each year, that's of course better than earning less or losing money. But inflation erodes the purchasing power of money. If earnings stay constant, the company's ability to grow decreases, because the value of its money will decline as a result of inflation.

Increase in Assets as Debts Are Stable or Decreasing

Increasing assets while decreasing debts (or at least stabilising them) is key to growing the book value of a company. *Book value* refers to the company's value as it appears on a balance sheet – equal to total assets minus liabilities. Book value usually differs significantly from market value (or market capitalisation) because market value is based on supply and demand of the company's shares in the marketplace. For example, a company may have a book value of £10 million (assets of £15 million less liabilities of £5 million) but a market value of £19 million (if, for example, it has 1 million shares that are currently trading at £19 per share). Usually, market value is higher (sometimes much higher) than book value.

Rising book value has a positive impact on market value, which, in turn, tends to drive the share price up as well. Therefore, it pays to watch book value. Rising book value can be accomplished in one of two basic ways:

- Debt stays level as assets rise
- Assets stay level as debts decline

When looking at a company's assets and debts, the best scenario you can find is assets rising and debts declining.

At the most basic level, total assets should exceed total debt. Preferably, the company should have a ratio of at least 2-to-1 or better in terms of assets to debt. A ratio of 3-to-1 is better, and so on. The less debt, the better.

The best way to figure out a company's asset to debt ratio is to look at the company's most recent balance sheet and compare it to its balance sheet from prior periods (such as the year before or the same quarter last year). By comparing the figures over three or more years, you can see a trend developing. If the asset to debt ratio has been stable or improving over these three balance sheets, the company is showing growing financial strength, which will help the company's share price increase in value.

Positive Publicity for Industry

When the media report that a company is doing well financially or that its products and services are being well received by both the media and the market, that news lets you know that this company's shares may be going places. This positive publicity ties in nicely with the other point made in this chapter about consumer acceptance for the company's products and services.

Positive press and consumer acceptance are important because they mean that the company is doing what's necessary to please its customers. The positive media coverage also may attract new customers to the company. Gaining customers means more sales and more earnings, which translates into a higher price for the shares. You can find corporate publicity on individual company Web sites and on the RNS (Regulatory News Service) run by the London Stock Exchange at `www.londonstockexchange.com`. Companies can also pay for their announcements to be flagged by the *Financial Times* on `www.ft.com/announce`.

Heavy Insider or Corporate Buying

Company insiders (such as the chief executive and the finance director) know better than anyone else about the health of a company. If insiders are buying shares by the boatload, then these purchases are certainly a positive sign for investors. Chapter 19 thoroughly covers insider trading, but I highlight the main points here. Insiders can do one of two things:

- ✔ **Buy shares for themselves:** If individuals such as the chief executive or the finance director are buying shares for their personal portfolios, you can assume that they think the shares are a good investment.

- ✔ **Buy shares as a corporate decision:** When the corporation buys its own shares, it's usually considered a positive move. The corporation may see its own shares as a good investment. Additionally, corporate share buy-backs reduce the number of shares available in the market, potentially pushing the share price higher.

All things being equal, either one should have a positive impact on the share price. The odds are that you won't see a stampede of insiders buying the shares in a day or week, but you will see it over a period of months. This is generally true simply because each insider has different circumstances, and insider buying is usually done on an individual basis. An accumulation of purchases tells you that members of the management team believe so strongly that the company will do well that they're willing to put their own money at risk.

More Attention from Analysts

During 2000-2002, analysts were criticised for being zealously optimistic about shares. We usually don't advise people to invest (or not invest) because of analysts' views, but they're important nonetheless. Many good analyst reviews, and the public's opinion of a single influential analyst, can make a share's price move dramatically.

Analyse a share according to its own merits first. Then watch the share's price as more and more analysts start to direct the public's attention to it. In a sense, they're promoting your shares, an action that tends to boost the share's price. Don't let the analyst's views sway you, though, because analysts may tout a share for unsavory reasons. Perhaps the company is a client of the brokerage firm, or maybe the brokerage firm owns a lot of the company's shares and wants to unload them. Analysts have to declare interests such as these if they have them.

Rumours of Takeover Bids

I never want anyone to base an investment decision on a rumour of a takeover bid, but it doesn't hurt if you were considering the shares anyway – basing your decision on a variety of other solid factors, of course, such as strong fundamentals, earnings growth, popular products or services, and so on. A company that's rumoured to be a takeover candidate (a company that may be potentially bought out by another company) may have an attractive aspect, such as a promising new patent or exclusive rights to certain properties, that could make it worthy for investors as well.

Rumours of a buyout are always welcome, but the bottom line is that it should alert you to a good value. Regardless of whether the buyout rumour proves true, you shouldn't even consider the shares if they aren't worth owning on their own merits. If it's a good company, the rumour tends to increase its visibility so that the chances of a takeover do, in fact, increase. Rumour or not, the attention does tend to increase the share price.

Praise from Consumer Groups

A company is only as good as the profit it generates. The profit it generates is only as good as the revenues that the company generates. The revenues are based on whether customers are accepting (and shelling out money for) the company's products or services. Therefore, if what the company offers is popular with consumers, it bodes well for profits and consequently higher share prices.

When you're ready to invest in shares, look for high consumer satisfaction. Review consumer publications and Web sites and read the surveys and consumer feedback information. Good publicity and word-of-mouth consumer satisfaction are things that investors should be aware of. Share-picking expert Peter Lynch (formerly of Fidelity Magellan fund fame) sees this popularity with consumers as very valuable share-picking information. He likes to see what consumers buy because that's where the company's success starts.

Strong or Improving Bond Rating

In Chapter 9, we point out that a poor or deteriorating bond rating is a warning sign for the company. The creditworthiness of a company is a critical factor in determining the company's strength. Most people presume that the bond rating is primarily beneficial for bond investors, and they're correct. However, because the bond rating is assigned according to the company's ability to pay back the bond plus interest, it stands to reason that a strong bond rating (usually a rating of AAA or AA) indicates that the company is financially strong.

The work of independent bond rating firms, such as Standard & Poor's and Moody's, is invaluable for investors in shares. For more about bond ratings, turn to Chapter 9.

Powerful Demographics

If you know that a company generates lots of profit from the teenage market and you find out that the teenage market is going to expand by 10 per cent per year for the foreseeable future, what would you do? Exactly – you'd buy shares in that company. If a company has strong fundamentals and appealing products or services and its market is expanding, that company has a winning combination.

Stay alert to growing trends in society. How are demographics changing? Which sectors of the population are growing? Shrinking? What shifts are expected in society in terms of age or ethnicity? Check out the data freely available at the Office of National Statistics. You can simply call up with a query or check out the latest census – taken in 2001 – at www.statistics.gov.uk/census.

For instance, the statistics show that people are living longer. Companies that aim their products and services at elderly consumers are increasing their earnings. Saga, founded by the son of a shoe factory worker from London's east end, has grown from a firm selling short breaks to the over 50s to a 'grey giant' selling insurance and travel services. It was bought by venture capitalists in October 2004 for £1.7 billion. In 2007 their investment was shown to be a sound one when motoring organisation the AA bought Saga in a deal which valued it at just under £3 billion.

A market that's growing in size isn't an indicator all by itself (in fact, no indicator gives you the green light all by itself anyway), but it should alert you to do some research. The fact that a strong company sees improving demographic shifts in its marketplace is a big plus.

Low P/E Relative to Industry or Market

The price to earnings (P/E) ratio is a critical number for investors. Value investors in particular scrutinise it. Because the share price's future ability to rise is ultimately tied to the company's earnings (profits), you want to know that you're not paying too much for the shares. A low P/E ratio (low relative to some standard, such as the industry's average or the average P/E for the S&P 500) is generally considered safe, and the shares are a potential bargain.

If the industry's P/E ratio is 20 and you're looking at a share that has a P/E of 15, all things being equal, that's great. The company has room for growth, and you are getting good value.

Chapter 23

Ten Ways to Protect Yourself from Fraud

· ·

In This Chapter

▶ Looking to the FSA for help

▶ Adopting a skeptical attitude

▶ Steering clear of scams

· ·

Making money is tough enough without worrying about who is out to get your cash. The usual suspects, such as the HMRC and other government agencies, are trying to take your money legally. Fortunately, most of that money goes to apparently beneficial pursuits. However, others are out to take your money by illegal methods. Fraud and theft schemes have always been there. Scammers are most prevalent during two economic conditions: When times are really, really good and when times are really, really bad. During the Great Depression, and a manic bull market alike, fraudsters were part of the human condition. Bottom line: Be alert and use the tips in this chapter to avoid being scammed.

Be Wary of Unsolicited Calls and E-mails

Phone calls or e-mails out of the blue to solicit money from you are always a bit questionable, but if they offer investments, you need to be particularly careful. But you knew that, right? You've read countless consumer reports warning you about investing via call centres and bogus emails. If the investment that's being pitched is so good, why is someone calling to sell you on it? Hasn't the financial press reported it? It probably has, but only as a warning to turn down any such offers. Find out more at Web sites such as www.scambusters.co.uk and www.thisismoney.co.uk.

Get to Know the FSA

Long before you invest your first pound, whether in shares or any other financial investment, get to know the Financial Services Authority (FSA). It's there primarily to protect investors from fraud and other unlawful activity designed to fleece them. The UK government created the FSA during the late 1990s to bring together several organisations that regulated different types of financial transactions and the people who carried them out. The aim of the FSA was to crack down on abuses that harmed consumers and the reputation of financial services companies.

The FSA has an excellent Web site at www.FSA.gov.uk The site offers plenty of great articles and resources for both novice and experienced investors to help you watch out for fraud and better understand the financial markets and how they work. You can call the FSA to ask if any broker or company you are dealing with is regulated and if any action has been taken against them. The FSA carries on a number of activities designed to help you invest with confidence. If it has penalised a company for regulatory failures it makes the sanction or fine public. And it maintains a database on file about fines levied against brokers and companies that have committed fraud or other abuses against the investing public.

Your tax pays for this important agency. Find out about its free publications, services, and resources before you invest. If you've already been victimised by unscrupulous operators, call the FSA for assistance and advice.

Don't Invest If You Don't Understand

Investments frequently can come in complicated forms that promise a great return but can be hard to understand. The premise of the investment – how it works and how it will create a great return on your money – may be hard to figure out. Scammers count on people being overwhelmed by the details to the point that they ignore the mechanics of the deal. Don't fall for such approaches. You should understand exactly what you're investing in, how it makes money, and what the risks are. If you still can't understand the investment (even if it's legitimate), then you're better off not plunging in with your hard-earned money.

If the investment still sounds intriguing, then at the very least get a second opinion by reviewing the details with advisors you trust.

Question the Promise of Extraordinary Returns

In good times and bad, people want to make as much money as possible with their investments. Hey, who doesn't? If your money is in a bank account earning a paltry 2 per cent, what's wrong with putting some of it into some investment earning 17 per cent compounded hourly? The extraordinary returns promised either end up being illusory or the result of great risk.

Misrepresenting or inflating promises of a great return on your money is common; sometimes even good brokers can unwittingly make them. Higher returns mean more exposure to loss.

If the investment is bona fide and is quoted as having a high rate of return (either in income or capital gains potential), then you can expect commensurate risk. The risk may not be immediately apparent, but it's there. As the broken record that we are in this chapter, we recommend that you seek independent third parties for an informed second opinion. Appendix A has an extensive list of places and people to turn to.

A notable investment pro once remarked, 'Sometimes, a return *on* your money is not as important as a return *of* your money.' In other words, until you pick up more investing knowledge, keeping your original investment safe is better than risking it for questionable, pie-in-the-sky promises.

Verify the Investment

If anyone asks you to invest, first verify that the investment exists. Sounds weird, huh? Not really. Yes, many people have lost money in a bad or dubious investment, but you'd be surprised at how many people have been willing to fork over hard-earned money for phantom investments.

Most share investment scams are perpetrated by so-called boiler rooms. This is a set up which appears to be legit but which exists solely to dupe hapless – a probably greedy – punters from their money. Most are sold over the phone but increasingly e-mails are being used to push these dodgy investment 'opportunities'.

When someone offers you an investment and you're not certain what type of investment it is or where it's traded, ask questions of the person presenting the investment and of third parties who can offer verification. Here are some questions to ask:

- ✔ What exchange or market is this investment traded or sold on?

- ✔ What government agency oversees this investment, and how can I contact that agency?

- ✔ Have articles on this investment been published by major media sources, such as *The Financial Times* and *Investor's Chronicle* magazine?

- ✔ Can I find documents filed by this company on RNS – Regulatory News Service – or one of the other approved services.

- ✔ What literature do I have that I can present to my accountant and lawyer, if I need to?

Check Out the Broker

Sometimes the investment is legitimate, but the broker or dealer isn't. Scammers don't let the absence of a licence stop them. When an unfamiliar financial products marketer contacts you, do some homework first. Contact one of the following to check the status of a broker or dealer:

- ✔ **The FSA:** Are these marketers properly registered? The FSA can inform you about whether these marketers have been penalised or banned from further activity.

- ✔ **Professional associations:** Do you want to know whether a marketer is a member in good standing? Associations help the public deal with unethical parties in the industry.

- ✔ **The London Stock Exchange (LSE):** Visit its great Web site at www.londonstockexchange.com. This site informs the public about the stockbrokers who are members of the exchange.

Beware of the Pump-and-Dump

The pump-and-dump is a classic scam that usually shows up in bull markets. The scam works best with small-cap or (even better) penny shares – in other words, small companies that have relatively few shares or small capitalisation. Scams are at their most effective when they can play on the two most overworked emotions in the financial markets: greed and fear. In the pump-and-dump, greed is the operative emotion. In this example, the investor to be plucked is called Jim Nicebutdim (no relation to the popular comic character Tim Nicebutdim).

The insiders at the dubious company first try to promote the shares as a 'hot investment.' The company activates the 'pump' when insiders and/or a stock-broker, in cahoots with the insiders, call up investors such as Mr Nicebutdim to tout this fantastic opportunity. They promise an opportunity to get into a profitable share that will skyrocket in value. As a result of the high-pressure sales tactics, investors start buying the shares. This demand pushes up the price easily because so few shares are available on this thinly-traded company. Perhaps Mr Nicebutdim didn't bite the first time the broker called, but the broker calls again.

'Hello again, Mr Nicebutdim! This is Barry Kuda, account representative from the brokerage firm of Fleecem & Scarper. Do you remember that share investment I brought to your attention last week? That's right . . . Titanic Bio-Tech, Inc. Have you seen the way its price has zoomed since then? When I last spoke to you, it was at £3 a share. Now it's already at £47! Our respected research department tells me it should be at £93 by lunchtime and will probably triple again before the weekend. You don't want to miss this opportunity of a lifetime! Now how many shares would you like?'

Indeed, the price certainly went up dramatically as Mr Kuda said it would. Mr Nicebutdim puts the order in immediately while pound signs dance in his head. The 'pump' is working very well. After the fraudulent operators see that the share has gone as high as possible, they immediately sell their shares at grossly inflated prices. The 'dump' is complete, and they disappear into the woodwork. Mr Nicebutdim and the other investors watch as their 'hot' investment turns stone cold and the shares plummet to pennies in the pound. Investors were so blinded by their greed that the pump-and-dump scam has successfully been done even in cases when no shares existed at all!

How can I do a warning about something legal in a chapter about fraud? Actually, isn't this entire chapter a warning? Yes, but sometimes you need a warning for things that aren't immediately apparent. As odd as this sounds, I want to warn you about something that technically isn't fraud. What is it? Well, a legal version of the pump-and-dump scheme does exist. It's not unusual for brokers and analysts to 'pump' up a share in the media. For example, a celebrated market strategist or high-profile CEO may talk up the wonderful potential of XYZ shares on a financial show. Then later you find out (through RNS filings, for instance) that while these people were recommending that people buy the shares, they had actually been furtively selling their holdings in the shares! You were hearing 'buy, buy', yet they were really saying 'bye-bye'.

Watch Out for Short-and-Abort

Short-and-abort works on the same premise as pump-and-dump. The difference is that instead of playing on the greed emotion, the con works on the fear emotion. To understand this scam, you should keep in mind that one can profit even when a share falls in price by 'going short.' Chapter 17 goes into detail about making money from going short on shares, but here I want to briefly describe it.

Going short is a strategy that an investor can use in a margin account with a broker. An investor may consider going short on a share if she expects the share's price to fall. Say that you think the shares of the company Plummet PLC. (at £50 per share) will sink fast. When you tell the broker that you want to go short on 100 shares of Plummet PLC., the broker borrows 100 shares from the market, sells those shares, and credits £5,000 to your account (100 shares at £50 per share). Because this transaction is based on 'borrowed shares' , sooner or later you have to return the shares. Say that the share price falls to £30; you could then instruct your broker to 'close out the position'. This order means that the broker debits your account for £3,000 (to buy 100 shares at £30) and returns the shares to the source. In this case, you make a £2,000 profit (the original £5,000 less the £3,000).

In the case of short-and-abort, the scammers want to make money from a share's plummeting price. They may contact shareholders directly or plant phoney stories or press releases in the media to cause concern and panic over a company's prospects. Naturally, shareholders in that particular company get anxious over their investment and decide to sell. The sudden, mass selling causes the share's price to fall. The scammer then closes out the short position, takes the money, and runs.

Remember That Talk Is Cheap (Until You Talk to an Expert)

A fertile area for misleading investors is in the world of independent, third-party information sources. As the bull market reached its zenith in late 1999, some people were selling expensive share-investing seminars and newsletters that promised get-rich-quick results. One promoter in the US sold basic information (some of which was inaccurate) in a £5,000 seminar program. After many complaints, the authorities investigated and found out that the presenters made a lot of money from their seminars, but they actually lost money on their investment strategies! (It figures.)

Another information marketer published an expensive newsletter that promised lucrative share picks. It was discovered that he wasn't recommending shares found through diligent and honest research; but recommended shares which companies had paid him to tout.

Seminars and newsletters are excellent sources of information and expertise on a given topic, but you should stay away from marketers that use hard-sell approaches for outrageously priced seminars and other information products. If you're considering expensive seminars and information products, check with such sources as `www.fool.co.uk` and its online message board for any complaints.

Recovering (If You Do Get Scammed)

If, despite your best efforts to invest wisely, you have that sinking feeling that you've been conned, it's time to gain assistance from the authorities. The FSA is a good place to start, but you can turn to other agencies, too.

If a scheme was promoted by phone, especially on a premium rate line, you can contact ICSTIS the regulatory body for the premium rate telecommunications industry. It has the power to fine companies abusing premium phone lines or supplying misleading content. See `www.icstis.org.uk` for more information,

Local trading standards offices will always be interested to hear of scams being carried out in their areas. You can also contact the Office of Fair Trading (`www.oft.gov.uk`) if you think issue is more than a local one. See Appendix A for more resources.

Chapter 24

Ten Challenges and Opportunities for Stock Market Investors

. . . .

In This Chapter

▶ The most pressing concerns for stock market investors

▶ Other markets that can affect shares

▶ The big picture and shares

▶ Hidden opportunities with new economic megatrends

. . . .

*O*ver the years, we have found that the easiest way to make money with shares (or the easiest way to avoid losing money on shares) was to simply be aware of the economic environment in which they operate. Shares can be the best (or worst) investment given the economic/political environment. There are many economic challenges facing the stock market and they include what is happening with government policy, societal trends, and national/international geopolitical conditions. You need to be aware of 'The big picture' by staying in touch with the news and regularly checking in with great Web sites such as Breaking Views (www.breakingviews.com), Bloomberg (www.bloomberg.co.uk), and the Mises Institute (www.mises.org). See Appendix A for more resources.

In this chapter, I discuss the most important issues or megatrends that can affect you and your loved ones as well as your share investments.

Debt, Debt, and More Debt

In early 2007, the United Kingdom's Gross Domestic Product (GDP) topped the £305 billion mark. Great! However, the total level of debt in the country hit £1.2 trillion. Ugh . . . NOT great. What has kept the economy afloat and 'growing' during the past eight to ten years has been massive and pervasive debt that must be dealt with. Debt in just about every category is at record levels. This includes mortgage, consumer, margin and corporatedebt. The problem is that this debt must be either paid off or wiped out through bankruptcy. Either one will have its negative consequences for the economy. Either one can do great harm to shares in general and/or your portfolio in particular.

Make sure that you are dealing with your debt level now. Reduce it as much as possible and make sure that you are analyzing your shares in the same light. Companies that carry too much debt will be at great risk. If the company sinks, your shares will follow. If the company goes into bankruptcy, your share's value will be vaporised.

If you want to see something fascinating (and scary at the same time), check out the total debt figures which are regularly reported in the press and listed on Web sites such as the National Statistics site at www.statistics.gov. uk. Charities such as Citizens Advice and Consumer Credit Counselling Service are constantly warning of the dangers of too much debt. It is sobering stuff!

Derivatives

Deriv . . . what? You might say 'what the hell are they?' unless, of course, you're a vicar. Derivatives are the largest financial market in the world. As of November 2006, the total dollar value of the global market hit $370 trillion. It easily dwarfs the world economy. Easily! Now, you don't have to understand them but you should be aware of what could go wrong if a derivatives problem occurs. The once-mighty Enron imploded very quickly primarily due to tragic errors in their derivatives portfolio. Derivatives 'accidents' such as the collapse of Barings Bank have dotted the financial landscape over the past 10 to 15 years and they had (and will continue to have) the potential to do major damage to the stock market.

There's no use fretting about derivatives. While you're at it, you might as well worry about falling meteors, electoral campaigns, and the chance you might get Ozzy Osbourne as your neighbour. Just take common sense approaches to protect your portfolio as you grow your wealth. Look into diversifying, trailing stops, and myriad strategies throughout this book and in the resources cited.

Property

In much the same way that everyone was enamoured with shares a few years ago, the same is true with property circa 2007. The property mania has turned into a dangerous bubble and it is an ominous development for the economy and yes . . . shares. The expansion of the money supply, excessive credit and debt growth, and the lowering of lending standards have acted like rocket fuel for the residential and commercial property markets causing prices to rise beyond reasonable market value. Millions of homeowners, investors, and speculators could be adversely affected. And listen, we're not just talking about property owners. The tentacles of the housing bubble reach far beyond bricks and mortar. Mortgages in the billions have been packaged and resold as securities and purchased by many funds, insurance companies, Fortune 500 companies, and pension plans. Because a huge chunk of these are *sub-prime* (risky) debt, that means huge problems as interest rates rise, the economy sags, and so on.

The message to you is clear: Make sure you have your mortgage under control and your debt at manageable levels. Make sure that you avoid shares in companies that are overly exposed to what could be a bubble to dwarf the dot.com bubble of 1998-2002.

Inflation

The last time inflation was a major problem was the late 1990s and . . . you guessed it . . . the market was having a rough time. Interest rates soared to close to 10 per cent and it was economic headaches for everyone. Although inflation was generally tamed during the 90s, it is showing renewed life during this decade. The *Consumer Prices Index* (CPI) is one of several indices used by the Office of National Statistics to measure our daily cost of living. It is worth paying close attention to this data when it is released each month because the release that comes with the headline figure breaks down inflation into industry sectors. The Retail Prices Index, also worth watching, is quoted in two forms: Including mortgage costs and excluding them. The difference that including mortgage costs can make may surprise you – another sign of the power of debt!

For share investors, inflation shows that having your money grows is more important than ever. Understanding the pernicious effects of inflation should be factored into your share choices. Some shares are more likely to suffer (mortgage companies with fixed-debt portfolios) while others (precious metals mining companies) are more likely to prosper.

Pension Crisis

You've seen all the headlines: 'Pensions black hole', 'Pension crisis means we must work til we drop', 'People are living longer lives', 'People are not saving enough for retirement.' Many governments and large companies will experience shortfalls in their financial ability to meet retirement plan obligations. Millions of people will, at the very least, not get as much as they expect when they retire. We've already seen thousands of workers left without any pensions when their companies went bust. And although the Financial Assistance Scheme is now in place to help pay minimum pensions when this happens in future, many pensioners will still suffer serious hardship.. Action by companies to plug the deficits in their pension schemes has made a big difference and the stock market has played its part. According to actuaries at accountants Deloitte, the combined final salary pension scheme deficits of FTSE 100 companies was £21 billion in March this year. This might sound a lot but it was the lowest deficit for five years. Only a month before when the stock market took a tumble the deficit jumped by another £20 billion. This is not just a UK issue: America, Europe, Japan, and even China are in the same (or worse!) predicament.

The message is clear: People need to save and invest more to fill in the financial gaps that seem to be inevitable. Shares are wealth-building tools well suited to long-term needs such as your retirement concerns. Start now because the future has a way of sneaking up on you faster than you think.

Government's Unfunded Liabilities

Social Security and the National Health Service are certain to be gigantic challenges during the next few decades. In 2007-2008, the UK government estimates that it will spend £100 billion on healthcare. Governments in the future will face rising pressure to curb spending on healthcare and get the patients (you and me) to foot the bill themselves. There are already calls to restrict access to the most expensive treatments to those who are 'responsible' for their illnesses – perhaps because they smoke or have a wild lifestyle. Benefits paid to those who have low incomes are also likely to be further restricted in future. And there is always the chance that state pensions will be limited in future. Current beneficiaries will probably not be affected, but anyone under 65 may well be. Let's face it: We're living longer than ever before and we will need to be more proactive about our personal responsibility in our senior years. To find out more, review your rights and responsibilities with the Department of Works and Pensions (www.dwp.gov.uk).

Recession and Depression

History tells us that share investing during a recession or depression is best avoided. Declines in economic growth always follow artificial economic booms.

In this decade, the likelihood of a recession or depression is remarkably high due to the fact that economic problems and imbalances (such as debt, the housing bubble, and so on) need to be addressed, and that means a significant downturn. Become more aware about economics and how it operates. Find out more at reader-friendly sites such as Motley Fool (www.fool.co.uk). In rough economic times, the best shares are defensive (food and drink, utilities, and so on) because people will buy these things no matter how good or bad the economy is. Cyclical shares will get beaten down so it might be a good idea to shop around for real value after the economy turns around. In the meanwhile, play it safe and protect your money with solid, financially sound companies and deploy protective strategies with your money.

Commodities

A shrewd man once said, 'History may not repeat but it can often rhyme' (Okay, it was Paul!). In many respects, part of this decade has resembled the 1970s. Shares were having a dreadful time as inflation, the energy crisis, and international tensions escalated. However, it was a great time to invest in energy, precious metals, and commodities. Gold and silver hit all-time highs by the end of the decade. Share investors that scooped up shares of companies in these specific industries racked up tremendous gains. The lesson for us to understand is that conditions in this decade offer opportunities in natural resources that mirror the late 1970s. In addition, China and India are growing and they will need more commodities (grains, base metals, energy, water, and so on) for their expanding economies and populations.

As demand continues to outpace supply, the shares of companies that provide products and services in natural resources will shine.

Energy

The world's appetite for energy (oil, gas, and so on) has caused prices to hit record highs, and the coming years promise more demand. The energy markets have seen a sea of change that makes current conditions far more different and more serious than we've seen in recent decades. We have entered the age of 'Peak Oil' (see more about this at www.peakoil.net), which means that cheap and readily available energy is a thing of the past. In 2006, oil topped $72 per barrel and petrol prices moved close to £1 a litre at the pumps across the country. All of a sudden, $100 oil and petrol at more than £1 a litre doesn't seem so far-fetched. Supply and demand is nowhere more evident than the world's energy market.

For share investors, this at least means the chance to grow your money both directly (energy companies, obviously) and indirectly (alternative energy companies). If we want our wealth to grow, then we need to understand the impact that energy will have on our portfolios. To get some excellent information on the energy sector, try a resource such as Doug Casey's Energy Speculator (www.caseyresearch.com). For more information, check out Chapter 13. Also look out for initiatives which help companies become *carbon neutral* – reducing and offsetting their carbon emissions – because this is one of the biggest trends in business at the moment.

Dangers from Out of the Blue

Blimey, after being beaten up by the previous nine points, what else is needed? Investing in shares is a brave, new world fraught with dangers for the clueless, but filled with wealth-building opportunities for the 'clued in.' The fact is that no one knows what will hit our economy and society from out of the blue. Events such as 9/11, the tsunami in Asia, Hurricane Katrina, and the London bombings of July 7 certainly tell us the world has unseen perils for us and our prosperity. The point is that terrorism and other factors will have an impact. Fortunately, you can make changes . . . even slight changes . . . that can protect or grow your wealth.

Whether you're talking about healthcare shares that boom in response to new health threats or concerns (bird flu, and so on) or shares in companies that prosper due to security issues, your share investing programme can survive and thrive. Stay informed and understand that successful share investing doesn't happen in a vacuum.

Part VI
Appendixes

"You want to see Mr. Pargeter about your investments — I'm afraid he's just left the building."

In this part . . .

Check out the appendixes for resources that aid you in making informed investment decisions. Whether the topic is share investing terminology, economics, or avoiding capital gains taxes, we include a treasure trove of resources for you. Whether you go to a bookshop, the library, or the Internet, Appendix A gives you some great places to turn to for help. In Appendix B, we explain financial ratios. These important numbers help you better determine whether to invest in a particular company's shares.

Appendix A

Resources for Investors in Shares

• •

*G*etting and staying informed is an ongoing priority for investors in shares. The lists in this appendix represent some the best information resources available.

Financial Planning Sources

To find a financial planner to help you with your general financial needs, contact the following organisations. Be sure to ask for a financial planner who specialises in investing.

Independent Financial Adviser Promotion (IFAP): 2nd Floor, 117 Farringdon Rd, London, EC1R 3BX. Tel: 0207 833 3131, Fax: 0207 833 3239, Web site: www.unbiased.co.uk.

The Institute of Financial Planning (IFP): Whitefriars Centre, Lewins Mead, Bristol BS1 2NT. Tel: 0117 945 2470, Fax: 0117 929 2214, Web site: www.financialplanning.org.uk

Association of Independent Financial Advisers (AIFA): 2-6 Austin Friars House, Austin Friars, London, EC2N 2HD. Technical help line: 020 7826 9048, General enquiries: 020 7628 1287, Web site: www.aifa.net.

The Language of Investing

The New Penguin Dictionary of Business: By Evan Davis, Paul Trott, Graham Bannock, and Mark D. Uncles. Published by Penguin Reference Books. A nicely laid out A-to-Z publication for investors mystified by financial terms. It explains the important investing and business terms you come across every day.

Investor Words: (www.investorwords.com) One of the most comprehensive sites on the Internet for beginning and intermediate investors for learning words and phrases unique to the financial world.

Investopedia: (www.investopedia.com):Another excellent site with plenty of information on investing for beginners and intermediate investors.

Textual Investment Resources

Share investment success is not an event; it's a process. The periodicals and magazines listed (along with their Web sites) have offered many years of guidance and information for investors, and they're still top-notch. The books and pamphlets provide much wisdom that is either timeless or timely (covering problems and concerns every investor should be aware of now).

Periodicals and magazines

These publications offer a wide range of news, analysis, and investment, whether online or in print. We give youbthe web addresses here to get you started.

Barron's: www.barrons.com

Forbes: www.forbes.com

Investor's Chronicle: www.investorschronicle.co.uk

Money Management: www.ftadviser.com

Moneywise: www.moneywise.co.uk

Investment Week: www.investmentweek.co.uk

The Financial Times: www.ft.com

Books and pamphlets

Austrian Economics for Investors by Mark Skousen, published by Pickering & Chatto Ltd.

The Financial Times Guide to Using the Financial Pages by Romesh Vaitlingam (Fifth edition), published by FT Prentice Hall

Guide to Analysing Companies by Bob Vause, published by Economist Books

How to Pick Stocks Like Warren Buffett: Profiting from the Bargain Hunting Strategies of the World's Greatest Value Investor by Timothy Vick, published by McGraw-Hill Professional Publishing

The Intelligent Investor: A Book of Practical Counsel by Benjamin Graham (preface by Warren Buffett), published by HarperCollins

Investments Made Clear: Guide from the Financial Services Authority (download), www.fsa.gov.uk, one of several publications providing basic information to help investors from the UK's financial watchdog.

Investor's Guide to Analysing Companies & Valuing Shares by Michael Cahill, published by FT Prentice Hall

The Investors Guide to Understanding Accounts, by Robert Leach, published by Harriman House Publishing

Magic Numbers for Stock Investors by Peter Temple, published by John Wiley & Sons, Ltd.

Online Stock Market Investing: The Definitive 20-Day Guide by Alexander Davidson, published by Kogan Page

Standard & Poor's Stock Guide (available in the library reference section) Ask your reference librarian about this excellent reference source, which gives one-page summaries on the major companies and has detailed financial reports on all companies listed on the New York Stock Exchange, American Stock Exchange, and major companies in Nasdaq

Special books of interest to share investors

These titles provide more in-depth information for Chapters 13 and 23.

Ethical Money: How to Invest in Sustainable Enterprises and Avoid the Polluters and Exploiters by John Hancock, published by Kogan Page

The Coming Crash in the Housing Market: 10 Things You Can Do Now to Protect Your Most Valuable Investment by John R. Talbott, published by McGraw-Hill

Bubbles and How to Survive Them by John P Calverley, published by Nicholas Brealey Publishing.

Hot Commodities: How Anyone Can Invest Profitably in the World's Best Market by Jim Rogers, published by Random House

Twilight in the Desert: The Coming Saudi Oil Shock and the World Economy, by Matthew R. Simmons, published by John Wiley & Sons, Inc.

Investing Web sites

How can any serious investor ignore the Internet? You can't and you shouldn't. The following are among the best information sources available.

General investing Web sites

Bloomberg www.bloomberg.com

Digital Look www.digitallook.co.uk

Breaking Views www.breakingviews.com

Motley Fool www.fool.co.uk

Stock investing Web sites

Advfn www.advfn.com

AIMQuoted.com www.aimquoted.com

Biospace.com www.biospace.com

Compeer www.compeer.co.uk

Economist www.economist.com

Global-investor.com www.global-investor.com

Interactive Investor www.iii.co.uk

Standard and Poor's www.standardandpoors.com

World Gold Council www.gold.org

Yahoo! Finance www.finance.yahoo.com

Investor Associations and Organisations

Financial Ombudsman Service: South Quay Plaza, 183 Marsh Wall, London, E14 9SR. Tel: 0207 964 1000 (switchboard); Web site: www.financial-ombudsman.org.uk

Financial Services Compensation Scheme: 7th floor, Lloyds Chambers, Portsoken Street, London E1 8BN Fax: 020 7892 7301; Web site: www.fscs.org.uk

The United Kingdom Shareholders Association (www.uksa.org.uk): Outspoken independent organisation representing private shareholders

Stock Exchanges

London Stock Exchange(and Alternative Investment Market): www.london stockexchange.com

Nasdaq: www.nasdaq.com

New York Stock Exchange: www.nyse.com

Ofex: www.plusmarkets.com

ShareMark: www.share.com/sharemark

Finding Brokers

The following sections offer both sources to help you evaluate brokers and an extensive list of brokers (Web sites and telephone numbers) so that you can do your own shopping.

Choosing brokers

Compeer (www.compeer.com): This firm is a specialist in competitor analysis and benchmarking. Its Private Client Stockbroking and Fund Management Survey is particularly useful.

Thisismoney (www.thisismoney.co.uk): Does a comprehensive review and comparison of stockbrokers pricing regularly.

Brokers

Abbey Sharedealing (www.abbeysharedealing.com): 0800 389 2324

Barclays Stockbrokers (www.barclays-stockbrokers.co.uk): 0845 601 7788

James Brearley & Sons (www.jbrearley.co.uk)

Cave & Sons Limited (www.caves.co.uk): 01604 621421

E*trade (www.uk.etrade.co): 0845 234 34 34

Fastrade (www.fastrade.co.uk): 0845 345 5922

Halifax (www.halifax.co.uk/sharedealing): 0870 242 5588

Hargreaves Lansdown (www.h-l.co.uk): 0845 345 0800

Hoodless Brennan (www.hoodlessbrennan.com): 0207 538 1166

iDealing (www.idealing.com): 0207 422 1685 or 07732 015 717

Norwich & Peterborough (www.npss.co.uk): 0151 242 3570

Redmayne Bentley (www.redmayne.co.uk): 0113 243 6941

The Share Centre (www.share.com): 01296 414141

TD Waterhouse (www.twdtrader.co.uk): 0845 607 6002

Virgin Money (www.virginmoney.com): 08456 021 501

Investment Sources

The following are fee-based subscription services. Many of them also offer excellent free e-mail newsletters tracking the stock market and related news.

Michael Walters (www.michaelwalters.com): Former Daily Mail journalist's share tipping news

Growth Company Investor (www.growthcompany.com): Tracks the fortunes of more than 2,000 companies in 10 issues each year.

Techinvest (www.techinvest.ie): Hi-tech stocks newsletter.

Red Hot Penny Shares (www.fleetstreetpublications.co.uk): Tip sheets for the adventurous.

Trendwatch: (www.trend-watch.co.uk)

Motley Fool: (www.fool.co.uk)

The Value Line Investment Survey (www.valueline.com): 800 654 0508

Dividend Reinvestment Plans

Lloyds Registrars (www.shareview.co.uk)

Motley Fool (www.fool.co.uk)

Sources for Analysis

The following sources give you the chance to look a little deeper at some critical aspects regarding stock analysis. Whether its earnings estimates and insider selling or a more insightful look at a particular industry, these sources are among my favorites.

Earnings and earnings estimates

Hemscott (www.hemscott.com)

Thomson Financial's First Call (www.firstcall.com)

Zacks Summary of Brokerage Research (www.zacks.com)

Industry analysis

Hoover's (www.hoovers.com)

Mergermarket (www.mergermarket.com)

Standard & Poor's (www.standardandpoors.com)

Factors that affect market value

Understanding basic economics is so vital to making your investment decisions that I had to include this section. These great sources have helped me understand 'the big picture' and what ultimately affects the stock market.

Economics and politics

The Bank of England (www.bankofengland.co.uk): *Note:* Learn how the Monetary Policy Committee decides on interest rates. This can give you a great insight into the predictions of the UK's foremost economists.

They Work for You (www.theyworkforyou.com)

Office for National Statistics (www.statistics.gov.uk): Here you will find all the numbers that count – from the government's official bean counters.

Securities and Exchange Commission (SEC) (www.sec.gov): The SEC has tremendous resources for investors who have shares in companies listed in theUSA. In addition to information on investing, the SEC also monitors the US financial markets for fraud and other abusive activities. For stock market investors, it also has EDGAR (Electronic Data Gathering, Analysis, and Retrieval system), which is a comprehensive, searchable database of public documents that are filed by public companies.

Changing laws

Go to any of these sites to find out about new and proposed laws. The on-site search engines will help you find the laws that are likely to affect your investments.

UK Government (www.direct.gov.uk): Find out what the government has been up to

10 Downing Street (www.number-10.co.uk)

House of Lords and House of Commons (www.publications. parliament.uk)

Technical analysis

Stock Charts (www.stockcharts.com)

Trader Tom (www.zanet.co.uk/tradertom)

UK Society of Technical Analysts (www.sta-uk.org)

Directors' sharedealing and other tips

Digital Look (www.digitallook.com)

Breaking Views (www.breakingviews.com)

T1ps.com (www.t1ps.com)

Michael Walters (www.michaelwalters.com)

Tax Benefits and Obligations

Some handy sites telling you what you have to pay, and giving you some advice on how to go about it.

HM Revenue & Customs (www.hmrc.gov.uk)

TaxationWeb (www.taxationweb.co.uk)

Grant Thornton (www.taxsolve.co.uk)

Tax café (www.taxcafe.co.uk)

Fraud

A selection of sites to help you ensure that no-one gets their hands on your money who shouldn't.

Financial Services Authority (www.fsa.gov.uk): Investing publications for consumers from the Consumer Information Center catalogue are available for downloading at this Web site at no charge.

Serious Fraud Office (www.sfo.gov.uk): Responsible for prosecuting cases of illegal insider dealing and other serious frauds.

The Fraud Advisory Panel (www.fraudadvisorypanel.org)

CIFAS (www.cifas.org.uk) The UK's Fraud Prevention Service

Cardwatch (www.cardwatch.org.uk)

Appendix B

Financial Ratios and Accounting Terms

• •

*A*s dull or cumbersome as the topic sounds, financial ratios are indeed the 'meat' of analysing shares. Sadly, most investors don't exercise their due diligence when it comes to doing some relatively easy things to make sure that the company they're investing in is a good place for their hard-earned investment pounds. This appendix lists the most common ratios that investors should be aware of and use. A solid company doesn't have to pass all these ratio tests with flying colours, but at a minimum, it should comfortably pass the ones regarding profitability and solvency:

✔ **Profitability:** Is the company making money? Is it making more or less than it did in the previous period? Are sales growing? Are profits growing?

You can answer these questions by looking at the following ratios:

- Return on Equity
- Common Size Ratio (P&L)
- Return on Capital Employed

✔ **Solvency:** Is the company keeping debts and other liabilities under control? Are the company's assets growing? Is the company's net equity (or net worth or shareholders' funds) growing?

You can answer these questions by looking at the following ratios:

- Debt-to-Equity
- Working Capital
- Quick Ratio

While you examine ratios, keep these points in mind:

✔ Not every company and/or industry is the same. A ratio that seems problematic in one industry may be just fine in another. Investigate.

✔ A single ratio isn't enough on which to base your investment decision. Look at several ratios covering the major aspects of a company's finances.

 ✔ Look at two or more years of a company's numbers to judge whether the most recent ratio is better, worse, or unchanged from the previous year's ratio. Ratios can give you early warning signs regarding the company's prospects.

Liquidity Ratios

Liquidity means the ability to quickly turn assets into cash. Liquid assets are simply assets that are easier to convert to cash. Property, for example, is certainly an asset, but it's not liquid because converting it to cash could take weeks, months, or even years. Current assets such as cheque accounts, savings accounts, marketable securities, accounts receivable, and stock are much easier to sell or convert to cash in a very short period of time.

Paying bills or immediate debt takes liquidity. Liquidity ratios help you understand a company's ability to pay its current liabilities. The most common liquidity ratios are the current ratio and the quick ratio; the numbers to calculate them are located on the balance sheet.

Current ratio

The current ratio is the most commonly used liquidity ratio. It answers the question 'Does the company have enough financial cushion to meet its current bills?' It's calculated as follows:

Current ratio = total current assets ÷ total current liabilities

If Holee Guacamolee PLC. (HG) has £60,000 in current assets and £20,000 in current liabilities, the current ratio is 3 because the company has £3 of current assets for each pound of current liabilities. As a general rule, a current ratio of 2 or more is desirable. A current ratio of less than 1 is a red flag that the company may have a cash crunch that could cause financial problems. Although many companies strive to get the current ratio to equal 1, we like to see a higher ratio (in the range of 1-3) to keep a cash cushion should the economy slow down.

Quick ratio

The quick ratio is frequently referred to as the 'acid test' ratio. It's a little more stringent than the current ratio in that you calculate it without taking into account stock. We'll use the current ratio example discussed in the preceding section. What if half of the assets are stock (£30,000 in this case)? Now what? First, here's the formula for the quick ratio:

Quick ratio = (Current assets less stock) ÷ current liabilities

In the example, the quick ratio for HG is 1.5 (£30,000 divided by £20,000). In other words, the company has £1.50 of 'quick' liquid assets for each pound of current liabilities. This amount is okay. *Quick liquid assets* include any money in the bank, marketable securities, and accounts receivable. If quick liquid assets at the very least equal or exceed total current liabilities, that amount is considered adequate.

The acid test that this ratio reflects is embodied in the question 'Can the company pay its bills when times are tough?' In other words, if the company can't sell its goods (stock), can it still meet its short-term liabilities? Of course, you must watch the accounts receivable as well. If the economy is entering rough times, you want to make sure that the company's customers are paying invoices on a timely basis.

Operating Ratios

Operating ratios essentially measure the company's efficiency. 'How is the company managing its resources?' is a question commonly answered with operating ratios. If, for example, a company sells products, does it have too much stock? If it does, that could impair the company's operations. The following sections present common operating ratios.

Return on equity (ROE)

Equity is the amount left from total assets after you account for total liabilities. (This can also be considered a profitability ratio.) The shareholders' funds (also known as net equity, or net worth) is the bottom line in the company's balance sheet, both geographically as well as figuratively. It's calculated as

Return on equity (ROE) = operating profit ÷ shareholders' funds

The operating profit (from the company's income statement) is simply the total income less total expenses. Operating profit that isn't spent or used up increases the company's net equity. Looking at operating profit is a great way to see whether the company's management is doing a good job growing the business. You can check this out by looking at the shareholder's funds from both the most recent balance sheet and the one from a year earlier. Ask yourself whether the current net worth is higher or lower than the year before. If it's higher, by what percentage is it higher? Use the ROE in conjunction with the ROA ratio (see the following section) to get a fuller picture of a company's activity.

Return on capital employed (ROCE)

The ROCE may seem similar to the ROE, but it's actually a widely used measurement of management performance expressed as a percentage. The formula for working out ROCE is

Return on capital employed (per cent) = (pre-tax profit × 100) ÷ capital employed

The ROCE reflects the relationship between a company's profit and the assets used to generate it. If the company HG makes a profit of £10,000 and has used assets of £100,000, the ROCE is 10 per cent. This percentage should be as high as possible.

Say that the company has an ROE of 25 per cent but an ROCE of only 5 per cent. Is that good? It sounds okay, but a problem exists. If the ROCE is much lower than the ROE, it indicates that the higher ROE may have been generated by something other than total assets – debt! The use of debt can be a leverage to maximise the ROE, but if the ROCE doesn't show a similar percentage of efficiency, then the company may have incurred too much debt. In that case, investors should be aware that it could cause problems (see the section, 'Solvency Ratios' , later in this appendix).

Solvency Ratios

Solvency just means that the company isn't overwhelmed by its liabilities. Insolvency means 'Oops! Too late'. You get the point. Solvency ratios have never been more important than they are now. Solvency ratios look at the relationship between what the company owns and what it owes. Here are two of the primary solvency ratios.

Debt to equity ratio

The debt to equity ratio is an indicator of the company's solvency. It answers the question 'How dependent is the company on debt?' In other words, it tells you how much the company owes and how much it owns. You calculate it as follows:

Debt to equity ratio = total debt ÷ shareholders' funds

But it is also sometimes calculated as:

Debt to equity ratio = total debt ÷ (shareholders' funds + total debt)

Using the first calculation method, if the company HG has £100,000 in debt and £50,000 in net worth, the debt to equity ratio is 2. The company has two pounds of debt to every pound of net worth. In this case, what the company owes is twice the amount of what it owns. Whenever a company's debt to net equity ratio exceeds 1 (as in the example), that isn't good. In fact, the higher the number, the more negative the situation. If the number is too high and the company isn't generating enough income to cover the debt, the company runs the risk of bankruptcy. But be sure of how this ratio is being calculated before you make any decisions based on it.

Working capital

Technically, working capital isn't a ratio, but it does belong to the list of things that serious investors look at. *Working capital* means what the company has in current assets and its relationship to current liabilities. It's a simple equation:

Working capital = total current assets – total current liabilities

The point is obvious: Does the company have enough to cover the current bills? Actually, you can formulate a useful ratio. If current assets are £25,000 and current liabilities are £25,000, then that's a 1-to-1 ratio, which is cutting it close. Current assets should be at least 50 per cent higher than current liabilities (say, £1.50 to £1.00) to have enough cushion to pay bills and have some money for other purposes. Preferably, the ratio should be 2 to 1 or higher.

Common Size Ratios

Common size ratios offer simple comparisons. You have common size ratios for both the balance sheet (where you compare total assets) and the profit and loss account (where you compare total sales or turnover):

- ✔ **To get a common size ratio from a balance sheet,** the total assets figure is assigned the percentage of 100 per cent. Every other item on the balance sheet is represented as a percentage of total assets. For example, if Holee Guacamolee PLC. (HG) has total assets of £10,000 and debt of £3,000, you know that total assets equal 100 percent, while debt equals 30 per cent (debt divided by total assets or £3,000 ÷ £10,000, which equals 30 percent).

- ✔ **To get a common size ratio from an income statement (or profit and loss account),** you compare total sales or turnover. For example, if a company has £50,000 in total sales and a net profit of £8,000, then you know that the profit equals 16 per cent of total sales.

Keep in mind the following points with common size ratios:

- ✔ **Net profit:** What percentage of sales is it? What was it last year? How about the year before? What percentage of increases (or decreases) is the company experiencing?

- ✔ **Expenses:** Are total expenses in line with the previous year? Are any expenses going out of line?

- ✔ **Shareholders' funds:** Is this item higher or lower than the year before?

- ✔ **Debt:** Is this item higher or lower than the year before?

Common size ratios are used to compare the company's financial data not only with previous balance sheets and income statements but also with other companies in the same industry. You want to make sure that the company is not only doing better historically but also as a competitor in the industry.

Valuation Ratios

Understanding the value of a share is very important for investors. The quickest and most efficient way to judge the value of a company is to look at valuation ratios. The type of value that you deal with throughout the book is the *market value* (essentially the price of the company's shares). You hope to buy it at one price and sell it later at a higher price — that's the name of the game. But what's the best way to determine whether what you're paying for now is a bargain or is fair market value? How do you know whether your share investment is undervalued or overvalued? The valuation ratios in this appendix can help you answer these questions. In fact, they're the same ratios that value investors have used with great success for many years.

Price-to-earnings ratio (P/E)

The price-to-earnings ratio can also double as a profitability ratio because it's a common barometer of value that many investors and analysts look at. We cover this topic in Chapter 10, but because it's such a critical ratio, we also include it here. The formula is

P/E ratio = price (per share) ÷ earnings (per share)

For example, if a company's share price is £10 and the earnings per share are £1, the P/E is 10 (10 divided by 1).

The P/E ratio answers the question 'Am I paying too much for the company's earnings?' Value investors find this number to be very, very important. Here are some points to remember:

✔ Generally, the lower the P/E ratio, the better (from a financial strength point of view). Frequently, a low P/E ratio indicates that the shares are undervalued (or the company is failing).

✔ A company with a P/E ratio significantly higher than its industry average is a red flag that its share price is too high (or that it is growing faster than its competitors).

✔ Don't invest in a company with no P/E ratio (it has a share price, but the company experienced losses). Such a share may be good for a speculator's portfolio but not for your retirement account.

✔ Any shares with a P/E higher than 40 should be considered a speculation and not an investment. Frequently, a high P/E ratio indicates that the shares are overvalued.

When you buy a company, you're really buying its power to make money. In essence, you're buying its earnings. Paying for a share that's priced at 10 to 20 times earnings is a conservative strategy that has served investors well for nearly a century. Make sure that the company is priced fairly and use the P/E ratio in conjunction with other measures of value (such as the other ratios in this appendix).

Price to sales ratio (PSR)

The price to sales ratio (PSR or P/R) is another method for valuing the company. It helps to answer the question 'Am I paying too much for the company's shares based on the company's sales?' This is a useful valuation ratio that we recommend using as a companion tool with the company's P/E ratio. You calculate it as follows:

PSR = share price (per share) ÷ total sales (per share)

This ratio can be quoted on a per-share basis or on an aggregate basis. For example, if a company's market value (or market capitalisation) is £1 billion and annual sales are also £1 billion, the PSR is 1. If the market value in this example is £2 billion, then the PSR is 2. For investors trying to make sure that they're not paying too much for the shares, the general rule is that the lower the PSR, the better. Shares with a PSR of 2 or less are considered undervalued.

Be very hesitant about buying a share with a PSR greater than 5. If you buy a share with a PSR of 38, that means you're paying £38 for each pound of sales – not exactly a bargain.

Price to book ratio (PBR)

The *price to book ratio* (PBR) is yet another valuation method. This ratio compares the market value to the company's accounting (or book) value. Recall that the book value refers to the company's net equity or shareholders' funds (assets minus liabilities). The company's market value is usually dictated by external factors such as supply and demand in the stock market. The book value is indicative of the company's internal operations. Value investors see the PBR as another perspective to valuing the company to determine whether you're paying too much for the shares. The formula is

Price to book ratio (PBR) = share price ÷ shareholders' funds per share

An alternate method is to calculate the ratio on a capitalisation basis, which yields the same ratio. If the company's share price is £20 and the book value (per share) is £15, then the PBR is 1.33. In other words, the company's market value is 33 per cent higher than its book value. Investors seeking an undervalued share like to see the market value as close as possible to (or even better, below) the book value.

Keep in mind that the PBR may vary depending on the industry and other factors. Also, judging a company solely on book value may be misleading because many companies have assets that aren't adequately reflected in the book value. Software companies are a good example. Intellectual properties, such as copyrights and trademarks, are very valuable yet aren't fully covered in book value. Just bear in mind that, generally, the lower the market value is in relation to the book value, the better for you (especially if the company has strong earnings and the outlook for the industry is positive).

Other Useful Accounting Terms

The more you read up on shares and investment the more likely you are to come across new accounting terms that are likely to bamboozle rather than bedazzle you.

EBITDA

The first mouthful you might encounter is EBITDA which is pronounced as a word (EE- Bit - Dah). It stands for *E*arnings *B*efore *I*nterest, *T*ax, *D*epreciation, and *A*mortisation. While it sounds very important it is pretty meaningless – except to highlight what could be an investment to avoid. Analysts in the US used EBITDA to value the telecommunications group WorldCom. This was not considered such a good move when an $11billion accounting fraud was revealed in June 2002 and the company filed for bankruptcy protection a month later. However some seasoned share pickers still take note of EBITDA when making selections.

Gearing

Gearing is not about fashion but you should pay attention to the gearing on your Primark and New Look shares. It is a ratio which expresses the company's level of borrowing. It is calculated by dividing the percentage of interest-bearing loans and preference share capital by ordinary shareholders' funds. Take care if the gearing is more than 50 per cent.

Index

Notes

Notes

FOR DUMMIES®

Do Anything. Just Add Dummies

PROPERTY

UK editions

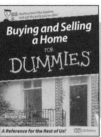

Buying and Selling a Home
978-0-7645-7027-8

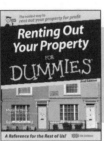

Renting Out Your Property
978-0-470-02921-3

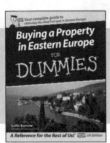

Buying a Property in Eastern Europe
978-0-7645-7047-6

PERSONAL FINANCE

Investing
978-0-7645-7023-0

Personal Finance & Investing All-In-One
978-0-470-51510-5

Bookkeeping
978-0-470-05815-2

BUSINESS

Starting a Business
978-0-7645-7018-6

Marketing
978-0-7645-7056-8

Business Plans
978-0-7645-7026-1

Answering Tough Interview Questions For Dummies (978-0-470-01903-0)

Being the Best Man For Dummies (978-0-470-02657-1)

Body Language FD (978-0-470-51291-3)

British History For Dummies (978-0-470-03536-8)

Buying a Home on a Budget For Dummies (978-0-7645-7035-3)

Buying a Property in Spain For Dummies (978-0-470-51235-77)

Cognitive Behavioural Therapy For Dummies (978-0-470-01838-5)

Cricket For Dummies (978-0-470-03454-5)

CVs For Dummies (978-0-7645-7017-9)

Detox For Dummies (978-0-470-01908-5)

Diabetes For Dummies (978-0-470-05810-7)

Divorce For Dummies (978-0-7645-7030-8)

DJing For Dummies (978-0-470-03275-6)

eBay.co.uk For Dummies (978-0-7645-7059-9)

Economics For Dummies (978-0-470-05795-7)

English Grammar For Dummies (978-0-470-05752-0)

Gardening For Dummies (978-0-470-01843-9)

Genealogy Online For Dummies (978-0-7645-7061-2)

Green Living For Dummies (978-0-470-06038-4)

Hypnotherapy For Dummies (978-0-470-01930-6)

Life Coaching For Dummies (978-0-470-03135-3)

Neuro-linguistic Programming For Dummies (978-0-7645-7028-5)

Parenting For Dummies (978-0-470-02714-1)

Personal Developmet All-In-One For Dummies (978-0-470-51501-3)

Pregnancy For Dummies (978-0-7645-7042-1)

Retiring Wealthy For Dummies (978-0-470-02632-8)

Self Build and Renovation For Dummies (978-0-470-02586-4)

Selling For Dummies (978-0-470-51259-3)

Sorting Out Your Finances For Dummies (978-0-7645-7039-1)

Starting a Business on eBay.co.uk For Dummies (978-0-470-02666-3)

Starting and Running an Online Business For Dummies (978-0-470-05768-1)

The Romans For Dummies (978-0-470-03077-6)

UK Law and Your Rights For Dummies (978-0-470-02796-7)

Writing a Novel & Getting Published For Dummies (978-0-470-05910-4)

Available wherever books are sold. For more information or to order direct go to www.wiley.com or call 0800 243407 (Non UK call +44 1243 843296)

FOR DUMMIES®

Do Anything. Just Add Dummies

HOBBIES

978-0-7645-5232-8

978-0-7645-5395-0

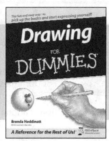

978-0-7645-5476-6

Also available:

Art For Dummies
(978-0-7645-5104-8)

Aromatherapy For Dummies
(978-0-7645-5171-0)

Bridge For Dummies
(978-0-471-92426-5)

Card Games For Dummies
(978-0-7645-9910-1)

Chess For Dummies
(978-0-7645-8404-6)

Improving Your Memory
For Dummies
(978-0-7645-5435-3)

Massage For Dummies
(978-0-7645-5172-7)

Meditation For Dummies
(978-0-471-77774-8)

Photography For Dummies
(978-0-7645-4116-2)

Quilting For Dummies
(978-0-7645-9799-2)

EDUCATION

978-0-7645-5434-6

978-0-7645-5581-7

978-0-7645-5422-3

Also available:

Algebra For Dummies
(978-0-7645-5325-7)

Astronomy For Dummies
(978-0-7645-8465-7)

Buddhism For Dummies
(978-0-7645-5359-2)

Calculus For Dummies
(978-0-7645-2498-1)

Cooking Basics For Dummies
(978-0-7645-7206-7)

Forensics For Dummies
(978-0-7645-5580-0)

Islam For Dummies
(978-0-7645-5503-9)

Philosophy For Dummies
(978-0-7645-5153-6)

Religion For Dummies
(978-0-7645-5264-9)

Trigonometry For Dummies
(978-0-7645-6903-6)

PETS

978-0-470-03717-1

978-0-7645-8418-3

978-0-7645-5275-5

Also available:

Labrador Retrievers
For Dummies
(978-0-7645-5281-6)

Aquariums For Dummies
(978-0-7645-5156-7)

Birds For Dummies
(978-0-7645-5139-0)

Dogs For Dummies
(978-0-7645-5274-8)

Ferrets For Dummies
(978-0-7645-5259-5)

Golden Retrievers
For Dummies
(978-0-7645-5267-0)

Horses For Dummies
(978-0-7645-9797-8)

Jack Russell Terriers
For Dummies
(978-0-7645-5268-7)

Puppies Raising & Training
Diary For Dummies
(978-0-7645-0876-9)

FOR DUMMIES®

The easy way to get more done and have more fun

LANGUAGES

978-0-7645-5193-2

978-0-7645-5193-2

978-0-7645-5196-3

Also available:

Chinese For Dummies
(978-0-471-78897-3)

Chinese Phrases
For Dummies
(978-0-7645-8477-0)

French Phrases For Dummies
(978-0-7645-7202-9)

German For Dummies
(978-0-7645-5195-6)

Italian Phrases For Dummies
(978-0-7645-7203-6)

Japanese For Dummies
(978-0-7645-5429-2)

Latin For Dummies
(978-0-7645-5431-5)

Spanish Phrases
For Dummies
(978-0-7645-7204-3)

Spanish Verbs For Dummies
(978-0-471-76872-2)

Hebrew For Dummies
(978-0-7645-5489-6)

MUSIC AND FILM

978-0-7645-9904-0

978-0-7645-2476-9

978-0-7645-5105-5

Also available:

Bass Guitar For Dummies
(978-0-7645-2487-5)

Blues For Dummies
(978-0-7645-5080-5)

Classical Music For Dummies
(978-0-7645-5009-6)

Drums For Dummies
(978-0-471-79411-0)

Jazz For Dummies
(978-0-471-76844-9)

Opera For Dummies
(978-0-7645-5010-2)

Rock Guitar For Dummies
(978-0-7645-5356-1)

Screenwriting For Dummies
(978-0-7645-5486-5)

Songwriting For Dummies
(978-0-7645-5404-9)

Singing For Dummies
(978-0-7645-2475-2)

HEALTH, SPORTS & FITNESS

978-0-7645-7851-9

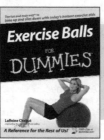

978-0-7645-5623-4

978-0-7645-4233-6

Also available:

Controlling Cholesterol
For Dummies
(978-0-7645-5440-7)

Diabetes For Dummies
(978-0-470-05810-7)

High Blood Pressure
For Dummies
(978-0-7645-5424-7)

Martial Arts For Dummies
(978-0-7645-5358-5)

Menopause FD
(978-0-470-061008)

Pilates For Dummies
(978-0-7645-5397-4)

Weight Training
For Dummies
(978-0-471-76845-6)

Yoga For Dummies
(978-0-7645-5117-8)

Available wherever books are sold. For more information or to order direct go to www.wiley.com or call 0800 243407 (Non UK call +44 1243 843296)

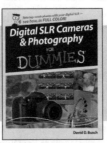